LAW OF THE EUROPEAN UNION

Second Edition

Penelope Kent

LL B, LL M, Solicitor
Senior Lecturer in Law
Middlesex University Business School

M&E
PITMAN
PUBLISHING

PITMAN PUBLISHING
128 Long Acre, London WC2E 9AN

A Division of Pearson Professional Limited

First published in Great Britain as *European Community Law* 1992
Second edition published in Great Britain as *Law of the European Union* 1996

© Pearson Professional Limited 1996

A CIP catalogue record for this book can be obtained from the British Library.

ISBN 0 7121 0851 3

10 9 8 7 6 5 4 3 2 1

Typeset by WestKey Limited, Falmouth, Cornwall
Printed and bound in Great Britain by Bell & Bain, Glasgow

The Publishers' policy is to use paper manufactured from sustainable forests.

CONTENTS

Part One
THE DECISION-MAKING PROCESS IN THE COMMUNITY

PREFACE

Great changes have taken place in Europe since the first edition of this book. The single market has been largely completed. The Maastricht Treaty has been ratified, but only after considerable opposition. Agreements have been signed with many of the former Soviet states as a prelude to full membership of the European Union. Austria, Finland and Sweden have joined the EU following the creation of the European Economic Area. In 1996 an intergovernmental conference will review the changes introduced at Maastricht.

The change of title of the book to *Law of the European Union* reflects the creation of the political entity known as the European Union. However the focus of the book remains on the legal regime of the European Community, one of the three 'pillars' of the union (the others being the Common Foreign and Security Policy, and Justice and Home Affairs).

While the second edition continues to cover both the constitutional and the substantive law of the EC, there has been some reordering of material to enable the chapters on actions and remedies in the Court of Justice to follow the consideration of the *Francovich* decision on state liability. Chapter 17 covers the free movement of capital and economic and monetary union. Chapter 26 has been expanded to introduce key policy areas arising from the Maastricht Treaty such as the environment. Chapter 27 outlines the likely main considerations for the 1996 IGC.

EC law has become a compulsory area of study within the academic stage of professional legal education. It is hoped that this book will provide an accessible introduction to the subject not only to law students but to students from other disciplines and to professionals whose work has a European dimension.

Grateful thanks are due to my husband David for his support throughout the writing of this second edition and to John Cushion, at Pitman, for his patience and attention to detail in editing this book. Any errors or omissions, of course, remain my own responsibility. I should also like to thank the Information Office of the Commission and the European Parliament for supplying the photographs.

The law is as stated on 31 August 1995 although a few later points are considered.

Penny Kent
November 1995

Note: A reference in the text such as *see* **10** refers to numbered section 10 of that chapter. A reference such as 5.**10** refers to numbered section 10 of chapter 5.

The citation of an author in the text such as *see* Wyatt and Dashwood p. 20 is a reference to the work of an author listed in Further Reading on p. 282.

ABBREVIATIONS

CAP	common agricultural policy
CCT	common customs tariff
CET	common external tariff
CFI	Court of First Instance
CMLR	Common Market Law Reports
COROPER	Committee of Permanent Representatives
DG	Directorate General
EC	European Community/Communities
ECJ	European Court of Justice
ECR	European Court Reports
ECSC	European Coal and Steel Community
ECU	European currency unit
EEA	European Economic Area
EEC	European Economic Community
EFTA	European Free Trade Association
EMS	European Monetary System
EMU	European Monetary Union
EP	European Parliament
ERM	Exchange Rate Mechanism
EU	European Union
Euratom	European Atomic Energy Authority
GATT	General Agreement on Tariffs and Trade
JO	*Journal Officiel* (French version of *Official Journal*)
OJ	*Official Journal*
SEA	Single European Act
TEU	Treaty on European Union

TABLE OF EUROPEAN COMMUNITY TREATIES

TABLE OF UNITED KINGDOM STATUTES

TABLE OF EUROPEAN COMMUNITY SECONDARY LEGISLATION

TABLE OF CASES IN THE COURT OF JUSTICE AND THE COURT OF FIRST INSTANCE

TABLE OF CASES BEFORE THE NATIONAL COURTS

TABLE OF COMMISSION DECISIONS

Part One

THE DECISION-MAKING PROCESS IN THE COMMUNITY

1

THE HISTORICAL BACKGROUND TO THE EUROPEAN COMMUNITY

1. The inspiration

The inspiration for the three institutions that came to be known as the European Community (EC) derived from the plan devised in 1950 by Robert Schuman, the French Foreign Minister, and Jean Monnet who was responsible for overseeing France's economic recovery after the war. The plan involved the pooling by France and Germany of their production of coal and steel.

2. The proposal

The proposal evolved out of the need to reconstruct Europe after the Second World War. The formulators of the plan believed that Germany should be helped to rebuild, but only if bound politically and economically within an organisation of European states so that a further war in Europe would be unlikely.

3. European Coal and Steel Community (ECSC)

As a result of this initiative the Treaty of Paris was signed in 1951 creating the European Coal and Steel Community (ECSC). The original six member states were France, Germany, Italy, Belgium, the Netherlands and Luxembourg. The objective of the ECSC was the creation of a common market in the production of coal and steel.

4. Creation of the EEC and Euratom

In 1957 the six member states signed two further treaties in Rome creating the European Economic Community (EEC) and the European Atomic Energy Authority (Euratom) modelled on the ECSC. Euratom resembles the ECSC in that it covers a limited sector, namely the nuclear industry in the EC, whereas the EEC was intended from the outset to evolve towards 'ever closer union among the peoples of Europe' (Preamble to the EEC Treaty).

5. Institutional framework

Initially, the ECSC, EEC and Euratom held only two institutions in common: the Assembly (or Parliament) and the Court. However, a single Council and a Commission were formed from the merger of the separate institutions including the High Authority: Merger Treaty 1965. After the merger the three communities functioned separately but with shared institutions. This book concentrates on the role of the EEC, later to become known as the EC, the community of widest interest and importance.

6. Sovereignty and the Treaty of Rome (EEC Treaty)

The EEC was concerned with general economic integration achieved by merging the separate interests of the member states into a common market where goods, persons, services and capital could circulate freely. The creation of the EEC required a pooling of sovereignty in areas covered by the EEC Treaty. It reflected a federalist ideal reminiscent of Churchill's vision of a 'United States of Europe', not as a single territory under the control of a federal authority but as a supranational organisation capable of making policies and rules which bound the member states. The founders of the EEC saw the gain in peace, stability and economic development as outweighing the inevitable loss of sovereignty.

7. Objectives of the EEC

The general objectives of the EEC under the Treaty of Rome were to promote throughout the community a harmonious development of economic activities, a continuous and balanced expansion, an increase in stability, an accelerated raising of the standard of living and closer relations between the states belonging to it (Article 2, EEC Treaty). These objectives were to be achieved by establishing a common market and progressively approximating (harmonising) the economic policies of the member states. As a result of the Single European Act 1986 the EC adopted measures to complete the internal market by 31 December 1992. The Treaty on European Union (TEU) developed the objectives further to provide for economic and monetary union: *see* Chapter 17.

8. The position of the United Kingdom

At the time the EEC Treaty was signed the United Kingdom was not prepared to sacrifice national sovereignty to join. Instead it proposed the creation of a free trade area in Europe within which tariff barriers would be dismantled but control of trade with non-members left to the member states. In 1959 the European Free Trade Association (EFTA) was founded by the UK, Norway, Denmark, Sweden, Austria, Portugal, and Ireland as an associate and, later, a full member. However, when the UK realised its growing economic isolation, it applied (unsuccessfully) for full membership of the Communities in 1961.

9. The first enlargement

In 1967 the UK re-applied for membership, again followed by Denmark, Norway and Ireland, leading to the signing of the Treaties of Accession in 1972 and 1973 after which the UK, Ireland and Denmark joined the Communities. Norway decided not to proceed to membership following a referendum. This negative decision was repeated in 1994 when Norway voted in a second referendum against membership. Greenland withdrew after a similar result in 1982.

10. 'Mediterranean' enlargement

Following its return to democracy Greece joined the EC in 1981, followed by Spain and Portugal in 1986. Turkey, Malta, and Cyprus have applied for membership. A favourable opinion has been given on future membership by Cyprus and Malta, with a commitment to include both countries in the next round of enlargement.

Turkey's position is more complex due to its lower level of economic development and human rights record. The Commission stated in 1989 that accession negotiations should not begin in the immediate future. Instead, the emphasis should remain on the achievement of the customs union under the 1964 association agreement.

11. The unification of Germany

Following unification of the German Democratic Republic (GDR) and the Federal Republic of Germany (FRG), the former GDR became a full legal member of the EC without the need for formal enlargement of the EC on 3 October 1990. Since that date EC law has applied in principle to the former GDR. The Council and the Parliament have approved special powers to enable the Commission to supervise the application of EC law in the GDR. The Commission has drawn up a package of proposals covering matters such as technical rules, professional qualifications, the Common Agricultural Policy (CAP), transport, the environment and trade with Eastern Europe. Agreement was reached at the Edinburgh Summit in 1993 to increase the number of German MEPs from 81 to 99.

12. EFTA, the EEA and further enlargement

The EFTA states with the exception of Switzerland signed the European Economic Area (EEA) Agreement which came into force on 1 January 1994, extending the application of the single market to the territory of the signatory states. The EEA Agreement set up its own institutions and was seen as a prelude to full membership of the European Union (of which the EC had become part under the TEU: *see* 15 below). The EU was enlarged on 1 January 1995 by a further Act of Accession as a result of which Austria, Finland and Sweden became full members of the EU. Unlike previous enlargements which involved extensive transitional arrangements the three EEA states acceded to the full body of EC law (the 'acquis communautaire') with limited temporary derogations. In 1995 only Norway, Iceland and Liechtenstein remain members of the EEA. EFTA continues to exist, but its future is uncertain.

13. The EU and Eastern Europe

In 1989 the collapse of the former Soviet Union was complete. Partnership and Co-operation Agreements were signed in 1994 between the EU and the Russian Federation, the Ukraine and Moldova. (Note: the agreement with the Russian Federation is currently suspended in response to the conflict in Chechnia.) These agreements cover the importance of democratic values, respect for human rights and the principles of the market economy. Trade barriers are gradually to be lifted and a regular political dialogue between the parties to be maintained. Negotiations are continuing with the Commonwealth of Independent States (the association of states covering much of the territory of the former USSR).

The Copenhagen Summit of 1993 paved the way for 'Europe Agreements' which have since been signed with many East European states to promote convergence, integration and regional co-operation. These agreements provide for a structured relationship with the EU when economic and political conditions are satisfied. Europe Agreements have been signed with Poland, Hungary, the Czech and Slovak Republics, Bulgaria, Romania, and the Baltic states.

14. The Single European Act

The Single European Act (SEA), signed in 1986, represented the first major revision to the EEC Treaty. The SEA followed a number of unsuccessful attempts to change the institutional balance within the EC such as the draft Treaty on European Union, put forward by the European Parliament in 1984: see Charlesworth and Cullen pp. 5–6. These attempts had failed largely because they were perceived as too federalist, particularly by the UK which opposed the further loss of sovereignty to the EC. The Single Market initiative, however, carried the support of all member states including the UK.

The rationale for the SEA had emerged as a result of a 1985 White Paper issued by the Commission which showed that many obstacles to trade between member states remained, to the detriment of the EC's global trading position. During the 1970s and early 1980s national self-interest predominated, impeding progress at EC level.

The SEA was signed in 1992, with the objective of removing all barriers, whether physical, technical or fiscal. A detailed and ambitious programme of directives was adopted under simplified voting procedures: see Chapter 2. The programme rekindled enthusiasm for European integration. By 1992 the single (or internal) market was largely complete. Member states defaulting on im-plementation could be subject to action in the Court of Justice (ECJ) and fined (following amendment to Article 171 by the TEU). The SEA was implemented in the UK by the European Communities (Amendment) Act 1986.

15. European Union and the Maastricht Treaty

An intergovernmental conference (IGC) was convened in 1990 to consider economic and monetary union (EMU). A second IGC examined political union (EPU). Several member states, notably Germany and France, believed that EMU could not be effective without EPU. The Treaty on European Union (TEU) providing for both forms of union was signed at Maastricht in the Netherlands in December 1991. The UK and Denmark 'opted out' of the third stage of EMU in a Protocol to the Treaty: *see* Chapter 17.

The structure created at Maastricht consists of three 'pillars':

(a) The three Communities (the ECSC, Euratom and the EC, as the EEC had been renamed), collectively known as the EC: *see* **18** below

(b) The Common Foreign and Security Policy (CFSP)

(c) Co-operation in Justice and Home Affairs.

Only the first pillar, the EC, is governed by EC Law. The second and third are administered through intergovernmental co-operation: *see* Chapter 27.

Other significant features of the TEU include the inclusion of:

(a) A new legal base for social policy in a Protocol annexed to the Treaty. The UK has refused to participate in these arrangements: *see* Chapter 24.

(b) The principle of subsidiarity (*see* Chapter 4) which provides for a form of devolved decision-making in areas outside the exclusive competence of the EC. The UK strongly supported the inclusion of subsidiarity in the TEU in the belief that it would act as a check on the EC institutions and the growth of federalism. This remains to be seen.

16. Objectives of the Union

The objectives of the Union as set out in Article B of the TEU reflect the activities to be pursued under the three pillars. In addition the Union is to maintain in full and build on the 'acquis communautaire'. This expression may be translated as the body of EC law in the founding treaties and the decisions of the Court of Justice.

The EC Treaty expresses its objectives in the form of 'Principles'. Article 2 adds to the original list of tasks the establishment of an economic and monetary union and the implementation of common policies of activities in Articles 3 and 3a (including the strengthening of social cohesion, a system to ensure that competition in the internal market is not distorted, environmental protection and a contribution to the strengthening of consumer protection). These principles are subject to the principle of subsidiarity: Article 3b.

17. Other changes introduced by the TEU

Other changes introduced by the TEU are considered in the subsequent chapters of this book where they occur. Certain institutional changes have been made including the new co-decision procedure which strengthens the role of the European Parliament without giving it direct legislative power: *see* Chapter 2.

The European Council (made up of the heads of state or government and the President of the Commission) is to meet at least twice a year: Article D TEU. It must provide the Union with 'the necessary impetus for its development' for which it must define the general political guidelines.

A new category of Citizenship of the Union is established for EU nationals: Article 8. A citizen of the Union (at least in principle) enjoys residence and various other civic rights throughout the EU. At present Article 8 is only partially implemented (in relation to right to stand or vote in municipal and European elections: *see* Chapter 14).

18. The EC, the EU and terminology

The TEU dropped the word 'Economic' from the 'European Economic Community' to signify a change of emphasis in its activities, but uncertainty remained about the correct designation of the various institutions. This has been clarified by guidance from the institutions. The EC, ECSC and Euratom, acting together under the first pillar, may be known collectively as the EC. Thus the expression 'EC law' refers to the legal regulation of activities under the first pillar. The European Union may be taken to cover the activities under the second and third pillars. While some commentators restrict the use of the term 'EU law' to these two pillars others use it to denote the regulation of all three pillars. The title of this book reflects the latter approach to indicate the significance of the changes introduced at Maastricht. However the main emphasis within the book will remain on the law of the EC until the second and third pillars are subject to legal rather than intergovernmental regulation.

The titles of the European Commission and European Parliament remain unaltered by the TEU, but the Council of Ministers is to be known as the Council of the European Union. Directives will be cited as no./year/EEC or no./year/EC depending whether they pre- or post-date the TEU. (In this book the final part of the citation, EC/EEC, is omitted.)

19. Ratification of the TEU

Ratification proved to be a fraught and lengthy process for several of the member states. There was considerable opposition in the UK before it was accepted by Parliament. The Danish people rejected the Treaty in a referendum, only accepting it in a second referendum after the Edinburgh Summit had allayed Danish fears on key policies such as subsidiarity and European citizenship. The Treaty came into force on 1 November 1993 when the ratification process was complete in all member states. The operation of the Treaty as amended by the TEU is due to be reviewed at an intergovernmental conference in 1996: *see* Chapter 27.

Progress test 1

1. What were the original institutional structures of the ECSC, EEC and Euratom? How were these structures changed by the Merger Treaty 1965?

2. Why did the EEC Treaty require member states to pool their sovereignty in certain areas?

3. How were the objectives of the EEC to be achieved?

4. Why was the UK not prepared to join the EEC at the outset?

5. What is the status of EC law in the former Federal Republic of Germany following reunification?

6. How has the most recent enlargement changed the composition of the EC?

7. What mechanisms has the EU adopted in its relation with the former Soviet bloc states?

8. How was completion of the internal market by 1992 largely achieved?

9. What are the 'three pillars' created by the TEU? Which pillar is regulated by EC law?

10. In what areas are the objectives of the EU after the TEU more ambitious than those of the EEC?

11. Which of the institutions is identified as an institution of the EU rather than the EC?

2

THE INSTITUTIONS OF THE EC: THE PARLIAMENT, THE COUNCIL, THE COMMISSION AND THE COURT OF JUSTICE

1. Introduction

The EC Treaty is a legal framework, providing for broadly stated objectives and obligations. It follows that enactment of detailed rules must be left to the Community institutions. The institutions of the EC are unique. They do not correspond to institutions at either national or international level. To understand the EC it is necessary to appreciate the changing nature of the balance of power between the institutions.

2. The four principal institutions

The four main institutions created by the Treaty (Article 4) are:

(a) the European Parliament

(b) the Council

(c) the Commission

(d) the Court of Justice.

All four institutions must act within the limits of the powers conferred by the Treaty: Article 4 EC. The same Article also provides for the setting up of an Economic and Social Committee (ESC) and a Court of Auditors. The Merger Treaty provides in Article 4 for the creation of the Committee of Permanent Representatives (COROPER). A new Court of First Instance (CFI) was established in 1988 under the Single European Act (SEA).

The Treaty on European Union (TEU) recognised as a separate institution the Court of Auditors, created in 1977 to audit the accounts of the EC institutions. Provision was also made under the TEU for the creation of a Committee of the Regions: Article 4(2) EC (*see* below). The TEU also recognised the European Investment Bank under Articles 198d and e EC, established as a non-profit-making basis in the less developed regions of the EC. Article 180d provides for the

European Central Bank (in the third stage of economic and monetary union: *see* Chapter 17) to take action against national banks which infringe EC law.

THE EUROPEAN PARLIAMENT

3. The Assembly

Under the EEC Treaty the Parliament was known originally as the Assembly. It was not democratically elected but was made up of nominees from the member states who were already members of their national parliaments. It had no direct legislative power but played a consultative and supervisory role.

4. The European Parliament

The Assembly came to be known as the European Parliament, and since the SEA has been officially known as the Parliament. In 1979 direct elections were held with varying representation according to the size of the member state. In all there are 626 Members of the European Parliament (MEPs), from 1 January 1995, made up as follows: Germany (99), France, Italy and the UK (87 each), Spain (64), Netherlands (31), Belgium, Greece and Portugal (25), Sweden (22), Austria (21), Denmark and Finland (16), Ireland (15) and Luxembourg (6). It is based in Strasbourg with some sessions held in Luxembourg and most committee meetings held in Brussels. Members are elected for five years.

5. Political groups

The Parliament is divided into political groups, with MEPs sitting in ten multi-lateral political groups. MEPs do not receive any voting mandate from their home state but vote on an individual and personal basis. As a majority of 314 votes is needed for a measure to pass the second reading stage there are many alliances which transcend political and national groupings. There are 18 Parliamentary Committees dealing with specific aspects of EC policy, e.g. transport and agriculture. The Parliament tends to align itself with the Commission against the Council in promoting European rather than national interests.

6. Parliament and the Budget

Under Article 203, EC Treaty, as amended by the Budgetary Treaty 1979, the Parliament has significant powers to amend and delay the Budget. Initially, the Commission draws up a preliminary draft Budget. This is sent to the Council which establishes the draft before sending it on to Parliament. If Parliament approves the Budget within 45 days it is adopted. In relation to non-obligatory expenditure (i.e. discretionary spending on areas such as education), Parliament may, however, suggest modifications or amendments, in which case the draft must be returned to the Council. The Council has a further 15 days in which to modify amendments. Parliament may select the modifications within a further

15 days on a majority of members with 315 votes cast. Finally, the Parliament may adopt the Budget or reject it as it did in 1979 and 1984. Where expenditure is obligatory (e.g. under the Common Agriculture Policy) the EP may propose modifications by majority. Amendments lapse unless accepted by the Council within 15 days.

The main contributors to the 1994 budget were: Germany 30 per cent, France 19 per cent, Italy 14 per cent, United Kingdom 12 per cent, followed in descending order by Denmark, Greece, Portugal, Ireland and Luxembourg. It can be seen from these figures that the 'big four' contribute approximately 75 per cent of the budget. The proportions for 1995 will differ, following the accession of Austria, Sweden and Finland, all net contributors to the budget.

7. Parliament and the Commission

The Parliament may question the Commission on its activities. It discusses the Commission's reports in open session, and parliamentary discussions are reported in the *Official Journal*. Parliament may censure the Commission, and has the power to dismiss the entire Commission: Article 144. This drastic power has been threatened but never actually carried, although a censure motion was proposed in 1990.

8. Parliament's role in the legislative process

Despite the pressure for greater legislative powers Parliament's (EP's) role is still largely consultative. Consultation is an essential procedural requirement in specific areas such as the implementation of the competition rules: Article 87. Failure to consult in *Roquette Frères SA* v. *Council* (Case 138/79) led to the annulment of the legislation in question.

The 'democratic deficit' whereby the unelected Council adopts legislation has gradually been eroded after the strengthening of the EP's role by the SEA and the TEU. There are currently three types of legislative procedure involving varying degrees of participation by the EP: consultation, co-operation and co-decision: *see* below.

9. Procedures: consultation, co-operation and co-decision

The co-operation procedure requires two hearings before the Parliament instead of the single hearing under the old-style consultation procedure (*see* Figs. 2.1 and 2.2 on pages 14 and 15).

(a) *Consultation procedure.* Proposed legislation is submitted by the Commission to the Council (*see* Fig. 2.1). Where the Treaty requires, the draft must be laid before the Parliament for the first reading. The draft is then considered in committee before an opinion is delivered. Any proposed amendments are referred back to the Council. The Council will adopt the final act after discussion in the Committee of Permanent Representatives (COROPER): *see* 17 below.

(b) *Co-operation procedure.* The co-operation procedure was introduced by the SEA to provide a straightforward mechanism for the adoption of internal market

Plate 1   The European Parliament Building

measures by qualified majority voting. Most of these measures are now covered by the co-decision procedure under Article 189b EC. Some measures (e.g. Article 1305(1) on the environment have been given a more substantial basis under the co-operation procedure in Article 189c EC. Other areas covered by Article 189c include the common transport policy (Article 75), health and safety (Article 118a), and vocational training policy (Article 127).

Where the co-operation procedure applies the Council will adopt a 'common position', either adopting the proposal by a qualified majority (54 votes) or drafting an amended proposal (on a unanimous vote): Article 189c EC. The draft is then sent for a second reading to the Parliament which has three months within which to:

(i)   accept (by a majority of votes cast)
(ii) reject (by an absolute majority of the votes of 260 (MEPs)
(iii) propose amendments (by an absolute majority) to the common position.

Acceptance will lead to final adoption by the Council in accordance with the common position. Failure to act within three months is deemed to be acceptance. Rejection of the common position is the Parliament's most significant legislative power. Amendment results in re-examination of the common position by the Commission which is not obliged to adopt the Parliament's amendments but

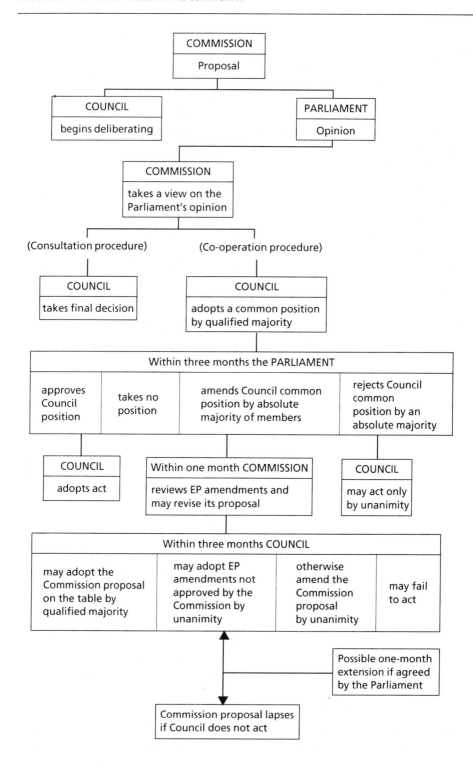

Figure 2.1 The co-operation procedure

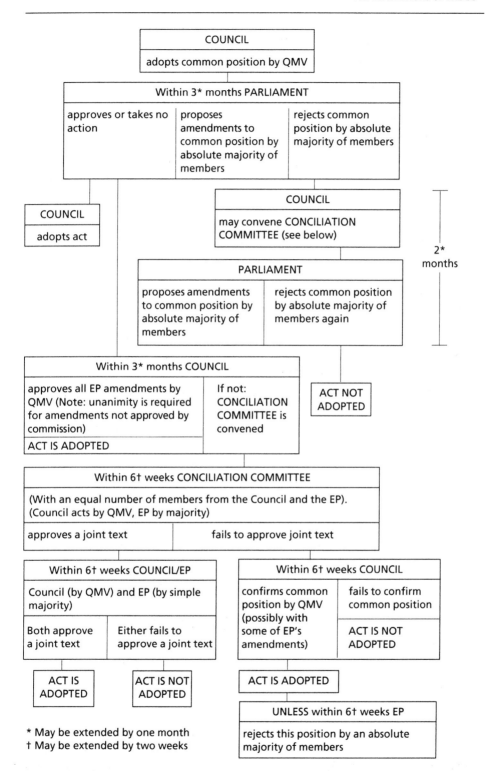

Figure 2.2 The co-decision procedure in the EC

may refer the draft to the Council in any event. The Council may then either accept the amended proposal (by qualified majority) or adopt a different version (by unanimous vote).

(c) *Co-decision procedure.* The objective of the co-decision procedure, introduced by the TEU, is to provide a new mechanism which recognises the joint involvement in the legislative process of the EP and the Council. It does not give direct legislative powers to the EP alone, the final adoption of measures being the responsibility of the Council, subject to the EP's right of veto: *see* below.

Under Article 189b the procedure follows the same route as the co-operation procedure until the point where the EP amends or rejects the Council's common position. In the event of rejection of the common position or refusal by the Council to accept the EP's amendments a Conciliation Committee composed of equal representation from the Council and EP must be convened. The objective of the Committee is to reconcile the two differing views, leading to the approval of a joint text which the EP may adopt by simple majority and the Council by qualified majority vote.

If the Committee cannot agree on a joint text the Council may confirm a text based on the common position, leading to the final adoption of the text unless the EP rejects by an absolute majority of MEPs. Thus the ultimate power of the EP is a negative one, the exercise of a veto (sometimes called 'negative assent').

Example In March 1995 the EP used its veto to reject the draft text agreed by the Conciliation Committee on the controversial directive on the protection of biotechnological inventions. Such action may fuel concern (*see* Shaw p. 82) that the EP may act as a 'destabilising influence', delaying the legislative process.

The co-decision procedure will apply in the following areas: free movement of workers (Article 49), freedom of establishment and mutual recognition of diplomas (Articles 54(2), 56(2), 57), internal market (Article 100a), incentive measures in education, culture and public health (Articles 126, 128, 129), consumer protection (Article 129a), Trans-European Networks (Article 129d), research and development framework programmes (Article 130i) and general action programmes on the environment which set out priority objectives (Article s (3)).

Note: A version of the co-decision procedure known as the assent procedure was introduced by the SEA and extended by the TEU. It requires the positive approval of both the EP and the Council before a measure may be adopted. Areas under the EC Treaty for which the assent procedure is required include applications for enlargement (Article 237), various categories of international agreements (Article 238), measures to facilitate the rights of European citizens (Article 8a) and acts regulating election to the EP (Article 106(5)).

10. Further changes under the TEU

Article 138 c EC enables the EP to set up temporary Committees of Inquiry to investigate alleged contraventions or maladministration in the implementation of EC law. Article 138d empowers any EU citizen or resident to petition the EP on any EC matter affecting him directly. Article 138e enables the EP to appoint an Ombudsman to receive complaints about maladministration by the EC institutions other than the ECJ.

THE COUNCIL OF MINISTERS

11. Composition

After the TEU the Council became known as the 'Council of the European Union.' It has a fluctuating membership of representatives at ministerial level, authorised to commit the government of each member state (Article 146) with membership depending on the issues under discussion. Only one voting delegate per member state is allowed. Meetings are held in private unless the Council unanimously decides otherwise. The office of the President is held by each state in turn for 6 months.

12. Functions

The task of the Council is 'to ensure that the objectives set out in this Treaty are attained': Article 145. It has a 'duty to ensure co-ordination of the general economic policies of the member states' and has 'power to take decisions'. Thus, although the Council is clearly a political body which may reflect the national interests of member states in legislative matters, it may usually act on a proposal from the Commission and is often required to consult Parliament and the Economic and Social Committees. A unanimous vote is required to override Parliamentary objections to a proposed measure under the co-operation and co-decision procedure. Unanimity is also required to amend a Commission proposal: Article 149. Adoption of the final decision on any legislative proposal rests with the Council, unless the EP vetoes the measure: *see* **9(c)** above.

13. Voting procedures

Under Article 148, as amended, voting may be by:

(a) simple majority (rare)

(b) qualified majority

(c) unanimity.

Qualified voting depends on a system of weighted votes. The largest member states France, Germany, the United Kingdom and Italy have 10 votes, Spain has 8 votes, Belgium, Greece, the Netherlands and Portugal have 5, Sweden and Austria have 4, Finland, Denmark and Ireland have 3, and Luxembourg 2. The minimum vote for a qualified majority is 62.

Under the original Treaty provisions many important areas, such as Article 100 on the approximation of laws, could only be implemented by unanimous vote. The intention of the Treaty was to move towards voting by qualified majority at the end of the transitional period (31 December 1965). Instead, as a result of a political crisis, the Luxembourg Accords were drawn up in 1966. The Accords do not have the force of law but have usually been followed. Under the Accords member states may insist on a unanimous vote where vital national interests are at stake. They remain in force but have an uncertain future after the commitment to integration implicit in the TEU.

In March 1994 the 'Ioannina Compromise' was agreed to allay fears expressed by the UK and Spain. As a result, if a dispute arises leading to a veto of 23 to 27 votes the measure is subjected to a 'reasonable delay' while a consensus is sought. Further discussion will take place at the 1996 IGC.

14. Effect of the SEA and the TEU

The need for a swift and effective voting mechanism was apparent when completion of the internal market was being considered. As a result the SEA increased the areas where voting by qualified majority is permitted to cover the internal market legislation. Any remaining areas of single market legislation were moved to the co-decision procedure under the TEU.

Unanimity is still required in some important areas including changing the number of judges in the ECJ (Article 165), agreeing the conversion rate at which national currencies will be fixed before replacement by the ECU (Article 109(4)), the general power to pass laws coming within the objectives of the EC (Article 235), the amendment of a Commission proposal (Article 189(a)(1)), and adopting a measure rejected by the EP under the co-operation procedure (Article 189(c)).

15. The European Council

The European Council should not be confused with the Council of Ministers. The European Council is a regular summit meeting of Heads of State and their Foreign Ministers, required to meet at least twice a year by the SEA (now under Article D2 TEU). The President of the Commission and one other Commissioner may attend.

16. Committee of Permanent Representatives (COROPER)

Since Council membership varies and is combined with full-time responsibilities in the home state, much of the work is carried out by the COROPER, a permanent body of representatives from the member states whose function is to examine and sift Commission proposals before a final decision is made by the Council.

THE COMMISSION

17. Features

Of the four institutions the Commission possesses the clearest supranational features. It was intended to express the Community interest and to promote further integration. While the Commission in some respects resembles a civil service, its role is wider encompassing the formulation and execution of EC policies and legislation. The Commission operates on a collegiate basis. It meets weekly in private, taking decisions by simple majority.

18. Composition

The present Commission was appointed on 1 January 1995 and consists of 20 members, chosen on the basis of general competence and 'whose independence is beyond doubt': Article 10, Merger Treaty. The Commissioners are appointed by agreement of the governments of the member states and must 'neither seek nor take instructions from any government or from any other body': Article 10, Merger Treaty. A Commissioner must be an EC national. The Commission must include at least one Commissioner from each member state. The President of the Commission holds office for a renewable term of two years.

Portfolios are allocated to individual Commissioners, each assisted by his own Cabinet, a group of officials appointed by and responsible to him. The Commission is divided into Directorates General (DGs) of varying importance covering matters such as external relations, competition and the internal market. There are also various specialised services such as the Legal Service which advises all the directorates general and represents the Commission in legal proceedings. The total staff of the Commission is over 10,000.

19. Functions

The Commission has three main functions:

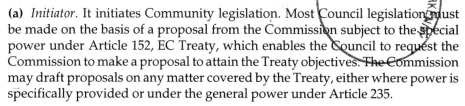

(a) *Initiator.* It initiates Community legislation. Most Council legislation must be made on the basis of a proposal from the Commission subject to the special power under Article 152, EC Treaty, which enables the Council to request the Commission to make a proposal to attain the Treaty objectives. The Commission may draft proposals on any matter covered by the Treaty, either where power is specifically provided or under the general power under Article 235.

(b) *Guardian of the Treaties.* The Commission acts as the guardian of the Treaties. Under Article 5 EC, member states must take all necessary steps to implement obligations imposed by the Treaty or by the institutions and to refrain from measures which could jeopardise the operation of the Treaty. The Commission has a duty to investigate and bring to an end infringements of EC law by the member states. It has the power to bring an action against a member state under Article 169. The Commission is solely responsible for the administration and enforcement of competition policy, with the power to penalise individuals in breach of EC law. A similar power exists for the enforcement of the law relating to state aids (financial subsidies provided by the state to the industries): Article 93, and the control of public undertakings: Article 90. The Commission also has considerable power to investigate alleged breaches under Article 213 and Regulation 17/62. A corresponding duty is placed on member states by Article 5 and on individuals by Regulation 17/62.

(c) *Executive.* The Commission acts as the executive of the Community, implementing policies decided on by the Council. This often involves drawing up detailed legislation which may require a final decision by the Council. Decisions may only be delegated under strict limits. In *Commission* v. *BASF AG* (PVC) (Case C-137/92 P) the ECJ upheld a decision by the CFI to annul a Commission decision which was defective in form (although not 'non-existent' as the CFI had held). The decision had been adopted by the Competition Commissioner in a number of translations additional to the originals adopted by the Commission. The CFI held that the Commission itself should have adopted each translation.

Where powers have been delegated by the Council to the Commission some measure of control is retained through the system of Comitology: *see* **20** below. The Commission also possesses its own power of decision under Article 155 where no reference to the Council is necessary, for example in the reinforcement of competition policy.

In addition the Commission possesses various representative and financial functions:

(a) *Representative*: in external relations it acts as the negotiator in the Treaty-making process, although agreements are concluded by the Council after consultation with the Parliament: Article 228.

(b) *Financial*: the Commission draws up the preliminary draft budget: *see* **6** above.

20. 'Comitology'

Comitology refers to the practice of decision-making by the Commission under powers delegated by the Council. Typically the Council will adopt a framework regulation, to be followed by detailed regulations or directives by the Commission (often under the CAP). The Commission's legislative activities are supervised by the Council under the system set out in the *Comitology* decision

Plate 2 The European Commission building

(D87/373). There are three categories of decision involving increasing levels of supervision:

(a) *Advisory Committees*: decisions of the Committee are not binding on the Commission but must be considered.

(b) *Management Committees*: the Committee may adopt measures by qualified majority voting which the Council may substitute for the Commission proposal.

(c) *Regulatory Committees*: failure by the Committee to adopt a measure leads to referral to the Council, but if the Council fails to act within three months the Commission may adopt the act.

Both the Commission and the EP object to the scope provided by Comitology for intervention by the Council. The system was unsuccessfully challenged before the ECJ in *Parliament* v. *Council* (Case 302/87). To avoid problems and delay draft measures are sent by the Commission to the EP for information before implementation.

THE COURT OF JUSTICE (ECJ)

21. Functions

The main functions of the Court of Justice are to ensure that Community law is enforced, to provide a forum for the resolution of disputes between member states and the EC and also between the institutions themselves, and to protect individual rights. After the TEU the ECJ may also review the acts of the EMU institutions, the European Investment Bank and the European Parliament where these acts have legal effect.

22. Composition

(a) *Judges*. The Court is composed of fifteen judges, one from each member state. Judges must be 'persons whose independence is beyond doubt': Article 167, and may be either judges or academics in their own country. The judges appoint a President for three years from among their own ranks and are assisted by nine advocates-general. Judges are appointed for staggered terms of six years. A judge may only be removed if all the other judges and advocates-general agree that he is no longer qualified or fit to hold office. This has never happened in all the years of the Court's existence. Judges must not be influenced by their own national origins but must strive for a Community approach in reaching a decision.

Decisions are taken by majority vote if the member state or institution concerned so require: Article 165. Actions brought by one of the member states or by the institutions are always heard in full court. However, straightforward actions may be heard in a chamber consisting of three or five judges.

(b) *Advocates-general*. Advocates-general must be qualified in the same way as judges. Their role is to assist the Court by presenting reasoned submissions on the facts and also recommendations for a decision. These submissions are objective and do not represent the views of either party. The advocate-general's submissions are the only part of the written record in which the legal issues are fully examined and are therefore helpful to the common lawyer unfamiliar with continental pleadings. While the submissions are persuasive they are not binding on the judges.

23. Judicial style in the ECJ

Procedures in the ECJ derive from the continental tradition and are mainly inquisitorial, with the emphasis on written rather than oral pleadings. However, the adversarial skills of the common lawyers are beginning to make an impact on the Court.

The judges produce a single judgment, formally and briefly expressed. There is no dissenting judgment, the nearest equivalent being the advocate-general's opinion where this has not been followed. Decisions of the ECJ are not subject to review. However, the Court does hear appeals from the new Court of First Instance: see 26 below.

24. The role of the Court of Justice

As the EC Treaty is a framework treaty, substance had to be given to its provisions by the ECJ. In its early years the Court adopted a dynamic approach to the integration of EC law into the legal systems of the member states, making full use of the Article 177 procedure for hearing preliminary references from the national courts: see 24. The European vision of the Court is clearly shown in such bold decisions as *Van Gend en Loos* (Case 26/62) in which the Court declared that '. . . The Community has created a new legal order in international law': see 5. While recent decisions such as *Marshall* v. *Southampton and South West Area Health Authority* (Case 152/84) show an apparently more conservative attitude, landmark decisions are still being made (see, for example, *Barber* v. *Guardian Royal Exchange Assurance Group* (Case 262/88)).

25. Procedures in the Court of Justice

Procedures in the Court are examined in more detail in Chapters 7–10. The Article 177 preliminary reference has been the most widely used procedure. However, the procedures under Articles 169 and 173 should also be noted. Under Article 169 proceedings may be brought by the Commission in the Court against a member state in breach of its obligations under the Treaty. Article 173 provides for the review of the legality of acts of the Council and the Commission other than recommendations or opinions.

26. The Court of First Instance (CFI)

The SEA provided for the creation of a new Court of First Instance to ease the workload of the Court of Justice: Article 168 EC. The CFI began sitting in September 1989, its jurisdiction limited to disputes between the EC and its staff

('staff cases'), competition and anti-dumping cases and certain matters relating to the ECSC and Euratom. Article 177 references are specifically excluded from its remit. Since 1993 (Decision 93/350) the CFI hears all cases brought by natural or legal persons, but not actions brought by the EC institutions or the member states. There is a right of appeal to the ECJ which may, if the appeal is allowed, give the final judgment itself or send the case back to the CFI.

27. Other bodies

(a) *The Economic and Social Committees (ESC).* The ESC plays a consultative role within the decision-making process of the EC and Euratom. The ECSC has an equivalent body called the Consultative Committee of the ECSC. Its 189 members who are appointed by the Council consist of representatives of groups such as farmers, trade unionists, producers and the general public. Consultation, where provided in the Treaty, is an absolute procedural requirement. The ESC gives its opinion by an absolute majority of members. The Committee may also be consulted by the Council and the Commission wherever they consider it appropriate and may advise the Council and Commission on its own initiative.

(b) *The Court of Auditors.* The Court of Auditors was set up in 1975 under the Budgetary Powers Treaty to control and supervise the implementation of the Budget. It became a full institution under the TEU.

Plate 3 The European Court of Justice

(c) *The European Central Bank (ECB).* Provision for the ECB to act as the Central Bank of the EU was made in a Protocol to the TEU: *see* Chapter 17. The ECB will act within the European System of Central Banks (ECSB) and will have responsibility for monetary policy within the EU. The ECB will be the only body entitled to issue ECU banknotes. It will be able to adopt regulations on monetary policy, take decisions, make recommendations and deliver opinions.

> *Note*: During the second (present) stage of EMU monetary policy will be under the control of the *Economic and Monetary Institute (EMI)*, based in Frankfurt. The EMI will be liquidated and its functions taken over by the ECB at the beginning of the third stage.

(d) *The Committee of the Regions.* The Committee of the Regions was set up in 1994 as an advisory committee by the TEU under Articles 189a–c EC. Its membership of 222 representatives is drawn from local and regional bodies (i.e. organisations, but not local or national governments). The function of the Committee is to provide an opinion in matters of particular concern to regions within the EU.

The Committee must be informed whenever an opinion is sought from the ESC. Consultation with the Committee is required under Articles 126 to 130b in matters of education, vocational training and youth, culture, public health, trans-European networks and social cohesion.

Progress test 2

1. What are the powers of the European Parliament in relation to the budget?

2. What are the powers of the Parliament over the Commission?

3. What is the 'democratic deficit' and to what extent is it remedied by the TEU?

4. What are the Luxembourg Accords? What status do the Accords have today?

5. Identify the main functions of the Commission.

6. What is the system known as 'Comitology' and how does it work?

7. What are the qualifications for appointment as a judge or advocate general in the ECJ?

8. What are the main differences in procedure between the ECJ and a court in the United Kingdom?

9. How has the Court of Justice made use of the Article 177 procedure to develop its jurisprudence?

10. What are the functions of the Court of First Instance?

3

THE SOURCES OF COMMUNITY LAW

1. Introduction

The sources of EC law are:

(a) The treaties creating the institutions

(b) Subsidiary treaties

(c) Secondary legislation

(d) The decisions, opinions and general principles of the ECJ.

THE TREATIES

2. The treaties creating the institutions

The European Community Treaty (EC Treaty) is a treaty of consolidation. It incorporates from 1993 the amendments in the Treaty on European Union (TEU) to the treaties creating the institutions listed below:

(a) ECSC Treaty 1951

(b) EEC Treaty 1957

(c) Euratom Treaty 1957

(d) Convention on Certain Institutions Common to the European Communities 1957

(e) Merger Treaty 1965

(f) Acts of Accession of 1972 (UK, Ireland, Denmark), 1979 (Greece), 1985 (Spain and Portugal) and 1994 (Austria, Finland and Sweden).

(g) Budgetary Treaties of 1970 and 1975

(h) Single European Act 1986.

(i) Treaty on European Union 1992 (the Maastricht Treaty).

These constitutive treaties have provided the legal framework of the Community as primary sources of EC law taking priority over conflicting legal obligations contained in subsidiary treaties or in secondary legislation, although this is not stated in the treaties themselves.

3. Subsidiary treaties

Subsidiary treaties (or conventions) form 'an integral part of Community law': *Haegeman* v. *Belgium* (Case 181/73). Such agreements may be concluded by the EC exclusively under powers conferred by the EEC Treaty (e.g. commercial agreements under Article 113), by the EC on succession to an earlier agreement (e.g. the General Agreement on Tariffs and Trade 1947, or GATT) or by individual member states under Article 220 (e.g. the Convention on Jurisdiction and Enforcement of Judgments in Civil and Commercial Matters 1968). The last category involving agreement between individual member states and non-EC members has only rarely been regarded as a source of EC law by the ECJ.

Note: the treaty-making powers of the EC are briefly outlined at the end of this chapter.

ACTS OF THE INSTITUTIONS

4. Legislative powers of the Council and the Commission

The Council and the Commission are empowered under Article 189: 'In order to carry out their task . . . in accordance with the provisions of this Treaty [to] make regulations, issue directives, take decisions, make recommendations or deliver opinions'. The measures, known as 'acts', are defined in Article 189:

A regulation shall have general application. It shall be binding in its entirety and directly applicable in all member states. A directive shall be binding, as to the result to be achieved, upon each member state to which it is addressed, but shall leave to the national authorities the choice of form and methods. A decision shall be binding in its entirety upon those to whom it is addressed. Recommendations and opinions shall have no binding force.

5. Regulations

A regulation sets out general rules which apply uniformly throughout the EC. As it is binding and directly applicable, it takes effect without further enactment and may be relied upon by individuals before the national courts: *see* Part Four.

6. Directives

A directive is binding 'as to the result to be achieved, upon each member state to which it is addressed', allowing states a discretion as to the means of implementation, legislation or administrative action. A directive may be addressed to some or all of the member states and is the main measure used in harmonisation, for example, in the 1992 Programme. While it appears to follow that a directive requires implementation to be legally effective, a number of directives have been held by the ECJ to be directly applicable: *see* 6:**15**.

7. Decisions

A decision of the Council or Commission, being an individual act, is addressed to specified persons, either states or individuals. As it is legally binding, it requires no further implementation: *see* 6:**12**.

8. Binding nature of secondary legislation

Only regulations, directives and decisions are legally binding. They must 'state the reasons on which they are based and shall refer to any proposals or opinions which were required to be obtained pursuant to this Treaty': Article 190. These procedural requirements are essential. Failure to comply with them may lead to annulment in the Court under Article 173 or 175: *see* Chapter 8. Recommendations and opinions are not legally binding although they are persuasive. However, they are not devoid of legal significance. In *Grimaldi* v. *Fonds des Maladies Professionelles* (Case C-322/88) the ECJ stated that national judges must consider relevant recommendations in dealing with cases before them particularly where they clarify the interpretation of other provisions of national or EC law.

9. Classification

The classification of acts, however, is not as straightforward as it appears from Article 189. The formal designation of an act as regulation, directive or decision may be misleading. This has led the ECJ to examine the substance of the act rather than its form, concluding on a number of occasions, for example, that where a regulation 'fails to lay down general rules', it may be relabelled a 'disguised decision': *see*, for example, *Confédération Nationale des Productions de Fruits et Légumes* v. *Council* (Cases 16 and 17/62), in which the ECJ held that a 'regulation' which failed to lay down general rules was in fact a 'disguised decision', giving rise to the right to challenge the act under Article 173. A similar conclusion was reached in *International Fruit Co.* v. *Commission* (Cases 41–44/70) in which another 'regulation' was held to be a 'bundle of decisions'.

DECISIONS OF THE ECJ AND CFI

10. The ECJ and CFI

Decisions of the ECJ and CFI are binding. Note also that the general principles and opinions of the ECJ on matters of EC law are also binding, giving the ECJ a unique role in the development of the EC legal system.

THE TREATY-MAKING POWERS OF THE EC

11. Express and implied powers

The EC's treaty-making powers may be divided into two categories: express powers and implied powers. Agreements are negotiated by the Commission and concluded by the Council, normally after consultation with the European Parliament.

(a) *Express powers* The two most clearly defined powers related to:

(i) *Commercial agreements* (Article 113). These powers cover the EC commercial policy as a whole, including tariff and trade agreements, export aids, credit, finance and development policy. As this power is exclusive, member states are no longer competent to conclude such agreements themselves.

(ii) *Association agreements* (Article 238). Association agreements are concluded with third countries either in preparation for full membership or as an alternative to membership.

(b) *Implied powers (the theory of 'parallelism')*. Under this theory the treaty-making or external competence of the EC should reflect its internal jurisdiction. The reasoning behind the theory is that if the EC possesses the powers to legislate internally it should also be competent to enter into international agreements in the same fields.

12. The European Road Transport (ERTA) Case

The theory gained approval in the *ERTA* case (*Commission* v. *Council*, Case 22/70). In 1962 five of the six member states had signed an agreement known as the first ERTA (European Road Transport Agreement) with certain other European states. As the agreement was not ratified by enough of the contracting states the member states began negotiations to conclude a second ERTA. Meanwhile the Council issued a regulation deriving from its internal power covering the same areas. The Commission objected to the Council's decision to allow negotiations to continue and sought to annul the resolution to that effect in the ECJ. The second ERTA was nevertheless concluded in 1970.

The ECJ held that the EC had authority to enter into such an agreement. Authority may arise not only out of express provision in the Treaty but also from other Treaty provisions and from secondary legislation. When the EC had adopted common rules to implement a transport policy in 1960 member states lost their competence to conclude international agreements in this area.

13. General powers under Article 235

The EC can thus be regarded as possessing wide-ranging treaty-making powers. After the *ERTA* decision particular use has been made of the so-called general powers provided by Article 235 which states that if action by the EC should prove necessary to attain, in the course of the operation of the common market, one of the objectives of the EC and that the Treaty has not provided the necessary powers, the Council shall, acting unanimously on a proposal from the Commission and after consulting the European Parliament, take the necessary measures.

14. Legal proceedings under Article 228

Article 228 (6) EC, as amended by the TEU, provides an important procedure under which the Council, the Commission or a member state may obtain an opinion of the ECJ on the compatibility of a proposed agreement with the Treaty. An adverse opinion ensures that the agreement may only come into force in accordance with Article N of the TEU. (This is the procedure for amending the Treaty and requires ratification by all member states.) It should be noted that the European Parliament has no power to request an opinion.

15. The European Economic Area (EEA) Case

The most significant opinion to date under Article 228 has been that relating to the draft agreement on the European Economic Area (EEA). The ECJ objected to the existence and jurisdiction of the proposed EEA Court (Opinion 1/91), holding that the EEA should not be able to determine the respective competences of the EC and the member states, these being matters for the exclusive jurisdiction of the ECJ under Article 219 of the EEC Treaty.

The draft EEA was fundamentally revised to comply with opinion 1/91. The EEA Court was abandoned. Instead it was proposed that the EFTA countries would establish an EFTA Court, operating separately from the ECJ, and an EEA Joint Committee composed of officials from the Commission, EC member states and the EFTA member states. The Joint Committee would review the decisions of the ECJ and the EFTA Court to ensure legal homogeneity throughout the EEA. The ECJ decided in Opinion 1/92 that the revised draft agreement was compatible with EC law provided a binding principle was adopted that decisions of the Joint Committee would not affect the ECJ. The EEA entered into force on 1 January 1994.

Progress test 3

1. What are the constitutive treaties? What is their relationship with subsidiary treaties and with secondary legislation?

2. What is a regulation and to what extent is it legally binding?

3. How does a directive differ from a regulation?

4. Do recommendations and opinions create any legal effects?

5. When is a 'regulation' not a regulation?

6. To what extent does the EC provide for the power to make treaties?

7. What is the significance of the *ERTA* case in relation to the doctrine of parallelism?

8. Explain the importance of the opinion of the ECJ in relation to the draft *EEA* Agreement.

4

GENERAL PRINCIPLES OF LAW

1. 'General principles of law'

The term 'general principles of law' has been liberally construed by the ECJ. While academic writers disagree over whether the expression covers the Treaties and EC secondary legislation there is agreement that it covers the unwritten law of the Community, namely the general principles of international law and the general principles of law common to the member states.

2. Role of the ECJ

The incorporation of general principles of law within the body of EC law is one of the essential features of the jurisprudence of the ECJ, representing a high degree of judicial activism. The ECJ has been encouraged to develop juris-prudence to fill many of the gaps left by the Treaty and by secondary legislation (*see* Steiner p.61):

(a) to interpret EC law (primary and secondary legislation in the EC and national implementation legislation)

(b) by states and individuals, to challenge EC action under Articles 169, 173, 177 or 184, or inaction under Articles 169 or 175

(c) to challenge the action of member states where the action arises out of a right or duty under EC law: *Hubert Wachauf* v. *Bundesamt für Ernährung und Forstwirtschaft* (Case 5/88)

(d) to support an action for damages against the EC under Article 215(2).

3. Legal authority

The legal authority for the incorporation of general principles of law derives from three Articles of the Treaty:

(a) Article 164 (role of the ECJ) provides that the ECJ shall ensure that in the interpretation and application of the Treaty 'the law' is observed. It is generally accepted that the word 'law' has a meaning which goes beyond the law in the Treaty, entitling the ECJ to take account of general principles formulated outside the Treaty.

(b) Article 173 gives the ECJ power to review the legality of acts of the Council and the Commission on grounds which include infringement of the Treaty or of any rule relating to its application.

(c) Article 215 provides that liability of the EC in tort is determined in accordance with the general principles common to the laws of the member states.

SOURCES OF GENERAL PRINCIPLES OF LAW

4. Introduction

General principles of law are found in international law (e.g. the European Convention on Human Rights), in the domestic legal systems of the member states and in the decisions of the ECJ. These three 'sources' are not mutually exclusive. What is regarded as a 'general principle' in the member states may represent a principle of international law, and may, in time, find its way into the jurisdiction of the ECJ.

To be accepted as a general principle by the ECJ the principle in question need not be common to all the member states. It is sufficient if the principle is accepted by the legal systems of most of the member states or conforms with the direction of legal developments in the member states. In the words of Advocate General Lagrange in *Hoogovens* v. *High Authority* (Case 14/61) at pp. 283–4, 'The Court . . . is not content to draw on more or less arithmetical "common denominators" between different national solutions, but chooses from each of the member states those solutions which, having regard to the objects of the Treaty, appear to be the best or . . . the most progressive'.

5. General principles in the legal systems of the member states

General principles are familiar to lawyers in continental legal systems: French administrative law has long been regulated by the general principles of law. In Germany the courts have held the principles of proportionality to underline Articles 2 and 12 of the Basic Law. To the UK lawyer the doctrine of general principles of law at first sight appears unfamiliar. However, the concept of reasonableness, the maxims of equity and the rules of natural justice are of equivalent importance and have influenced the development of general principles in the ECJ.

6. The role of general principles in EC law

General principles may be invoked to interpret EC law. They cannot, however, prevail over the express provision of the Treaty: *Sgarlata* (Case 40/64). The general principles of law have become an independent and important source of law. General principles include:

(a) Fundamental rights

(b) Proportionality

(c) Equality

(d) Legal certainty

(e) Procedural rights.

FUNDAMENTAL RIGHTS

7. Introduction

The development of fundamental rights in EC law owes much to the role of fundamental human rights in the post-war German constitution which empowers the Federal Constitutional Court to determine the constitutionality of legislation. German litigants in their national courts and in the ECJ argued that EC law should comply with the fundamental rights provisions of the constitution. Thus, 'fundamental rights' are not, in themselves, a self-contained legal principle but an approach which reflects other general principles such as proportionality.

8. The first statement on fundamental rights by the ECJ

As a response to the German constitutional arguments, the ECJ formulated its own doctrine of fundamental rights by which it declared that the ECJ would annul any provision of EC law which contravened human rights. This declaration was made in the case of *Stauder* v. *City of Ulm* (Case 29/69), a case which arose out of a Community scheme to provide cheap butter for recipients of welfare benefits. The applicant objected to the requirement to divulge his name and address on a coupon to obtain the butter and challenged the law as a violation of human rights (equality of treatment) in the German courts. A reference was made to the ECJ to determine the validity of the EC decision creating the scheme. The ECJ held that the scheme did not require the applicant's name on the coupon and found nothing in the scheme 'capable of prejudicing the fundamental human rights enshrined in the general principles of Community law and protected by the Court.'

9. Development of fundamental rights

The ECJ refined its approach further in *International Handelsgesellschaft* (Case 11/70), a dispute arising out of the CAP under which exports of certain agricultural products were only permitted if the exporter had first obtained an export licence and paid a deposit. The applicants objected to the forfeiture of their deposit for failure to carry out the export within the period of validity of the licence as contrary to the German constitution, particularly the principle of proportionality.

The ECJ decided that the scheme did not infringe fundamental rights and stated that Community measures may only be judged according to Community criteria and not by national standards, even those relating to fundamental human rights. However, the ECJ also added,

> Respect for fundamental rights forms an integral part of the general principles of law protected by the Court of Justice. The protection of such rights, whilst inspired by the constitutional traditions common to the member states, must be ensured within the framework of the structure and objectives of the Community.

10. Fundamental rights and general principles

The scope of fundamental rights was extended further in *J. Nold v. Commission* (Case 4/73). The applicant, a coal wholesale company in Germany, challenged a Commission decision under the ECSC Treaty on the ground that it violated the company's fundamental human rights (the right to the free pursuit of economic activity and property rights). While the ECJ considered that there was no breach of fundamental rights on the facts which concerned 'mere commercial interests or opportunities', it reiterated the principle that fundamental principles form an integral part of the general principles of law and continued:

> In safeguarding these rights, the Court is bound to draw inspiration from constitutional traditions common to the member states, and it cannot therefore uphold measures which are incompatible with fundamental rights recognised and protected by the constitutions of those states.
>
> Similarly, international treaties for the protection of human rights on which the member states have collaborated or of which they are signatories, can supply guidelines which should be followed within the framework of Community law.

It is clear from this statement that EC measures conflicting with fundamental rights enshrined in national constitutions may be annulled. Further, the ECJ is emphasising the importance of international law as a source of law.

11. International treaties

The European Convention on Human Rights 1953 (ECHR) is the most significant international treaty protecting human rights. All the EC member states are signatories although they differ in the degree of recognition accorded to the Convention in their own legal systems. The institutions of the EC issued a Joint Declaration in 1977 affirming their adherence to the principles of the ECHR. The ECJ has referred to the Convention on several occasions.

Examples
(1) *Rutili* (Case 36/75): restrictions which may be placed on human rights.
(2) *Hauer* v. *Rheinland-Pfalz* (Case 44/79): First Protocol, right to property.
(3) *National Panasonic* v. *Commission* (Case 136/79): Article 8, respect for home and correspondence.
(4) *R.* v. *Kirk* (Case 63/83): Article 7, non-retroactivity of penal provisions.

Article F of the TEU commits the EU to respecting fundamental rights as provided by the ECHR 'as they result from the traditions common to the member states'. This Article is unlikely to be justiciable before the ECJ and thus fails to provide a clear legal basis for the protection of human rights. (*See* Shaw p. 110.)

PROPORTIONALITY

12. The principle of proportionality

The principle of proportionality is one of the most important of the general principles recognised by EC law. It is derived from German law where it is regarded as one of the rights underlying the constitution: *International Handelsgesellschaft: see* above. The principle of proportionality is applied to administrative law. It operates as a constraint on public authorities which may not impose obligations beyond those which are appropriate and necessary to achieve the objective of the measure. This principle implies a clear relationship between the means and the ends of legislation: the means must be reasonably likely to achieve the objective and the advantage to the public must be greater than the disadvantage. The principle of proportionality is similar to the concept of reasonableness but involves more stringent criteria than the English concept. The ECJ has on occasion referred specifically to reasonableness: in *Chasse* (Case 15/57) the ECJ held that the High Authority must not exceed what is reasonable and must avoid, as far as possible, causing harm.

The principle of proportionality has been invoked frequently before the ECJ, particularly under Article 173 under which an administrative act may be annulled.

Example

An export company paid the Intervention Board for Agricultural Produce a deposit of £1,670,000 to support its application for an export licence. When the application was submitted to the Commission four hours late, the Commission ruled that the entire deposit was forfeit, as it was required to do under EC regulation. The ECJ, on an Article 177 reference from the English court, ruled that forfeiture of the entire deposit for a trivial breach of the deadline was a disproportionate act (*R. v. Intervention Board for Agricultural Produce, ex parte Man (Sugar)* (Case 181/84)).

13. The internal market

Proportionality has also been applied in relation to the provisions for limitation of the free movement of labour and persons which must be justified under Article 36 or Article 48(3). The ECJ in various cases has held that the measure must not exceed what is necessary to achieve the objective. The proportionality principle invoked in relation to Sunday trading (*Torfaen Borough Council* v. *B&Q* (Case 145/88) – *see* Chapter 5) in which the ECJ held that national measures banning Sunday trading must not exceed what was necessary to achieve the objectives in question.

14. Freedom of commercial activity

The principle of proportionality reflects the broader concept of freedom of commercial activity, a freedom which underlines the EC Treaty and which is protected in the German constitution. Freedom of commercial activity is a wide-ranging freedom which encompasses not only the principle of proportionality but also the freedom to pursue a trade or profession, the freedom from unfair competition and a general freedom to act where no legal prohibition applies.

All four principles were unsuccessfully invoked in *Walter Rau* v. *BALM* (Cases 133–136/85) and *ALBAKO* v. *BALM* (Case 249/85) in a dispute arising out of a Commission scheme in 1985 to increase butter consumption. Under the scheme the inhabitants of West Berlin were offered two blocks of butter for the price of one. Rau, an aggrieved margarine manufacturer, challenged the Commission decision before the ECJ under Article 173 and brought parallel proceedings in the German courts against BALM. The ECJ held that none of the four principles had been infringed, upholding its own earlier decisions on a cheap 'Christmas butter' scheme also involving Walter Rau (Cases 279, 280, 285 and 286/64).

EQUALITY

15. Introduction

The principle of equality implies that persons in similar situations should be treated in the same way unless there is objective justification for different treatment. The EC Treaty prohibits discrimination on grounds of:

(a) Nationality: Article 6 EC, Article 7 EEC

(b) Sex, in the context of equal pay for men and women: Article 119

(c) Against producers or consumers under the CAP: Article 40(3).

The ECJ has gone further than the Treaty and held that EC law recognises a general principle of non-discrimination. In a number of cases the ECJ has upheld the principle of equality (or non-discrimination), e.g. *Royal Scholten-Honig* (*'Isoglucose'*) (Cases 103 and 145/77) in which it held that the production levy system for Isoglucose 'will offend against the general principle of equality of which the prohibition on discrimination set out in Article 40(3) . . . is a specific expression.' In *Frilli* (Case 1/72) the ECJ held that equality of treatment is one of the fundamental principles of EC law.

Examples
    (1) A female official at the European Parliament was denied an allowance because she was not the 'head of the family'. Under the relevant provision of EC law it was only possible for a woman to be defined as a 'head of the family' in exceptional circumstance such as incapacity of the husband through illness. HELD: The provision was discriminatory and could not be upheld: *Sabbatini* v. *European Parliament* (Case 20/71).

    (2) A female EC official lost her expatriation allowance on marriage to an Italian under an EC rule which did not permit payment of the allowance to an official who acquired the nationality of the country in which she worked. (Foreign women marrying Italian men automatically acquired

Italian nationality on marriage although foreign men marrying Italian women did not.) HELD (ECJ): EC law may not take account of nationality which has been involuntarily acquired under a discriminatory national law: *Airola* v. *Commission* (Case 21/74).

(3) A Jewish woman sought annulment of a Council decision to hold a competitive examination for a post as an EC official on a Jewish festival. The applicant had not mentioned her religion on the application form and there was no specific evidence of religious discrimination. The Council accepted that freedom of religion was a general principle of EC law but argued that it was not in breach. HELD (ECJ): The appointing authority was not obliged to avoid holding the examination on a religious holiday since it had not been informed of the fact in advance. Where advance information is given, the appointing authority should try to avoid such dates: *Prais* v. *Council* (Case 130/75).

LEGAL CERTAINTY

16. Principle of legal certainty

Legal certainty is a wide-ranging and important principle underlying EC law and the legal systems of many of the member states. The concept can be sub-divided into two specific principles: non-retroactivity and legitimate expectations.

17. Retroactivity

Two rules govern the principle of non-retroactivity in EC law:

(a) In the absence of clear evidence to the contrary, there is a rule of interpretation that legislation is presumed not to be retroactive. The principle prevents EC secondary legislation from taking effect before publication.

In *Société pour l'Exportation des Sucres* v. *Commission* (Case 88/76) the Commission had passed a regulation on 30 June 1976 removing the right of exporters to cancel their export licences. The regulation was dated 1 July, the expected date of publication of the *Official Journal*. Owing to a strike the *Journal* did not appear until 2 July. The applicant applied for cancellation on 1 July but was refused on the basis of the regulation. The ECJ ruled that the regulation did not come into force until 2 July, the date of actual publication.

(b) Under substantive EC law, retroactivity is prohibited unless the measure could not otherwise be achieved, provided there is respect for legitimate expectations.

Examples
(1) A regulation establishing a system of levies and quotas for the production of isoglucose had been annulled for non-consultation with the European Parliament. Following the correct consultation procedure a further regulation was issued retrospectively regulating isoglucose. The ECJ upheld

the regulation on the basis that isoglucose producers should reasonably have expected the measure (*Société pour l'Exportation des Sucres* v. *Commission* (Case 88/76)).

(2) The captain of a Danish fishing vessel was charged with fishing in British waters. An EC regulation prohibiting such fishing was subsequently enacted. HELD (ECJ): Penal measures are presumed not to be applied retrospectively. The charge could not be upheld: *R.* v. *Kirk* (Case 63/83).

Note: In some cases the ECJ has limited the temporal effect of its own judgments: *see Defrenne* v. *Sabena (No. 2)* (Case 43/75), in which the ECJ ruled that considerations of legal certainty required that claims based on Article 119 could only be brought from the date of the judgment unless proceedings had already commenced. The *Defrenne* approach was reserved for exceptional cases where the ECJ introduced a new principle or when the judgment might cause serious difficulties in relation to past events, e.g. *Barber* v. *Guardian Royal Exchange* (Case C-262/88) (*see* Chapter 25).

18. Legitimate expectations

The principle of legitimate expectations (originally translated into English as 'protection of legitimate confidence') is another concept originating in German law. Under the principle EC measures must not violate the legitimate expectations of those concerned, in the absence of overriding public interest. The principle may be invoked as a rule of interpretation: *Deuka* v. *EVGE* (Case 78/74), and as the basis for an action in tort for damages: *CNTA* v. *Commission* (Case 74/74) (*see* chapter 9), and as a basis for annulment of an EC measure: *Töpfer* v. *Commission* (Case 112/77).

In *BASF AG and others* v. *Commission* (Cases T-79 etc./89) the ECJ has recently upheld a decision of the CFI in which legal certainty had been invoked as a reason to annul a Commission measure. The Commission had failed to create an authenticated version of the measure in contravention of its own procedural rules.

Notes: (1) An expectation will only be legitimate if it is reasonable, i.e. within the contemplation of a prudent person acting within the course of business. It does not cover speculative profiteering: *EVGF* v. *Mackprang* (Case 2/75). In this case a German grain dealer was prevented by a Commission decision from taking advantage of a fall in the value of the French franc which had made it profitable to buy grain in France and resell it to EVGF, the German grain intervention agency. Mackprang brought proceedings against EVGF in the German courts, claiming that he had a legitimate expectation of being able to sell the grain to the agency. The ECJ ruled in an Article 177 reference that the Commission decision did not infringe the principle of legitimate expectations but was a justified precaution against speculative activities. (*See also: Pardini* v. *Ministero con l'Estero* (Case 338/85).)

(2) A legitimate expectation does not arise from:

(a) incorrect acceptance by an official of a defective document: *Van Gend en Loos NV and Expeditieditiebedriff Wim Bosman BV* v. *Commission* (Joined Cases 98/83 and 230/83)

(b) incorrect calculation by an EC institution of a trader's previous profit: *Töpfer* v. *Commission* (Case 112/77).

It may be seen from the examples above that few cases claiming legitimate expectations have been successful.

PROCEDURAL RIGHTS

19. Procedural rights and EC law

Procedural rights in EC law are usually specifically provided in the relevant secondary legislation. Where they are not provided, the person affected may rely on general principles in the following areas:

(a) *The right to a hearing.* The right to a hearing derives from the English principle of natural justice. It was first raised in the ECJ in *Transocean Marine Paint Association* v. *Commission* (Case 17/74), a competition case under Article 85. The Commission had addressed a decision to the applicants without referring to a condition which was later applied. The applicants sought annulment of the decision as far as it related to this condition. Following Advocate-General Warner's submissions the ECJ held that there is a general principle of EC law that a person whose interests are perceptibly affected by a decision taken by a public authority must be given the opportunity to make his views known. As this had not been done, the condition was annulled. The decision was followed by the ECJ in *Dow Benelux* v. *Commission* (Case 85/87); *see also Al-Jubail Fertilizer* v. *Council* (Case C-49/88). The ECJ annulled a regulation imposing anti-dumping duty on certain products made in Libya and Saudi Arabia after a complaint by the applicants, Saudi Arabian manufacturers, that they had been denied a fair hearing.

(b) *The duty to give reasons.* The duty to give reasons was established in *Union Nationale des Entraîneurs et Cadres Techniques Professionels du Football (UNECTEF)* v. *Heylens* (Case 222/86). M. Heylens was a Belgian national, holding a Belgian football trainers' diploma. His application to the French authorities for recognition of the diploma was refused without any reason for the decision. M. Heylens was charged with practising in France as a football trainer without the necessary French diploma (or recognised equivalent). On an Article 177 reference the ECJ held that the right of free movement under Article 48 requires that there should be legal redress from a decision affecting access to employment and that reasons for the decision should be given.

(c) *The right to due process.* The right to due process is a corollary to the right to be supplied with the reasons for a decision. It was upheld in *Johnston* v. *Chief Constable of the Royal Ulster Constabulary* (Case 222/84), an Article 177 reference arising out of a refusal by the RUC to renew contracts of women members of the RUC Reserve (*see* Steiner p. 63). A decision had been taken that full-time Reserve members were to be fully armed. Women were neither issued with firearms nor trained to use them. Mrs Johnston, a full-time member, claimed that the measure contravened Directive 76/207 providing equal treatment for men and women in employment. The Secretary of State for Northern Ireland issued Mrs Johnston with a certificate stating that the purpose of the refusal was to safeguard national security and public order, 'conclusive evidence' of purpose under Article 53(2) of the Sex Discrimination (Northern Ireland) Order.

The ECJ stated that Article 6 of Directive 76/207 requiring member states to pursue their claims by judicial process after recourse to the competent authorities reflected a general principle laid down in Articles 6 and 13 of the ECHR. Further, member states must ensure effective judicial control of directly applicable EC law and national implementing legislation. The ECJ held that national legislation stating that a compliance certificate was conclusive deprived the individual of access to the courts to assert his rights under EC law, contrary to Article 6 of the Directive.

Thus, the ECJ in *Johnston* appears to have recognised the principle that the individual is entitled to effective judicial control of rights protected under EC law.

20. Other general principles

A number of other general principles have been identified by the ECJ including the right to be assisted by counsel: *Demont* (Case 115/80); confidentiality of communication between lawyer and client: *AM&S* (Case 155/79); and the right to exercise a profession: *Keller* (Case 234/85).

SUBSIDIARITY

21. Introduction

The principle of subsidiarity derives from theological and natural law traditions. It has not developed though the case law of the ECJ, but was inserted into the EC Treaty by the TEU. Subsidiarity is likely to prove of the utmost importance in the future as the responsibilities of the EC and the member states are resolved.

22. Subsidiarity under the EC Treaty

Article 3b of the EC Treaty states that 'the Community shall act within the limits of the powers conferred upon it by this Treaty and of the objectives assigned to it therein'. In the second paragraph it provides that:

> In areas which do not fall within its exclusive competence, the Community shall take action, in accordance with the principle of subsidiarity, only if and in so far as the objectives of the proposed action cannot be sufficiently achieved by the member states and can therefore, by reason of the scale or effects of the proposed action, be better achieved by the Community.

23. The Edinburgh Summit and the Commission guidelines

At the Edinburgh Summit in December 1992 the heads of state agreed on procedures and criteria for applying the subsidiarity principle. In 1993 the Commission produced guidelines from which it is clear that the principle does not apply to matters within the exclusive jurisdiction of the EC. (For a clear summary, *see* Weatherill and Beaumont pp. 778–82.) To decide whether action can be better achieved by the member states or by the EC the following considerations are set out in the guidelines:

(*i*) whether the issues in question have transnational aspects which cannot be satisfactorily regulated by the member states; and/or

(*ii*) whether actions by member states alone would conflict with the requirements of the Treaty; and/or

(*iii*) whether the Council is satisfied that action at EC level would produce clear benefits by reason of scale or effects compared with action at the level of member states.

Paragraph 3 of Article 3b states that 'Any action by the Community shall not go beyond what is necessary to achieve the objectives of the Treaty'. The Commission accepts that Article 3b represents a version of the principle of proportionality: *see* **12** above. The guidelines also make it clear that directives are to be preferred to regulations and framework directives to detailed directives.

24. Application of subsidiarity to legislation

The Council will examine every Commission proposal for compliance with the principle of subsidiarity. The Commission is required to submit an annual report on the application of the principle to the European Council and the European Parliament. The first full report was presented in December 1993. In it the Commission gave three undertakings:

(*i*) that a justification would be included in all new legislative proposals (this led to a reduction in new proposals in 1993);

(*ii*) that it would withdraw or revise certain pending proposals (15 proposals were withdrawn in 1993); and

(*iii*) that it would review existing legislation. This is the biggest task. Priority will be given to the review of old legislation. Legislation to be revised will be recast (i.e. modernised and reordered), simplified or repealed.

(a) *Rules and regulations to be recast.* These include many regulations and directives relating to customs (to be recast into two regulations), 11 directives and regulations on the right of residence (not in fact recast by the end of 1994) and a gradual recasting of measures on competition and state aids.

(b) *Rules and regulations to be simplified.* These include directives on technical standards, a possible framework directive on foodstuffs, the directives on mutual recognition of qualifications (to be gradually phased out), the environment, free movement of workers, VAT (by 1995) and consumer protection.

(c) *Rules and regulations to be repealed.* This category overlaps with the other two, as recasting and simplification will usually involve some repeal. In addition, measures on the right of establishment and the freedom to supply services will be repealed.

25. Can subsidiarity be invoked before the ECJ?

It remains to be seen whether subsidiarity is justiciable before the ECJ. The formulation of the principle is vague. Doubts have been expressed by academic writers and by a former judge at the ECJ, Lord Slynn (in *Introducing a New Legal*

Order at pages 25–26). It should, at least, be possible to invoke the principle as an aid to interpretation in the ECJ and the national courts. (*See* Wyatt and Dashwood pp. 658–59.)

Progress test 4

1. What is the legal basis for the incorporation of general principles of law?

2. Which general principles may be accepted as sources of EC law?

3. How did the doctrine of fundamental rights develop in German law and how has it been utilised in EC law?

4. Compare and contrast the principles of proportionality and reasonableness.

5. How has the ECJ used the principle of equality to extend the scope of the prohibition on non-discrimination under the EEC treaty?

6. What are the effects of the principle of non-retroactivity of EC law?

7. In which circumstances may the principle of legitimate expectations be invoked?

8. How has English law affected the development of procedural rights in EC law?

9. What is the significance of the principle of subsidiarity and what is its likely effect on EC legislation?

5

THE SUPREMACY OF COMMUNITY LAW

1. Introduction

The direction of European integration is a controversial issue for the European Union. Member states continue to debate whether the EU should proceed to federation with a centralised decision-making structure, a prospect not supported by the UK. The EC, the first pillar of the Union subject to regulation by the Treaty, has been evolving rapidly to suit the changing expectations of an ever-expanding membership. In recent years the debate has moved to the question of subsidiarity, now recognised in Article 3b of the EC Treaty: *see* 4:21–25. The supremacy of EC law over national law is an essential element in the EC legal order. Supremacy is not provided by the Treaty. The ECJ has been responsible for the development of the 'new legal order' based on supremacy and direct effect (*see* Chapter 6). In the seminal decision of *Costa* v. *ENEL* (Case 6/64) the ECJ stated that the precedence of EC law is confirmed by Article 189 which would be 'quite meaningless if a state could unilaterally nullify its effects by means of a legislative measure which could prevail over Community law'.

2. Incorporation of treaties

In terms of traditional international law the EC Treaty (and before it the founding treaties) are international agreements entered into by sovereign states. The EEC/EC Treaty does not provide for the supremacy of EC law over national law although some support is provided by Article 5 (known both as the principle of solidarity and of effectiveness).

In the event of a clash between EC and national law it is necessary to examine the method of incorporation of the Treaty into the legal system in question. There are two main approaches:

(a) *The monist approach*: the international treaty takes effect in the domestic legal system soon as the treaty is ratified (as e.g. in France and the Netherlands).

(b) *The dualist approach*: the international obligation does not take effect in the domestic legal system until incorporation by statute (as e.g. in Germany, Italy, Belgium and the UK which incorporated the EEC Treaty through the European Communities Act 1972). It may also be necessary to refer to the constitution (if written) and to the practice of the courts. Although the French constitution provides that treaties or agreements which have been ratified have authority superior to any national law the Conseil d'Etat only moved towards acceptance of this position in 1989.

THE ROLE OF THE COURT OF JUSTICE

3. The need for a uniform approach

To avoid disparities arising out of different national approaches to the incorporation of EC law and to ensure uniformity in its application, the Court of Justice has developed its own jurisprudence on the supremacy of EC law. The first statement of the Court on this issue was made in the *Van Gend en Loos* decision (Case 26/62): *see* 6:5. Other important decisions in which the Court has declared the supremacy of Community law over national law include *Costa v. ENEL* (Case 6/64), *International Handelsgesellschaft GmbH* (Case 11/70), *Simmenthal Spa No. 2* (Case 106/77) and *Factortame* (Case C-213/89): *see* below, all decided under the Article 177 procedure. The principle of supremacy was clearly stated in these decisions and has since been reiterated by the Court on a number of occasions, for example in relation to the Sunday trading cases: *see* below. The decisions in *Marleasing* (Case C-106/89) on the interpretation of indirectly effective EC law and in *Francovich* (Cases 6, 9/90) on state liability are also significant: *see* Chapter 6.

4. A new legal order

In the *Van Gend en Loos* case involving a clash between Article 12 of the Treaty and a prior Dutch law the Court held that Article 12 was directly effective. The real significance of the case, however, lies in the general words of the Court about the nature of Community law:

> . . . The Community constitutes a new legal order in international law, for whose benefits the States have limited their sovereign rights, albeit within limited fields.

5. Limitation of sovereign rights

In *Costa* v. *ENEL* (Case 6/64) the ECJ developed its reasoning in *Van Gend en Loos* on the limitation of sovereign rights. Mr Costa was a shareholder in the Italian electricity company which had been nationalised by a statute passed after the Italian Ratification Act incorporating EC law into Italian law. He refused to pay his electricity bill, claiming that the nationalising statute contravened various provisions of the EEC Treaty. The Italian court referred the question of priority to the Court of Justice. The Court held that the reception of Community law into the legal system of the member states made it impossible for the member state to give priority to a unilateral, subsequent national measure over EC law. The Court further stated that:

The transfer, by member states, from their national orders in favour of the Community order of the rights and obligations arising from the Treaty, carries with it a clear limitation of their sovereign right upon which a subsequent unilateral law, incompatible with the aims of the Community, cannot prevail.

6. EC law may not be invalidated by national law

The dispute in *International Handelsgesellschaft* v. *EVGF* (Case 11/70) arose out of an apparent clash between a requirement under the CAP for an export licence and German fundamental rights. The applicant sought annullment of the regulation in the German court, claiming that the German constitution which enshrines fundamental rights took precedence over EC law. In an Article 177 ruling the EC rejected this claim holding:

> Recourse to the legal rules or concepts of national law in order to judge the validity of measures adopted by the institutions … would have an adverse effect on the uniformity and efficacy of Community law. The validity of such measures can only be judged in the light of Community law.

7. Conflicting national legislation should not be applied

Simmenthal Spa (No. 2) (Case 106/77) involved a conflict between an Italian statute passed after the Ratification Act and Article 30 of the EEC Treaty on the free movement of goods. The Italian judge referred a question to the Court of Justice to see whether he should wait for the Italian constitutional court to declare the measure void (as it had declared it would do if the Italian law conflicted with EC law) or give immediate priority to EC law. The ECJ replied that a national court in such circumstances must refrain from applying the conflicting national legislation even if adopted subsequently and should not wait for the decision of a higher court before action.

8. National statutes may be set aside

In the leading case of great importance *R* v. *Secretary of State for Transport, ex parte Factortame (No. 2)* (Case C-213/89R) the ECJ followed *Simmenthal* and allowed an action for interim relief even though it meant setting aside a national statute (in this case a UK Act of Parliament), holding:

> The full effectiveness of Community law would be . . . impaired if a rule of national law could prevent a court seised of a dispute governed by Community law from granting interim relief in order to ensure the full effectiveness of the judgment to be given on the existence of those rights claimed under Community law. It follows that a court which in those circumstances would grant interim relief were it not for a rule of national law, is obliged to set aside that rule.

9. Interpretation of national law

The problems posed by supremacy may, in some circumstances, be avoided by recourse to the principle in *Marleasing*, extending the principle in the *Von Colson* decision (see 6:**18–20**). *Marleasing* requires national courts to interpret national legislation so as to comply with EC obligations whether the national law is passed before or after the relevant EC law. This obligation may not be applied retrospectively to penalise individuals: *Kolpinghuis Nijmegen* (Case 80/86).

10. Interpretation of differing language versions of EC measures

The need for a uniform interpretation of EC law is increased by the multiplicity of official languages in the Court. In *Milk Marketing Board of England and Wales* v. *Cricket St Thomas Estate* (Case C-372/88) (compensatory milk payments by producers to the Milk Marketing Board) the ECJ stated that the English language version of the Regulation in dispute could not provide the sole basis for interpretation, nor could it override the other language versions. Where there is a difference between the various language versions the provision must be interpreted by reference to the purpose and general scheme of the rules of which it forms a part.

11. The *Francovich* principle

The principle in the *Francovich* decision, discussed fully in Chapter 6, sets out the circumstances in which a state may be liable to its citizens in damages for breach of EC law. The decision has its origins in the supremacy of EC law over national law and reminds member states of the financial implications of failing to fulfil their obligations under EC law. It also makes it clear that liability may be applied where the EC law in question is not directly effective provided the three conditions set out in the decision are satisfied.

EC LAW IN THE UNITED KINGDOM – THE EUROPEAN COMMUNITIES ACT 1972

12. Introduction

The European Communities Act 1972 (ECA) was enacted to give effect to UK obligations under the EEC Treaty and came into force on 1 January 1973.

13. Direct applicability

Section 2(1) ECA provides for the direct applicability of EC law in the UK:

> All such rights, powers, liabilities, obligations and restrictions from time to time created or arising by or under the Treaties, as in accordance with the Treaties, are without further enactment to be given legal effect or used in the United Kingdom and shall be recognised and available in law, and be enforced, allowed and followed accordingly, and the expression 'enforceable Community right' and similar expressions shall be read as referring to one to which this subsection applies.

14. Indirect applicability

Section 2(2) ECA provides for the implementation of EC obligations which are not directly applicable by means of secondary legislation, subject to the provisos of Schedule 2.

15. Supremacy or rule of construction?

Section 2(4) ECA deals with the relationship between EC law and national law without expressly providing for the supremacy of EC law over national law. As a result there is doubt about whether s. 2(4) gives priority to EC law or is merely a rule of construction. (*See* Steiner pp. 54–57.) Section 2(4) states:

> any enactment passed or to be passed . . . shall be construed and have effect subject to the foregoing provisions of this section.

The UK Courts tend to favour the 'rule of construction' approach: *see* below.

16. Validity, meaning or effect

Section 3(1) ECA provides that any question about the validity, meaning or effect of any Community instrument shall be treated as a question of law and, if not referred to the Court of Justice, shall be determined according to the principles and decisions of the Court.

17. Uncertainty

Early decisions of the UK courts show uncertainty in the UK about the status of EC law: see e.g. *Bulmer* v. *Bollinger* (1974 CA). Despite a growing willingness to accept the supremacy of EC law the House of Lords in *Duke* v. *Reliance Systems Ltd* (1988 HL) refused to interpret part of the Sex Discrimination Act 1975 so as to give effect to the Equal Treatment Directive 76/207 because the statute predated the directive. Such an approach should no longer be followed after the *Marleasing* decision and the ruling of the House of Lords in *Factortame*: *see* **18** below.

18. The approach of the House of Lords

The 'rule of construction approach' to s. 2(4) was adopted by the House of Lords in *Garland* v. *British Rail Engineering Ltd*, another case involving a clash between the Equal Pay Act 1970 and Article 119, this time over the exemption of death and retirement from the equal pay provision under s. 6(4) of the Act. The House of Lords held that s. 6(4) must be construed so as to conform with Article 119.

The House of Lords went even further in this approach in *Pickstone* v. *Freemans plc* (1988), interpreting regulations amending the Equal Pay Act 1970 against their literal meaning to comply with EC law. Such national legislation must be interpreted 'purposively' to give effect to the broad intentions of Parliament: *see also* Litster v. *Forth Dry Dock Co.* (1989).

Thus, it appears that the House of Lords favours a liberal approach to s. 2(4) as a 'rule of construction' provided the UK legislation clearly intends to comply with EC law. Otherwise, in the unlikely event of the UK Parliament deliberately enacting legislation which contravenes EC law, the House of Lords would be likely to follow the national legislation. While this possibility is at present merely theoretical, such an approach cannot be consistent with the principle of direct effect.

Where the EC legislation in question is not directly effective the House of Lords has indicated in the *Litster* v. *Forth Dry Dock Engineering Co. Ltd* (1989) that the *Von Colson* compromise should be adopted: *see* 4:7. By this means, UK courts may accord 'priority' to EC law where it conflicts with UK law by interpreting the UK law 'purposively' to comply with the spirit and purpose of the relevant EC law. Since the House of Lords did not refer to the decision in *Duke* v. *Reliance Systems Ltd* the current approach of the House of Lords must be that expressed in *Pickstone* and *Litster*. Such an approach is consistent with s. 3(1) of the ECA which states that legal proceedings concerning the meaning of the Treaties and secondary legislation shall be treated as a question of law for determination by the Court of Justice or by other courts in accordance with the principles laid down by the Court (in cases such as *Costa* v. *ENEL* (Case 6/64). See also the ruling of Lord Bridge in *Factortame*: *see* above.

Lord Bridge in applying the *Factortame* ruling in the House of Lords stated unequivocally that, under the terms of the ECA 1972, 'It has always been clear that it was the duty of a United Kingdom court, when delivering final judgment, to override any rule of national law found to be in conflict with any directly enforceable rule of Community law.' After *Francovich* this recognition will need to extend more widely to cover EC law which is not directly effective: *see* 11 above.

19. Recent landmark decisions arising from the UK courts

(a) *'Quota hopping' and the Spanish fisheries cases*. The dispute in *R.* v. *Secretary of State for Transport, ex parte Factortame* (Case C-213/89) (and others on similar facts: *see R.* v. *Ministry of Agriculture, Fisheries and Food, ex parte Agegate Ltd* (Case C-3/87)) arose out of the introduction by the UK government of the Merchant Shipping Act 1988. The statute created stringent new rules against fishing in UK waters by vessels not registered as British. Under the nationality and evidence requirements of the new rules many Spanish vessels previously registered as British failed to qualify for registration and were thus unable to share the UK catch quota. The Queen's Bench Divisional Court referred several questions to the ECJ to enable the UK court to determine the compatibility of the new requirements with EC law. As a reference under Article 177 usually takes about two years and with major commercial interests at stake, the Divisional Court ordered the temporary suspension of the controversial provisions of the Merchant Shipping Act until the ruling was made.

The Court of Appeal, however, quashed the order for the temporary suspension of the legislation. An appeal against the decision was made to the House of Lords which referred further questions to the ECJ, reformulated by the ECJ as an enquiry as to whether a national court may disregard a national rule which precludes it from granting interim relief. The ECJ ruled that a national law should be set aside where it prevents the granting of interim relief in a dispute governed by EC law: *see* 8 above.

This ruling is of major constitutional significance. It means that the UK courts (and those of the other member states) have jurisdiction temporarily to suspend any provisions of national law which may be in breach of EC law. By the time the ruling was received the offending parts of the Merchant Shipping Act had already been suspended as a result of parallel proceedings brought by the Commission against the UK government: *Commission* v. *UK Re Merchant Shipping Rules* (Case 246/89R): *see* Chapter 7. For the decision of the House of Lords applying the ruling of the ECJ: *see R.* v. *Secretary of State for Transport, ex parte Factortame* (1990): *see* **18** above. The ECJ ruled on the substantive issues (on the right of the establishment) under Article 52 of the EEC Treaty in *R.* v. *Secretary of State for Transport ex parte Factortame* (Case C-221/89).

(b) *Sunday trading.* In recent years the lower courts have shown a greater willingness to make Article 177 references to the ECJ, moving away from strict adherence to the guidelines of Lord Denning in *Bulmer* v. *Bollinger: see* Chapter 10.

In *Torfaen Borough Council* v. *B&Q plc* (Case 145/88) the Cwmbran magistrates court referred questions to the ECJ to clarify whether Article 30 of the EEC Treaty permitted national measures (such as s. 47 of the Shops Act 1950) to ban Sunday trading. The Court ruled that Article 30 does not prohibit such a ban provided the legislation in question is not disproportionate to its objectives: *see* Chapter 12.

Acceptance of the supremacy of EC law over national law is clearly demonstrated in one of the many Sunday trading cases, *Stoke-on-Trent* v. *B&Q plc* (1990) in which Hoffman J stressed in the Chancery Division of the High Court that the EEC Treaty is: 'the supreme law of our country, taking precedence over Acts of Parliament. Our entry into the Community meant that Parliament had surrendered its sovereign rights to legislate contrary to the provisions of the Treaty on matters of social and economic policy which it regulated.'

EC LAW IN OTHER MEMBER STATES

20. Belgium

It is not entirely clear whether Belgium adopts a monist or dualist approach to international law. EC law is incorporated into Belgian law by statute. However, there is no provision in the constitution giving supremacy to international law. Thus the constitutional status of EC law in Belgium was uncertain until the decision of the Cour de Cassation in *Minister for Economic Affairs* v. *Fromagerie Franco-Suisse 'Le Ski'* (1972). The ECJ had ruled in Article 169 proceedings that import duties on dairy products contravened Article 12 of the EEC Treaty. The Belgian Parliament abolished the duties but passed a statute preventing the return of money already paid. The retention of the money was challenged in the Belgian courts. The Cour de Cassation ruled that the normal rule that a later statute repeals an earlier one did not apply to an international treaty, being a higher legal norm. It followed that in the event of a conflict between the EEC Treaty and domestic law, the Treaty must prevail.

21. France

There has been reluctance in the French courts to recognise the supremacy of EC law. For many years, the Cour de Cassation, the highest court of appeal, displayed a greater preparedness than the Conseil d'Etat, the supreme administrative court, to find legal solutions to the problems posed by EC law. Two cases illustrate these differing approaches:

Directeur Général des Douanes v. *Société Jacques Vabre* (1975, Cour de Cassation): Vabre, a coffee importer, had imported soluble coffee extract into France from the Netherlands. Under a French statute passed after membership of the EC, Vabre was required to pay customs duties, while coffee extract produced in France was taxed at a lower rate. Vabre claimed that the payment of these duties was contrary to that of Article 95, EEC Treaty. The Cour de Cassation upheld his claim. HELD: The Treaty had created a separate legal order binding on the member states. Further, any apparent lack of reciprocity in enforcement by the Netherlands was not a ground for refusing to apply EC law. (This approach was followed a year later by the Cour de Cassation in *Von Kempis* v. *Geldof* (1976) that the EEC Treaty also takes precedence over earlier French legislation.)

Cohn-Bendit (1975, Conseil d'Etat): Daniel Cohn-Bendit was a German citizen permanently resident in France where he was a student. As one of the leaders of the student uprising in 1968 he was deported following an order from the Minister of the Interior on the ground that he represented a threat to public policy ('ordre public'). In 1975 he sought to return to France to take up an offer of employment. The Minister, however, without giving any proper reason, refused to rescind the deportation order. Cohn-Bendit challenged this decision in the Tribunal Administratif which stayed the proceeding pending the result of a reference to the ECJ to determine the scope of the public policy proviso under Directive 64/221.

The Minister appealed to the Conseil d'Etat against the order of reference. Before judgment was given, the Minister revoked the deportation order. Despite the revocation, the Conseil d'Etat delivered its judgment and allowed the appeal. HELD: Under the EEC Treaty directives may not be invoked by individuals to challenge administrative decisions. Thus, as Cohn-Bendit could not invoke the directive, its interpretation was irrelevant.

While the Cour de Cassation acknowledged the full supremacy of EC law over French law, doubt remained after the *Cohn-Bendit* decision over the recognition of the direct effect of directives by the French administrative courts until the judgement (published on 20 October 1989) in a series of cases before the Conseil d'Etat: *Application of Georges Nicolo* (1989).

The cases concerned alleged irregularities in the elections to the European Parliament. The Conseil d'Etat declared that it was prepared to accept the supremacy of the EEC Treaty over the law of 7 July 1977 on the election of representatives to the European Parliament. See also *Boisdet* (Conseil d'Etat,

1991) where acceptance of the supremacy of EC law was based on the case law of the ECJ.

22. Germany

Initially, membership of the EC posed constitutional problems for Germany, exemplified in the *International Handelsgesellschaft* decision (1974): *see* Chapter 4. A potential challenge to the supremacy of EC law was posed by the Constitutional Court's statement that until fundamental rights were adequately protected in EC law, EC measures would be subject to the provisions of the German constitution. No such measures were in fact found to contravene the German Constitution and in 1986 the Constitutional Court ruled in *Wünsche Handelsgesellschaft* that provided the general protection of human rights in EC law remained adequate, it would hear no further test cases involving a comparison of EC law with the German constitution.

However, the supremacy of EC law is not universally recognised throughout the German courts. Apart from the Federal Constitutional Court, the final authority on constitutional matters, Germany has five separate systems of courts: the ordinary courts and specialised courts dealing with administrative matters, social security, labour and tax, each headed by a federal supreme court.

The Federal Tax Court has refused on two occasions, in 1981 and 1986, to recognise the direct effect of directives. Both cases arose out of claims by taxpayers for a tax exemption provided under a VAT directive which had not been implemented in Germany. In the second of these cases, *Kloppenburg* (Case 70/83), the Federal Tax Court contradicted a ruling of the ECJ in the same case that the directive was directly effective and refused the exemption. Kloppenburg appealed to the Constitutional Court which upheld the supremacy of EC law, annulling the decision of the Federal Tax Court as violating the German constitution which provides that no one shall be deprived of his 'lawful judge' (in this case, the ECJ). The Tax Court should either have followed the ECJ ruling or made a second reference.

23. Italy

The leading case on the constitutional position of EC law in Italy in recent years is *Frontini* (1974). In this case a cheese importer claimed that a levy imposed by an EC regulation contravened Article 23 of the Italian constitution which states that taxes may only be imposed by statute. Since Article 189 of the EEC Treaty provides for the direct effect of regulations, he argued that the EEC Treaty was incompatible with the Italian constitution, with the result that the Italian incorporation statute was unconstitutional. The Italian Constitutional Court ruled that EC law is separate from international law and from Italian law, and that the Italian constitution does not apply to legislation enacted by the EC institutions. Thus, Article 23 of the Italian constitution does not apply to EC measures. In subsequent decisions such as *Spa Beca* v. *Ammistrazione della Finanze* (*see* Charlesworth and Cullen p. 57) (1982) the Italian courts have shown clear support for the supremacy of EC law.

Progress test 5

1. How do different methods of incorporation of international treaties affect the application of EC law within the member states?

2. What is meant by the statement of the ECJ in *Van Gend en Loos* (Case 26/62) that 'The Community constitutes a new legal order in international law'?

3. What would be the legal position if one of the member states enacted legislation which contravened the EC law? Would it alter the legal position if the offending national legislation were enacted before or after the relevant EC law?

4. How does the European Communities Act 1972 provide for the relationship between EC law and UK law?

5. To what extent have the UK courts accepted the supremacy of EC law over national law? What is the constitutional importance of recent ECJ decisions in relation to the Spanish Fisheries and Sunday trading?

6. What is the significance of the Nicolo decision in the French Conseil d'Etat?

6

THE PRINCIPLES OF DIRECT APPLICABILITY AND DIRECT EFFECT

1. Supremacy of EC law

In order to give effect to the objectives of the EC and to ensure that EC law is applied uniformly throughout the member states it is essential that EC law takes precedence over national law.

2. Direct applicability and direct effect

The principle of the supremacy of EC law over national law is closely bound up with the allied principles of direct applicability and direct effect. While these two terms are not defined in the EEC Treaty and are frequently interchanged it may be useful to distinguish between them (*see Winter* (1992) CMLRev 425):

(a) 'Directly applicable' EC law means those provisions which take effect in the legal systems of the member states without the need for further enactment.

(b) 'Directly effective' EC law means those provisions which give rise to rights or obligations on which individuals may rely before their national courts. (The term used throughout the book is 'directly effective' except where legislation specifies otherwise.)

3. Article 189, EEC Treaty

The EEC Treaty provides in Article 189 that regulations (without mention of any other legal provisions) are 'directly applicable'. However, the Court of Justice has decided in a number of references under Article 177 that not only regulations but also Treaty articles, directives and certain provisions of international treaties are also directly effective: *see* **5, 6, 7** below.

4. United Kingdom

In the United Kingdom provision is made for the principle of direct effect in s. 2(1) of the European Communities Act 1972:

All such rights, powers, liabilities, obligations and restrictions from time to time created or arising by or under the Treaties, ... as in accordance with the Treaties are without further enactment to be given legal effect or used in the United Kingdom shall be recognised and available in law, and shall be enforced, allowed and followed accordingly; and the expression 'enforceable Community right' and similar expressions shall be read as referring to one to which the subsection applies.

TREATY ARTICLES

5. *Van Gend en Loos* (Case 26/62)

This was the first case in which the Court of Justice considered the direct effect of Treaty provisions. A private firm sought to rely on EC law against the Dutch customs authorities in proceedings before a Dutch tribunal. The Court of Justice held in an Article 177 reference that Article 12 (which prohibits member states from introducing new customs duties between themselves) was directly effective and could therefore be relied on before the Dutch Courts.

6. Requirements for direct effect

The Court in *Van Gend en Loos* stated the requirements for direct effect. These requirements have been modified by later decisions and can now be stated as follows: **(a)** the provision must be clear and unambiguous; **(b)** it must be unconditional; **(c)** it must take effect without further action by the EC or member states.

7. Application of the criteria

The three criteria have been fairly liberally applied to cover a Treaty provision where the meaning is not entirely clear or after the expiry of the implementation date (where implementation is required). The ECJ has found many Treaty provisions to be directly effective, in particular provisions on the free movement of persons: Articles 48 and 52, and goods: Articles 30 to 34, equal pay: Article 119, and competition: Articles 85 and 86. Thus rights in these significant areas may now be directly enforced by individuals in their national courts. However, Articles 1 to 4 of the Treaty expounding general principles relating to the role of the EEC are incapable of conferring individual rights: *Sacchi* (Case 55/73).

VERTICAL AND HORIZONTAL DIRECT EFFECT

8. Vertical direct effect

Where a Treaty obligation falls on a member state itself, the provision may create vertical direct effect, reflecting the relationship between the individual and the state. Such a provision may, therefore, only be enforced against the state and not against individuals. However, the concept has been extended to cover public authorities or 'organs of the state' (such as the Dutch customs authority in *Van*

Gend en Loos). The meaning of the term 'organ of the state' has been clarified by the ECJ in *Foster* v. *British Gas* (Case C-188/89): *see* below.

9. Horizontal direct effect

Horizontal direct effect arises where an obligation falls on individuals, reflecting the relationship between individuals. The precise scope of horizontal direct effect has been controversial.

> *Defrenne* v. *Sabena (No. 2)* (Case 43/75): an air hostess invoked Article 119 in an equal pay claim before the Belgian courts. Article 119 was intended to be implemented by the end of the transitional period (December 1961). This deadline was moved to the end of 1964 but was still not met by several member states. The Commission threatened to bring enforcement proceedings against any member state not complying by July 1973. This threat was not carried out and in February 1975 the Council issued the Equal Pay Directive for implementation by July 1976.
>
> HELD (ECJ Article 177): Article 119 was directly effective and was not limited to public authorities but also covered the relationship between individuals. Resolutions purporting to alter the implementation timetable were ineffective.

In theory, therefore, it should have followed in *Defrenne* that eligibility to back-pay in the UK would have arisen on the date of accession (1 January 1973) and in the other Member States from the end of the transitional period. However, the Court ruled that in the interest of legal certainty only those workers whose actions had already started before the *Defrenne* judgment could claim back-pay.

10. Regulations

Article 189 states that a regulation is of 'general application . . . binding in its entirety and directly applicable in all Member States'. Thus, it takes effect without further enactment and may be invoked either vertically or horizontally if the requirements for direct effect are met.

However, a regulation may not be regarded as directly effective if it is formulated too vaguely, leaving many important features to be devised and implemented by the member states. The general rule laid down by the ECJ is that implementation measures should not be required except where they are 'necessary': *see* the *Eridiana* decision (Case 230/78) in which the ECJ held that the directly applicable nature of regulations does not prevent them from containing provisions for implementation by the member states.

DIRECTIVES AND DECISIONS

11. Article 189

Article 189 states that a directive is '. . . binding, as to the result to be achieved, upon each Member State to which it is addressed, but shall leave to the national authorities the choice of form and methods'. A decision is binding '. . . in its entirety upon those to whom it is addressed'.

12. The *Grad* decision

Unlike regulations directives are not described in the Treaty as 'directly applicable'. However, the Court of Justice has held in *Grad* v. *Finanzamt Traustein* (Case 9/70) that, where the criteria for direct effects are satisfied, decisions and, by implication, directives may be directly effective. Doubt remains about whether a decision can create horizontal effects when addressed to a state.

The *Grad* case arose out of a challenge brought by a German company to a tax imposed by the German government which the company argued contravened an EC directive requiring member states to amend their VAT systems and a decision which set a time limit for implementation of the directive. The ECJ ruled that it would be incompatible with the binding nature of decisions (and, by implication, directives) to exclude the possibility of direct effect. Although the directive in *Grad* required implementation, once the time limit for implementation had expired, the directive could be directly effective.

13. Time limits for implementation of directives

Where a time limit has not expired a directive is not directly effective. In *Pubblico Ministero* v. *Ratti* (Case 148/78) Mr Ratti, an Italian solvent manufacturer, sought to defend himself against charges brought under Italian legislation on the labelling of dangerous products. He claimed that the products were labelled in accordance with two directives which had not been implemented by the Italian government. The time limit for implementation had expired in relation to one of the two directives. The ECJ held that only the directive in which the deadline had expired could be directly effective.

A directive may be invoked after implementation (*Verbond* v. *Nederlands Ondernemingen* (Case 51/76)) to allow individuals access to the courts to determine whether the implementing authorities have acted within their powers. In *Emmot* v. *Minister for Social Welfare* (Case C-208/90) the ECJ held that limitation periods under national law do not begin to run until full implementation of the relevant directive.

Note: In *Steenhorst-Neerings* (Case C-335/91) the ECJ held that the ruling in *Emmott* was justified on the particular facts (time bar had deprived applicant of opportunity to rely on the directive). In *Johnson* v. *CAO* (Case C-410/92) the ECJ held that it was compatible with EC law to apply a national rule limiting the period in which arrears of benefit may be claimed under Directive 79/7 even where the directive had not been properly implemented within the transposition period by the member state.

14. Implementation not required

Where implementation of a directive is not required it may take effect at once provided the criteria for direct effect are met. *Van Duyn* v. *Home Office* (Case 41/74) in which ECJ held that Article 3 of Directive 64/221 (the public policy proviso) was directly effective, as the three criteria were satisfied: *see* 12:**37**.

15. Direct effect of directives

The question of the direct effect of directives is a vexed one. There has been a reluctance among some of the member states to accept that directives may be directly effective. For many years this attitude was reflected in the ECJ which avoided ruling on whether a directive may create horizontal direct effect. The issue of the direct effect of directives came to a head in *Marshall v. Southampton and South West Area Health Authority (Teaching) (No. 1)* (Case 152/84). In this case Mrs Marshall challenged the different retirement ages (65 for men and 60 for women) permissible under the Sex Discrimination Act 1975 but forbidden under Article 5 of the Equal Treatment Directive 76/207. The Court of Justice, in an Article 177 reference from the Court of Appeal, ruled that a directive may produce vertical but not horizontal direct effects. This ruling has, however, created anomalies. Mrs Marshall succeeded in her claim under the directive because she was employed by an area health authority which was deemed to be a public body. Had she been employed in the private sector (that is by an employer who was not a 'public' body or 'organ of the state') her equal value claim based on the Directive would have failed. In contrast, an action for equal pay based on Article 119 could be brought against an employer in either the state or private sector since Treaty provisions are directly effective both vertically and horizontally.

Note: In *Marshall (No. 2)* (Case C-271/91) the ECJ held that the amount of damages available under a directly effective right in EC law may not be limited under a national statute.

16. Public bodies

Some doubts remain about which bodies can be considered to be 'public bodies'. In *Foster v. British Gas* (Case C-188/89) the ECJ held that Article 5 of the Equal Treatment Directive could be relied upon against a body made responsible for providing a public service under state control and which possessed special powers exceeding those normally applicable in relations between individuals. At the relevant time British Gas was still in public ownership. A privatised industry may still be considered a 'public' body if its powers and responsibilities bring it within the definition in *Foster*, as the High Court decided in *Griffin v. South West Water* (1995) in relation to a privatised water company.

However, in *Rolls Royce plc v. Doughty* the Court of Appeal applied the ruling of the ECJ in *Foster* and concluded that Rolls Royce did not possess the necessary special powers and responsibilities and was not a public body, despite being wholly owned by the Crown at the time. Other bodies which have been held to be public bodies include the Royal Ulster Constabulary: *Johnson v. RUC* (Case 224/84), local or regional authorities: *ECSC v. Acciaiera e ferrier Busseni* (Case C-221/88), and tax authorities: *Becker* (Case 8/81).

17. Indirect effect and the interpretation of national law

The ECJ established the principle that indirectly effective legislation should be interpreted in the light of the wording and purpose of the directive which it implements in *Von Colson* v. *Land Nordrhein-Westfalen* (Case 14/83) and *Harz* v. *Deutsche Tradax GmbH* (Case 79/83), two decisions of the Court of Justice prior to *Marshall*. Both plaintiffs had been rejected after applying for jobs, Miss Von Colson with the prison service and Ms Harz with a private company. The German court found in both cases that the rejection was based on sex but was justifiable and awarded damages limited to travelling expenses. The two plaintiffs claimed that these awards of damages contravened Article 6 of the Equal Treatment Directive 76/207 which requires member states to introduce the necessary measures to enable persons claiming breach of the principle of equal treatment to pursue their claims through the judicial process. Article 6 does not prescribe a specific sanction and was therefore held not to be directly effective.

The ECJ, instead of addressing the horizontal/vertical issue, concentrated on Article 5 of the EEC Treaty which requires member states to take all appropriate measures to fulfil their obligations under EC law. The Court stated that this obligation applies to all authorities, including the courts in the member states. National courts were also held to be bound under Article 189 to achieve the result stated in the directive. It followed that the national courts must apply national law so as to ensure an effective remedy under Article 6. The *Von Colson* approach has been confirmed by the ECJ in *Marleasing* (Case C-106/89) and *Faccini Dori* (Case C-91/92).

18. UK decisions on indirect effect

Problems remain about reliance on directives, particularly in the United Kingdom under the European Communities Act where there is doubt as to whether s. 2(1) covers Community law which is not directly effective. In *Duke* v. *Reliance Systems Ltd* (HL, 1987) the plaintiff sought damages under the Sex Discrimination Act 1975 which had been amended to comply with the Equal Treatment Directive 76/207. As the amendment was retrospective the House of Lords refused to allow a claim arising out of the period before amendment on the basis that the language of the statute was clear. The *Von Colson* approach was rejected as the basis for interpretation of a UK statute.

However, in *Litster* v. *Forth Dry Dock Engineering* (HL, 1989) the House of Lords interpreted a UK regulation implementing Directive 77/187 (which safeguards employees' rights if the undertaking is transferred) so as to comply with the directive. Thus, it follows that where the national legislation is enacted to give effect to EC obligations the national courts should adopt a 'purposive' approach to statutory interpretation, that is they should, wherever possible, construe the English law so as to comply with EC law, even if this involves departing from a strict, literal approach.

19. The duty of interpretation

The obligation on member states to interpret their own laws in the light of EC laws has been maintained since the *Von Colson* decision in cases such as *Marleasing* and *Faccini Dori*, both of which also show the ECJ's determination not to extend horizontal direct effects to directives.

Marleasing SA v. *La Comercial Internacional de Alimentacion* (Case C-106/89): M., a Spanish company, claimed that the defendant company was void under the Spanish Civil Code due to lack of cause. The defence of La Comercial was based on the lack of mention of lack of cause ground in Directive 68/151 which lists exhaustively the grounds for company invalidity. The ECJ under Article 177 held that the obligation to interpret national law in the light of the wording and purpose of the directive applies whether the law was adopted before or after the directive. This obligation derives from the need to achieve the result required by the directive according to Article 189.

Faccini Dori v. *Recreb Srl* (Case C-91/92): Ms. F.D. entered into a contract for a language correspondence without prior business arrangement at Milan Station. She changed her mind 4 days later and sought to cancel the contract within the 7-day cooling off period provided by Directive 85/577, a consumer-protection measure applying to contracts concluded away from business premises. The directive had not been implemented by Italy. The ECJ held that although the relevant parts of the directive were sufficiently clear, precise and unconditional they could not create horizontally enforceable rights. The ECJ then repeated its formulation in *Marleasing* on the national court's obligation to interpret its own law, whether before or after the directive, in the light of the directive (a formulation which would benefit only litigants other than Ms. F.D.).

The rulings in these two cases pose problems for national courts obliged to interpret a national statute which predates a directive. Wyatt and Dashwood (p. 76) suggest that the ECJ has confused the principle of consistent application with that of direct effect.

20. State liability for non-implementation of directives

The landmark decision in *Francovich* v. *Italy* (Cases C-6, 9/90) mitigated to some extent the lack of horizontal effect of directives. The case arose out of Italy's failure to implement Directive 80/987 on the protection of workers on the insolvency of their employer. The ECJ held that the directive was insufficiently precise in identifying the institution which was to guarantee compensation to beneficiaries under the directive. The Court continued its analysis by examining the duty to give effect to EC law under Article 5, deciding that effectiveness requires the opportunity for individuals to obtain compensation for a breach of EC law where the fault is attributable to a member state. The decision in *Francovich* has been upheld in *Faccini Dori* and in *Wagner Miret* (Case C-334/92).

Three conditions were laid down by the ECJ in *Francovich* before a member state may be found to be liable:

(a) The directive must confer rights for the benefit of individuals.

(b) The content of the rights must be identifiable from the directive.

(c) There must be a causal link between the damage suffered and the breach.

It is the responsibility of member states to determine the procedures and courts to enable individuals to pursue claims against the state. These must not make a remedy impossible and should be no less favourable than procedures to pursue a similar claim under national law.

21. Implications of the *Francovich* decision

While *Francovich* has obvious immediate implications for insolvency and employment law its scope is potentially very wide. It removes any incentive a member state may have for not implementing a directive on time. It provides a remedy, when the three conditions are satisfied, for individuals to claim against the state under directives which are not directly effective. Thus it complements, rather than replaces, the principle of direct effects. Further clarification of the *Francovich* decision is expected when the ECJ gives its ruling in the case of *Brasserie de Pecheur* v. *Germany* (Case C-46/93).

22. International treaties

No general rule may be formulated about the possible direct effect of international treaties. In *Kupferberg* (Case 104/81), in a case before Portugese accession, the ECJ found that Article 1 of the Free Trade Agreement between Portugal and the EC was directly effective. In *Bresciani* (Case 87/75) Article 2(1) of the Yaounde Convention was also found to be directly effective. Similar decisions were reached in relation to parts of several association agreements: see e.g. the agreement between the EC and Portugal: *ONEM* v. *Kziber* (Case C-18/90).

Although international agreements are judged by the same criteria as Treaty provisions they may be more strictly interpreted (Weatherill and Beaumont p. 308): see e.g. Opinion 1/91 on the Draft *EEA Agreement* in which the ECJ stated that the Agreement was intended only to create rights and obligations between the contracting parties (states) and provided no transfer of sovereign rights. In an earlier case, *International Fruit* (Cases 21–24/72) the ECJ had found Article XI of the GATT not to be directly effective.

23. General principles of law

The general principles of EC law are not usually binding on member states. They may be regarded as directly effective only in very limited circumstances, for example:

(a) In an action by an individual to challenge the use of a derogation such as the public policy proviso under Article 48(3) or Article 36 on the basis that it contravenes a general principle of EC law:

(b) Where a party to proceedings claims that an EC measure is invalid because it contravenes a general principle of EC law. Determination of such an issue would require a reference to the ECJ.

Progress test 6

1. What is the distinction between directly applicable and directly effective EC law? What are the requirements for Treaty provisions to be directly effective?

2. What is the distinction between horizontal and vertical direct effect? What did the following cases decide on the scope of direct effects: *Defrenne* v. *Sabena (No. 2)* (Case 43/75); *Marshall* v. *South West Area Health Authority (Teaching)* (Case 152/84); *Foster* v. *British Gas* (Case C-188/89)?

3. How did the ECJ avoid the question of the direct effect of directives in the *Von Colson* decision (Case 14/83)? How has this approach been applied by the House of Lords?

4. Which of the following are capable of creating direct effects: decisions, international treaties and general principles of law?

5. Does it make any difference to the interpretation of a national law whether it was passed before or after a relevant directive?

6. In what circumstances will a state be liable to an individual for non-implementation of a directive?

7

ACTIONS AGAINST MEMBER STATES: ARTICLES 169 TO 171, 93(2), 100A(4) AND 225

1. Introduction

In Chapters 7 and 8 the key procedures involved in the enforcement of EC law against member states, and in the judicial review of the acts of the institutions, are outlined. The main procedure for enforcement of EC law against member states by the Commission is provided in Article 169. A parallel procedure for action by member states is provided by Article 170. New remedies to support the enforcement procedures under Articles 169 and 170 are provided by Article 171 (as amended by the TEU). Article 93(2) enables the Commission to bring proceedings against member states for infringement of rules on state aids: *see* Chapter 23. Similar powers exist under Article 100A(4) in relation to wrongful use of the derogation procedure under that Article, and under Article 225 for measures taken to protect essential security interests or to prevent serious internal disturbances: *see* **13**.

ACTION UNDER ARTICLE 169

2. Power of the Commission under Article 169

Article 169(1) provides that if the Commission considers that a member state has failed to fulfil an obligation under the Treaty, it shall deliver a reasoned opinion on the matter after giving the state concerned the opportunity to submit its observations. Under Article 169(2), if the state concerned does not comply with the opinion within the period laid down by the Commission the latter may bring the matter before the ECJ.

3. Function of Article 169

Article 169 serves three main functions (*see* Steiner p. 343):

(a) It seeks to ensure that member states comply with their EC obligations

(b) It provides a useful non-contentious means of resolving disputes: *see* **8** below

(c) Where the ECJ is involved, it provides general guidance on EC law.

4. Failure to implement an obligation

Proceedings may be brought against any state or state agency. 'Failure' covers any breach of EC law, whether under the EEC Treaty, international agreements to which the EC is a party, secondary legislation or general principles of law. Such a breach may take the form of either act or omission, including non-implementation of EC law and retention of national laws which conflict with EC law.

5. Procedure

There are two stages to procedure under Article 169: the first stage which is administrative and the second stage which is judicial.

(a) *The administrative stage.* Having informed the state concerned of the grounds of complaint, the Commission invites it to submit its observations. The Commission issues a reasoned opinion recording the infringement and requiring the state concerned to take action to end the breach. If the state will not accept the opinion it may move on to the second stage before the ECJ. The reasoned opinion is not a binding act capable of annulment; it is merely a step in the proceedings: *Alfons Lütticke GmbH* v. *Commission* (Case 48/65). The Commission usually imposes a time-limit for compliance in the reasoned opinion. If not, a member state should comply within a reasonable time. While the ECJ may dismiss an action where the Commission has allowed insufficient time: *Commission* v. *Belgium Re University Fees* (Case 293/85), it may not change the limit imposed by the Commission: *Commission* v. *Italy* (Case 28/81). No party may require the Commission to act under Article 169. Failure to act is not a breach of Article 175: *Star Fruit* v. *Commission* (Case 247/87).

(b) *The judicial stage.* If a member state fails to comply with the reasoned opinion within the time limit in the reasoned opinion, the Commission has discretion as to whether to bring proceedings before the ECJ. The ECJ conducts a full examination into the case and may review the legality of the Commission's action: *Commission* v. *Belgium* (Case 293/85). While interested states have the right to be heard, individuals do not: *Commission* v. *Italy (Re Import of Foreign Motor Vehicles)* (Case 154/85R).

6. Defences

Defences raised to actions under Article 169 have rarely succeeded. Member states are required by Article 5 to implement EC law fully. Occasionally, a state establishes that it is not bound by the obligation (e.g. where the deadline for implementation of a directive has not yet expired). Unsuccessful defences have included: necessity, reciprocity and *force majeure*: *Commission* v. *Italy* (Case 101/84) (a bomb attack on the office of the Italian Ministry of Transport was held to be no justification for Italy's failure to submit statistical returns on carriage of goods by road); difficulties of a constitutional, institutional or administrative nature: *Commission v. Italy* (Case 28/81), or of a political nature: *Commission v. United Kingdom (Re Tachographs)* (Case 128/78); introduction of the obligation in practice but not in law: *Commission v. France (Re French Merchant Seamen)* (Case 167/73); failure to implement an obligation which is directly effective: *Commission v. Italy* (Case 104/86); failure by another state to comply with EC law: *Commission v. France (Lamb Wars)* (Case 232/78).

7. Parallel proceedings

It is becoming increasingly common for proceedings to be brought before a national court in which a question of EC law is raised leading to a referral to the ECJ under Article 177. At the same time, the Commission may instigate proceedings under Article 169 where it considers that there has been a breach of EC law. Interim measures may be ordered at the request of the Commission where there is a prima facie case and the matter is urgent.

Example
R. v. Secretary of State for Transport, ex parte Factortame (Case C-213/89): ECJ ruling on an Article 177 ruling from the House of Lords, and *Commission v. UK (Re Merchant Shipping Rules)* (Case 246/89R): Article 169 proceedings ordering the suspension of the Merchant Shipping Act 1988.

8. Volume of actions under Article 169

There has been a considerable increase in the number of actions brought under Article 169 in recent years. While the total number of enforcement actions from 1953 to 1982 was only 166, there were 734 actions from 1983 to 1993: *see* Brown and Jacobs (p. 426). The UK's record of compliance is relatively good with a total of 34 actions against it from 1973 (accession) to 1993.

The best record of compliance with EC law is held by Denmark, followed by the UK and the Netherlands. Between 1988 and 1990, 15 actions were brought against the UK under Article 169 compared with 143 against Italy. By December 1992 both Italy and Belgium had failed to implement 59 measures to complete the single market (cf. 22 measures not implemented by Denmark).

Non-implementation by Italy should improve as a result of the procedure adopted in 1989 to transpose all applicable EC laws directly (i.e. literally and fully). However this is proving to be a slow process.

It will be interesting to see what impact the *Francovich* decision will have on non-implementation (*see* Chapter 6) and on the imposition of penalties by the ECJ under Article 171: *see* below.

The increased use of the Article 169 procedure has been criticised on the grounds that 'Excessive use of the procedure might risk diluting its dissausive effect and even undermining the Court's judgement' (Brown and Jacobs p. 107).

ACTION UNDER ARTICLE 170

9. Action by member states: Article 170

Under Article 170(1) a member state which considers that another member state has failed to fulfil an obligation under the Treaty may bring the matter before the ECJ. Member states bringing an action are subject to a similar procedure to that created by Article 169, namely notification to the Commission: Article 170(2), followed by the delivery of a reasoned opinion by the Commission: Article 170(3), with the right to bring the matter before the ECJ: Article 170(1).

Under Article 170(3) both parties have the right to submit their case orally and in writing. Failure by the Commission to deliver an opinion within three months does not prevent the matter being brought before the ECJ.

10. Action before the ECJ

Only one case has been brought under Article 170: *France* v. *United Kingdom (Re Fishing Net Mesh Sizes)* (Case 141/78). In an action brought by France against the UK, the UK was found to be in breach of its Treaty obligations in relation to net mesh sizes by the Commission. France took the matter before the ECJ, the Commission intervened in support of France and the ECJ upheld the Commission opinion.

It is clearly preferable for member states to avoid direct confrontation. As a result, actions under Article 170 are more likely to be threatened than brought.

11. Voluntary procedure: Article 182

Article 182 provides an alternative mechanism for the resolution of disputes under which states may agree to submit any dispute concerning the subject matter of the Treaty to the ECJ.

12. Sanctions against member states under Article 171

The original wording of Article 171 EEC was declaratory in nature, with no sanction attached. It provided that if the ECJ found that a member state failed to fulfil an obligation under the Treaty the state must take the necessary measures to comply with the judgment of the ECJ.

Article 171 was amended by the TEU. The declaratory provision was retained but strengthened by a new procedure. As a result the Commission may issue a reasoned opinion specifying non-compliance with a judgment of the ECJ after giving the member state the opportunity to submit its observations. The Commission may initiate proceedings in the ECJ if the state fails to take the necessary measures to comply within the time limit laid down by the Commission. If the ECJ finds that the state has not complied it may impose a lump sum or penalty payment.

SPECIFIC ENFORCEMENT PROCEDURES: ARTICLES 93(2), 225 AND 100A(4)

13. State aids: Article 93(2)

Under Article 93(2) the Commission may issue a decision which requires the state concerned to change or abolish the illegal aid within a set time. Failure to comply entitles the Commission or any other interested state to bring the matter before the ECJ. Decisions under Article 93(2) (unlike opinions under Article 169 or 170) may be challenged before the ECJ under Article 173: *Commission* v. *Belgium* (Case 156/77). *See*, for example, *Commission* v. *United Kingdom* (Cases 31/77 and 53/77R) in which the Commission issued a decision to UK pig producers to end a subsidy forthwith. In the absence of action by the UK, the Commission brought the matter before the ECJ under Article 93(2). The ECJ upheld the Commission decision in the same terms, cf. *British Aerospace and Rover Group Holdings plc* v. *Commission* (Case C-292/90) in which failure by the Commission to observe the rights of interested third parties led to annulment of the Commission decision. This decision had required the UK to recover payments which the Commission considered were illegally made to Rover in the takeover by British Aerospace.

14. Measures to prevent internal disturbances: Article 225

Article 225 enables the Commission to challenge the action of a member state under Articles 223 and 224, following an expedited procedure, where it considers that the state concerned is acting improperly. The ruling of the ECJ is given in camera. (Articles 223 and 224 enable member states to disregard obligations under the Treaty in the essential interests of its security, internally or internationally, where these interests involve arms production or the withholding of information.)

Note: The ECJ has the power under Article 186 in any cases before it to prescribe any necessary interim measures. This power may be used, for example, in conjunction with Articles 93 or 225 to enable the ECJ to grant an interim injunction.

15. Improper use of powers under Article 100A(4)

Article 100A(4) (para. 1) empowers a member state after adoption of a harmonisation measure to apply stricter national measures under Article 36 or relating to the protection of the environment or working environment. Article 100A(4) (para. 3) enables the Commission or a member state to use a similar procedure to that under Article 225 where it considers that a state is making improper use of its powers under Article 100A(4).

Progress test 7

1. In what circumstances may the Commission bring an action against a member state under Article 169? Why, in recent years, has the number of actions brought under Article 169 increased?

2. What are the main defences to an action under Article 169?

3. Why are actions under Article 170 infrequent?

4. What is the significance of the amendment of Article 171 by the TEU?

5. In what circumstances is the Commission entitled to bring an action against a member state under Article 225?

8

JUDICIAL REVIEW: ANNULMENT UNDER ARTICLE 173, FAILURE TO ACT UNDER ARTICLE 175, AND INDIRECT REVIEW UNDER ARTICLE 184

1. Introduction

The system of judicial review under Articles 173 and 175 is based on French administrative law. Under Article 173 the ECJ may examine the activities of the institutions to determine the validity of their legislation, whereas under Article 175 (which complements Article 173) the ECJ may consider the inactivity of the institutions when they are under a legal duty to act. Article 184 provides a means of indirect review where the 'plea of illegality' is invoked: *see* below.

ACTION FOR ANNULMENT: ARTICLE 173

2. Scope of Article 173

Article 173(1) of the EEC Treaty (prior to amendment by the TEU) provided that the ECJ shall review the legality of acts of the Council and the Commission other than recommendations and opinions. For this purpose the ECJ had jurisdiction in actions brought by member states, the Council or the Commission on grounds of lack of competence, infringement of an essential procedural requirement, infringement of the EEC Treaty or of any rule of law relating to its application, or misuse of powers. Article 173(2) provides that, in certain circumstances, any natural or legal person may challenge a decision before the ECJ, provided the proceedings are instituted within the time limits specified in Article 173(3).

An important amendment was made to Article 173 by the TEU as a consequence of the decision of the ECJ in *Partie Ecologiste 'Les Verts'* v. *European Parliament* (Case 294/83). The wording of the decision was adopted verbatim in the amendment. Under Article 173 EC the ECJ is now permitted to review 'the legality of acts adopted jointly by the European Parliament and the Council, . . .

and of acts of the European Parliament intended to produce legal effects vis-à-vis third parties.'

3. Five essential questions

Five questions must be considered in relation to Article 173, namely:

(a) Which acts may be challenged?

(b) Who has the right to challenge?

(c) What are the relevant time limits?

(d) On which grounds may the acts be challenged?

(e) What are the effects of annulment?

ACTS WHICH MAY BE CHALLENGED

4. Reviewable acts

Reviewable acts are not limited to regulations, directives and decisions. The ECJ is concerned with substance rather than form and will consider all measures taken by the institutions which are designed to have legal effect: *Commission v. Council (Re European Road Transport Agreement)* (Case 22/70). The following have been held to be reviewable acts:

Examples
   (1) 'Discussions' of guidelines before the signing of the ERTA: *Commission v. Council (Re ERTA)* (case 22/70).
   (2) A 'communication' in the form of a registered letter from the Commission issued under the competition rules (stating that the company was no longer immune from fines): *Re Noordwijk's Cement Accord* (Cases 8–11/66).

The following have been held not to be renewable acts:

Examples
   (1) A reasoned opinion under Article 169: *Pigmeat* (Case 7/61).
   (2) A letter from the Commission to an undertaking under Regulation 17 containing a statement of objections: *IBM* v. *Commission* (Case 60/81).
   (3) Preliminary observations by the Commission in a competition investigation: *Automec* v. *Commission* (Case T-64/89).

Although Article 173 EEC prior to amendment by the TEU referred only to acts of the Council and the Commission, the ECJ held in *Luxembourg* v. *European Parliament* (Case 230/81) and in *Partie Ecologiste 'Les Verts'* v. *European Parliament* (Case 294/83) that the Parliament's acts could also be challenged (because the acts of the EP had legal force in relation to third parties). *Luxembourg* v. *European Parliament* arose out of a challenge by Luxembourg to the Parliament's resolution to move from Luxembourg to Brussels and Strasbourg and, in *'Les Verts'* v. *European Parliament* (Case 294/83), from the allocation of campaign funds to the Green Party for the 1984 elections. The wording in *'Les Verts'* is now reflected in the amended version of Article 173: *see* **2** above.

But *see 'Les Verts'* v. *European Parliament* (Case 190/84) in which a further challenge to the budget (relating to acts authorising and implementing expenditure) already the subject of a challenge in Case 294/83 was held to be inadmissible on the ground that the acts in question had only internal effect. The acts in question authorised and implemented expenditure.

THE RIGHT TO CHALLENGE

5. The right to challenge (*locus standi*)

Before amendment of Article 173 of the EEC Treaty by the TEU the right to challenge was limited to:

(a) member states, the Council and the Commission

(b) individuals, in certain circumstances.

(a) *Member states, the Council and the Commission ('privileged applicants').* Article 173(1) expressly gave the right to bring an action to member states, the Council and the Commission. No such right was granted to the Parliament which was, however, allowed to intervene.

In *Parliament* v. *Council (Chernobyl)* (Case C-70/88) the ECJ recognised that the EP has limited rights to safeguard its own prerogatives under Article 173. In the *Chernobyl* decision the EP challenged the legal basis of a Council regulation on the permitted level of radioactive contamination in foodstuffs. The decision partly overruled the decision in *Parliament* v. *Council (Comitology)* (Case 302/87) that the EP may challenge an Act under Article 175 but not Article 173. The wording of Article 173 EC (as amended by the TEU) reflects the decision of the ECJ in *Chernobyl*: 'The Court shall have jurisdiction . . . in actions brought by the European Parliament and by the ECB for the purpose of protecting their prerogatives . . .'

(b) *Individuals.* A natural or legal person is only entitled to challenge a decision addressed to himself or a decision in the form of a regulation or a decision addressed to another person, which is of direct and individual concern to himself.

Many successful challenges to decisions concerning individuals have been brought in competition cases: *see*, for example, *Consten and Grundig* v. *Commission* (Case 56 & 58/64). However, there are problems where the decision is addressed to another person (held to include member states: *Plaumann* (Case 25/62)). In such a case or where a regulation is involved it is essential to satisfy two criteria for an action to be admissible:

(a) The measure must be equivalent to a decision

(b) It must be of direct and individual concern to the person himself.

6. The measure must be equivalent to a decision

A 'true' regulation may not be challenged: *Calpack* (Case 789/89). The ECJ has stressed that the nature and content of an act rather than its form should be considered: *Confédération Nationale des Productuers de Fruits et Légumes* v. *Council* (Cases 16 and 17/62). A regulation applies generally and objectively to categories of persons whereas a decision (or a regulation which is a disguised decision) binds those to whom it is addressed, i.e. named (or identifiable) individuals.

Examples

(1) A regulation was held to be a disguised decision where it prescribed the number of import licences for a particular period on the basis of previous applications and so applied only to a finite number of people: *International Fruit NV* v. *Commission (No. 1)* (Cases 41–44/1970).

(2) A company exporting watches was held to have *locus standi* where its behaviour had been taken into account in a regulation imposing anti-dumping duties: *Timex* v. *Commission* (Case 264/82).

Note: Some regulations are considered to be 'hybrid', i.e. of general application, but operating as a decision for identifiable individuals: *Japanese Ball Bearings Cases* (Cases 113 and 118–121/77).

7. The measure must be of direct and individual concern to the applicant

A measure is of direct concern to the applicant when his position is decided by the act itself, without further implementation by the member state concerned: *SA Alcan* v. *Commission* (Case 69/69). Individual concern may be established by showing that the act in question affects the applicant in the same way as if it had been addressed to him, either alone or as a member of a closed class.

Most importers have not been regarded as directly concerned under Article 173. However in *Extramet Industrie SA* v. *Council* (Case C-358/81) the ECJ held that an anti-dumping measure may individually concern importers. It is not clear whether this interpretation will be extended to non-dumping measures.

Examples

(1) The applicant, an importer of cereals, had requested a licence from the German government to enable him to import cereals from France into Germany. The Commission decision confirmed the government refusal of a licence. As the decision affects only existing applicants it was thus of individual concern to the applicant: *Toepfer KG* v. *Commission* (Cases 106 and 107/63).

(2) The applicant, a major importer of clementines, claimed to be individually concerned in a Commission decision addressed to the German government refusing permission to the government to reduce customs duties on clementines from outside the EC. Refusing to accept that the applicant had *locus standi* (clementines could be imported by anyone), the ECJ held that to establish individual concern, the applicant must prove that the decision affects him because of factors which are peculiarly relevant to

him, and not merely because he belongs to a class affected by the act: *Plaumann & Co.* v. *Commission* (Case 25/62).

The ECJ adopted a highly restrictive view over the question of individual concern: *see*, for example, *Spijker Kwasten NV* v. *Commission* (Case 231/82) in which the Commission had issued the Dutch government with a decision permitting the Dutch government to ban the import of Chinese brushes. Despite the fact that the applicant had previously applied for an import licence for Chinese brushes, the ECJ held that the decision was *not* of individual concern to the applicant. However, in *AE Piraiki-Patriki* v. *Commission* (Case 11/82) the applicants who manufactured and exported cotton yarn sought to challenge a decision addressed to the French government authorising the imposition of an import quota on Greek cotton yarn. The decision applied generally. The ECJ held that the decision *was* of individual concern to those who had entered into contracts before the decision for performance subsequently.

In *Sofrimport* v. *Commission* (Case C-152/88) the ECJ held that importers whose goods were in transit at the time a Commission regulation was adopted were individually concerned. The regulation banning the importation of fruits into the EC had been adopted under a Council regulation which required the EC to have regard for the interests of importers with goods in transit.

Note: In *TWD Textilwerke* v. *Germany*, T. failed to challenge a Commission decision to refuse state aid despite notification in writing by the German government of the decision and the right to challenge it. HELD: T. could not plead invalidity of the decision in the national courts.

TIME LIMITS

8. What are the relevant time limits?

Under Article 173(3) an applicant, whether a privileged applicant or an individual, must bring a claim for annulment within two months of:

(a) publication of the measure; or
(b) notification of the measure to the applicant; or
(c) the day in which it came to the knowledge of the applicant (in the absence of notification).

As Article 191 requires regulations to be published, time will run from the date of publication. In the case of directives and decisions time will run from the date of notification. The date of knowledge is the date on which the applicant became aware of the measure. A limited extension of the two-month limitation period takes account of the distance of the applicant's place of residence from the ECJ (10 days in the case of the UK).

After the expiry of the two-month period, the measure may not be challenged by other means such as Article 184: *Commission* v. *Belgium* (Case 156/77) or Article 175: *Eridania* v. *Commission* (Cases 10 and 18/68). But *see Commission* v. *French Republic* (Cases 6 and 11/69) in which a late action after two months was permitted under Article 173.

GROUNDS FOR CHALLENGE

9. Grounds for annulment

Article 173 provides four grounds for annulment:

(a) Lack of competence

(b) Infringement of an essential procedural requirement

(c) Infringement of the EEC Treaty or of any rule relating to its application

(d) Misuse of power.

These actions derive from French administrative law where they are known respectively as *incompetence, vice de forme, violation de la loi* and *détournement de pouvoir*. The grounds for annulment are not mutually exclusive but overlap, making it possible to plead more than one ground.

10. Lack of competence

This ground is the equivalent of the English doctrine of *ultra vires* in substantive law. The institutions may adopt measures only where they are empowered to act by the EC Treaty or secondary legislation. Thus, a measure may be challenged on the ground that the adopting institution lacked the necessary legal authority. *See* the *ERTA* decision (Case 22/70) in which the Commission brought an action (unsuccessful on the facts) against the Council over the latter's participation in the formulation of the road transport agreement (where Article 228 gives the Commission the power to negotiate and the Council power to conclude international agreements). In *France v. Commission* (Case C-303/90) France successfully challenged a Commission measure under a requirement for the application of structural funds under Article 130 EC.

11. Infringement of an essential procedural requirement

This ground, the equivalent of *ultra vires* in procedural matters, is based on the requirement that institutions adopting binding measures must follow the correct procedures. Procedures may be laid down either in the EEC Treaty or in secondary legislation. A number of actions have invoked Article 190 which provides that decisions of the Commission shall state the reasons on which they are based.

Examples
(1) An application by Germany to the Commission to import wine for blending for domestic consumption was partially unsuccessful, the Commission giving as its reason that information showed a sufficient production of such wines already within the EC. The ECJ annulled the decision on the ground of vagueness. HELD: Reasons must not be too vague or inconsistent. They must set out in a clear and relevant manner the main issues of law and fact on which they are based to enable: (i) the parties to defend their rights, (ii) the ECJ to exercise its supervisory functions and (iii)

member states and interested nationals to be informed: *Germany* v. *Commission (Re Tariff Quotas on Wine)* (Case 24/62).

(2) The Commission challenged two regulations adopted by the Council under the General System of Preferences (tariffs to developing countries). HELD (ECJ): Failure to state the legal basis infringed an essential procedural requirement under Article 190: *Commission* v. *Council* (Case 45/86).

Note: An action does *not* lie where the result of applying the measure is unaffected by the defect: *Distillers Co. Ltd* v. *Commission* (Case 30/78), nor where the defect is trivial.

Failure to consult the European Parliament where this is required by the Treaty has also been held to constitute an essential procedural requirement: *Roquette Frères SA* v. *Council* (Case 138/79) and *Maizena GmbH* v. *Council* (Case 139/79).

Consultation with the EP has in some cases been denied by choice of an incorrect legal basis for the legislation. In the *Titanium Dioxide* case (Case C-300/89) (*Commission* v. *Council*) the Council based a measure to harmonise the regime for titanium dioxide waste on Article 130 (the consultation procedure requiring unanimity) rather than on Article 100a (the co-operation procedure requiring a qualified majority). The ECJ held that a single legal base, Article 100a, should have been used enabling the EP to influence decision-making in environmental issues. After amendment by the TEU, environmental measures now require the conciliation and veto procedure under Article 189b.

It is arguable whether choice of incorrect legal basis is an infringement of an essential procedural requirement or an infringement of the Treaty. Aspects of both are present. The choice of legal base is likely to become increasingly controversial as a result of new areas and procedures added by the TEU.

12. Infringement of the Treaty or of any rule relating to its application

This ground for annulment is widely drafted to cover the provisions of *all* relevant Treaties, secondary legislation adopted under the Treaties and general principles common to the laws of the member states: *see*, for example, *Transocean Marine Paint Association* (the principle of natural justice) (Case 17/74). For further examples relating to general principles: *see* Chapter 4.

13. Misuse of powers

This ground is known in English law as abuse of power, misuse of power or bad faith. However, the term has been interpreted by the ECJ to include improper (though not illegal) use of powers. In *French Republic* v. *High Authority* (Case 1/54) the High Authority of the ECSC took several decisions under Article 60 ECSC which could have had the effect of reducing prices generally although the stated purpose was to prevent price discrimination. The ECJ held that where the main purpose of the act complained of was legitimate, there was no abuse of powers even if an improper object were incidentally achieved. *See also Werner A. Bock KG* v. *Commission* (Case 62/70) (decision annulled for breach of the principle of proportionality).

EFFECTS OF ANNULMENT

14. Effects of annulment

Article 176 requires the institutions whose act has been declared void to take the necessary measures to comply with the judgment of the ECJ. In some cases, only part of the measure is declared invalid: *see*, for example, *Consten and Grundig* v. *Commission* (Cases 56 and 58/64). Where the act for annulment is a regulation, Article 174(2) empowers the ECJ to declare which parts of the measure annulled shall be considered as definitive: *see*, for example, *Commission* v. *Council* (Case 81/72) in which the ECJ ordered that staff salaries should still be paid under a regulation which had been annulled until a new regulation was issued.

In *Parliament* v. *Council* (Case C-295/90) the EP obtained annulment of Directive 90/366 which provided for the right of residence for students on the grounds of incorrect legal base. Nevertheless the ECJ ordered that the provisions of the directive should remain in force until correctly based legislation was adopted. This was achieved by Directive 93/96.

ACTION FOR INACTIVITY UNDER ARTICLE 175

15. Introduction

Article 175 complements Article 173 by providing a remedy where an EC institution has failed to act. Inconsistency between the provisions of Articles 173 and 175 may be resolved by applying the 'unity principle', i.e. the same approach to both Articles: *Chevalley* v. *Commission* (Case 15/70). But *see Parliament* v. *Council 'Comitology'* (Case 302/87) in which this approach was rejected: *see* **5** above.

16. The provision

After amendment by the TEU Article 175(1) EC states that if the EP, the Council or the Commission fail to act in infringement of the Treaty, the member states and the other institutions of the EC may bring an action before the ECJ to have the infringement established. (A similar action lies under Article 35 ECSC.) Prior to amendment by the TEU no specific provision was made to the EP. No claims for inactivity against the EP were brought in the ECJ.

17. Scope of Article 175

Failure to act must be an infringement of the Treaty. Such a failure includes failure to act where the institution was under a legal obligation. In *Parliament* v. *Council* (Case 13/83) the Parliament brought an action under Article 175 complaining of the Council's failure to implement a common transport policy. The ECJ upheld the action in part but rejected the complaint where the obligation was too vague to be enforceable.

THE RIGHT TO COMPLAIN (*LOCUS STANDI*)

18. 'Privileged applicants'

As privileged applicants under Article 175(1) the EC institutions including the EP after amendment by the TEU may challenge any omission on the part of the Council or the Commission to adopt a binding act where there is a legal duty to act. While the Council and the Commission were specifically accorded this right under the EEC Treaty the ECJ recognised that the Parliament as one of the 'other institutions' is also privileged: *European Parliament* v. *Council* (Case 13/83).

19. Individuals

Article 175(3) gives natural and legal persons the right to complain to the ECJ that an institution had failed to address to that person any act other than a recommendation or an opinion.

Where the decision is addressed to a third party the legal position is not clear. By analogy with Article 173, it would be consistent if an applicant could challenge an omission in relation to a third party where he is directly and individually concerned. Such a right was implied by the ECJ (although the claim failed) in *Bethell* v. *Commission* (Case 246/81) in which the requirement was stated to be that the institution had failed to adopt a measure which the applicant was legally entitled to claim. See also *Mackprang* v. *Commission* (Case 15/71).

Where the applicant succeeds in establishing his right to complain, resulting in a decision addressed to a third party, he will be considered to be directly and individually concerned in that decision with entitlement to review under Article 173: *Timex Corporation* v. *Council and Commission* (Case 264/82).

20. Procedure

No action may be brought under Article 175 unless the institution in question has first been called upon to act. Following such a call, the institution has two months in which to act in accordance with the request or to define its position. If the institution fails to comply, the applicant may bring an action before the ECJ within two months.

Where the institution has defined its position but has not adopted a measure, the applicant may not invoke Article 173. No further action may be taken under Article 175. In *Lütticke GmbH* v. *Commission* (Case 48/65) the ECJ held that a definition of position by the institution ends its failure to act. *See* also *GEMA* v. *Commission* (Case 125/78).

21. Effects of successful action

Article 176 lays down the effects of a successful action under both Articles 173 and 175. In both cases the institution concerned will be required to take the necessary measures to remedy its failure in accordance with the judgment of the ECJ. No sanctions are available, although a further action may be brought under Article 175.

INDIRECT REVIEW UNDER ARTICLE 184

22. Introduction

Like the grounds for annulment under Article 173, the plea of illegality (or *exception d'illégalité*) also derives from French law. Under Article 184 an applicant may challenge the legality of a general act on which a subsequent act or omission is based without restrictive time limits.

23. The provision

Article 184 provides that, notwithstanding the expiry of the time limit laid down in Article 173(3), any party may, in proceedings in which a regulation of the Council or the Commission is in issue, plead the grounds specified in Article 173(1), in order to invoke before the ECJ the inapplicability of that regulation.

24. Scope of the provision

The plea of illegality does not give rise to an independent cause of action but may only be invoked in the context of proceedings already before the ECJ: *Wöhrmann* v. *Commission* (Cases 31 and 33/62), e.g. under Article 173 (or in equivalent provision, Article 35 ECSC: *SNUPAT* v. *High Authority* (Cases 42 and 49/59)). However, the ECJ refused to consider a plea under Article 184 in the context of Article 177 proceedings: *Hessische Knappschaft* v. *Maison Singer et Fils* (Case 44/65).

A plea under Article 184 may be brought by either the applicant, or by the defendant provided there is a direct judicial link between the act or omission affecting the applicant and the general measure in question: *Italy* v. *Council and Commission* (Case 32/65).

25. *Locus standi*

Article 184 gives the right to bring an action to 'any party'. Doubt remains over the entitlement of the institutions to bring an action. While the issue has not been decided by the ECJ it has been raised in cases such as *Italy* v. *Council and Commission* (Case 32/65) and *Commission* v. *Belgium* (Case 156/77). It appears likely, however, that the liberal wording of Article 184 would enable the institutions to act.

26. Reviewable acts

Article 184 is stated to apply only to regulations. However, to be consistent with the approach adopted under Article 173 where the substance rather than the form determined the remedy, the ECJ held in *Simmenthal SpA* v. *Commission* (Case 92/78) that a general notice of invitation to tender (the basis of a decision to the Italian government in which the applicant was directly interested) could be challenged. As a result the decision was annulled.

27. Grounds of review

The grounds of review under Article 184 are the same as those for annulment under Article 173.

28. Effects of a successful action

A successful action under Article 184 will result in the regulation in question being declared inapplicable. Any subsequent measure based on the inapplicable regulation will be void.

Progress test 8

1. Which acts of the EC institutions may be challenged under Article 173?

2. When do individuals have the right to challenge under Article 173?

3. What are the grounds for annulment of an act under Article 173? How do these grounds reflect principles in English law?

4. What is the relationship between Articles 173 and 175? Is the European Parliament subject to proceedings under Article 175?

5. When are individuals entitled to complain to the ECJ under Article 175?

6. What is the main advantage of the Article 184 procedure over the Article 173 procedure?

7. Who is entitled to bring proceedings under Article 184?

9

CONTRACTUAL AND NON-CONTRACTUAL LIABILITY OF THE COMMUNITY

CONTRACTUAL LIABILITY

1. Introduction

Article 215 EC distinguishes between contractual and non-contractual liability. Contractual liability is governed by the national law applicable to the contract in question: Article 215(1). As a result litigation arising from a contract will be determined by the relevant national court.

2. Jurisdiction

Jurisdiction rests exclusively with the national courts. The ECJ has no jurisdiction in contractual matters (cf. Article 178 in relation to non-contractual liability) unless accorded in an arbitration clause under Article 181. The EC may, however, be made a party to a dispute before a court or tribunal of a member state.

3. Staff disputes

Disputes concerning the contracts of employment of EC staff are not covered by Articles 178 and 215, having a separate head of jurisdiction under Article 179. Staff cases are now dealt with by the CFI.

NON-CONTRACTUAL LIABILITY

4. The Treaty provisions

In contrast to contractual liability, Article 178 gives the ECJ jurisdiction in disputes relating to compensation for damage provided for in Article 215. The explanation for this distinction apparently lies in the need for careful deliberation by the ECJ over the non-contractual liability of a public body, whereas contractual liability may be left to the national courts of the member states.

In the case of non-contractual liability Article 215(2) provides that the Community shall, in accordance with the general principles common to the laws of the member states, make good any damage caused by its institutions or by its servants in performance of their duties. This liability now extends to the ECB following amendment to Article 215 by the TEU.

5. *Locus standi* and limitation

There are no restrictions on the persons who may bring an action under Article 215(2). A five-year limitation period, however, starts to run from the event giving rise to liability: Article 43, Protocol on the Statute of the Court of Justice. However, time will only start to run when all the requirements for liability have arisen: *De Franceschi SpA Monfalcone* v. *Council and Commission* (Case 51/81). The generous scope of Article 215(2) makes it possible to avoid the limitations of Article 173 and obtain a declaration of invalidity in proceedings arising out of non-contractual liability: *Aktien-Zuckerfabrik Schoppenstedt* v. *Council* (Case 5/71). (*See* Steiner p. 389.)

6. Elements of non-contractual liability

Three basic elements in establishing non-contractual liability were laid down by the ECJ in *Alfonse Lütticke GmbH* v. *Commission* (Case 4/69):

(a) a wrongful act or omission by a community institution ('faute de service') or its servants ('faute de personne')

(b) damage to the plaintiffs

(c) a causal connection between the two.

7. Categories of wrongful acts or omissions

Wrongful acts or omissions fall into three main categories:

(a) Failures of administration, e.g. giving misleading information: *Richez-Paris* v. *Commission* (Case 19 etc. /69) in which the applicants, EC officials, had resigned, relying on incorrect information about their pensions. The ECJ held that the failure to correct the information was 'faute de service' under Article 215(2).

(b) Negligent acts by a servant in performance of his duties; this category is hard to satisfy. In *Sayag* (Case 5/68) an engineer employed by Euratom caused an accident while driving to work. The ECJ held under Article 177 that the use of a private car only constituted performance of his duty in exceptional circumstances (such as a serious emergency).

(c) The adoption of wrongful acts having legal effect or the wrongful failure to adopt a binding act when under a duty to do so.

8. Wrongful acts having legal effect

Most wrongful acts or omissions fall into category (c). Although the ECJ in *Plaumann & Co* v. *Commission* (Case 25/62) refused to allow the applicant who lacked *locus standi* in Article 173 proceedings to invoke Article 215(2), it reached a different decision in *Alfons Lütticke GmbH* v. *Commission* (Case 4/69). In *Lütticke* the ECJ held that although the action failed under Article 175, a separate action under Article 215(2) was admissible. The ruling established that an action for damages under Articles 178 and 215(2) was established as 'an independent form of action with a particular purpose to fulfil'. The *Lütticke* approach was upheld in *Zuckerfabrik Schoppenstedt* v. *Council* (Case 5/71) in which the ECJ stressed the restrictive nature of the remedy under Article 215(2). The requirement came to be known as the '*Schoppenstedt*' formula.

> Note: The formula applies only to legislative measures, not to individual acts such as decisions.

THE 'SCHOPPENSTEDT' FORMULA

9. The requirements of the formula

The formula lays down three essential requirements:

(a) The legislative measure in question must concern choices of economic policy.

(b) There must be a breach of a superior rule of law for the protection of the individual, e.g. proportionality, equality or legitimate expectation. The principle of legitimate expectations was successfully invoked in *Sofrimport SARL* v. *Commission* (Case C-152/88). An EC measure failed to provide for goods in transit, thus depriving importers affected by it of the opportunity to mitigate their loss by making alternative arrangements for apples entering the EC from Chile.

'Individual' may include a class of people where legislation was designed to protect that class: *Firma E. Kampffmeyer* v. *Commission* (Cases 5, 7 and 13–24/66). (*See* Steiner pp. 392–393.)

(c) The breach must be 'sufficiently serious', i.e. where a sufficiently flagrant violation of a superior rule of law for the protection of the individual has occurred: *Schoppenstedt*. This requirement has been narrowly construed in *Bayerische HNL Vermehrungsbetriebe GmbH & Co. KG* v. *Council and Commission* (Cases 83 and 94/76, 4, 15 and 40/77) in which it is stated that liability is only incurred in a legislative field characterised by the exercise of discretion where the institution in question has manifestly and gravely disregarded the limits on the exercise of its power. In *Amylum* v. *Council and Commission* (Cases 116 and 124/77) the ECJ held that only conduct 'verging on the abnormal' was covered.

10. The merits of the case

The requirements of the '*Schoppenstedt*' formula are so strict that few cases succeed on the merits. Two different approaches have been used in applying these requirements, usually in the context of the CAP, examining: (*a*) the conduct of the defendant and (*b*) the effect of the breach. Both factors were emphasised by the ECJ in the recent decision in *Mulder* v. *Commission and Council* (Cases C-104/89 and 37/90). A Council regulation had fixed exemption on levies on dairy products by reference to the previous year's sales figures. As no products had been sold the previous year the applicants were refused an exemption. While the breach was sufficiently serious, a later change in EC rules prevented actual loss. The application failed.

CAUSATION AND DAMAGES

11. Causation

The damages must not be too remote: *Lütticke*, and must be a sufficiently direct consequence of the unlawful conduct of the institution in question: *P. Dumortier Fils SA* v. *Council* (Cases 64 and 113/76, 167 and 239/78, 27, 28 and 45/79) in which refunds withheld as a result of an illegal regulation were recovered but not damages for reduced sales. Applicants must, however, act as reasonably prudent business people: *Compagnie Continentale* v. *Council* (Case 169/73), in this case in relation to handling misleading information.

12. Contributory negligence

The ECJ does not usually take contributory negligence into account. However, it did so in *Adams* v. *Commission (No. 1)* (Case 145/83), a decision which shows that an action complaining of a wrongful administrative act is more likely to succeed than one alleging the adoption of a wrongful measure of general application. In *Adams* damages for financial loss and emotional distress arising out of a breach of confidence by the Commission were reduced by 50 per cent as a result of the plaintiff's failure to protect himself: 21:**10**.

There is a duty on the applicant to mitigate his loss: *Raznoimport* v. *Commission* (Case 120/83). In *Mulder* v. *Commission and Council* (Cases C-104/89 and C-37/90) damages were reduced by the amount the applicants would have earned from alternative commercial activities while they were unable to produce and sell dairy products.

The applicant is unable to recover a loss which he could have passed on to his customers: *Interquell Stark-Chemie GmbH* v. *Commission* (Cases 261/78 and 262/78).

DAMAGE

13. Recoverable damage

Actual damage (or imminent damage which is foreseeable with sufficient certainty: *Kampffmeyer*) must be established. Damages for economic loss are recoverable, but only where such losses are specific, e.g. arising out of cancelled contracts already concluded or loss due to currency fluctuations: *Kampffmeyer* v. *Commission* (Cases 5, 7 and 13–24/66). Damages are payable in the national currency of the plaintiff at the rate applicable on the date of judgment under Article 215(2), from which date interest is also payable: *Dumortier.*

In each case the ECJ states the basis on which damages should be calculated and orders the parties to try to reach agreement within a specified period on the amount of compensation. If the parties cannot agree they must submit a statement with supporting figures: *see*, for example, *Adams* v. *Commission*. Interest is payable from the date of judgement: *Sofrimport.*

Damages were *not* recovered in the following cases:

Examples

(1) A regulation which infringed the principle of legitimate expectations deprived the plaintiff of export refunds. Currency fluctuations, however, prevented actual loss: *CNTA SA* v. *Commission* (Case 74/74).

(2) French farmers were not entitled to damages for alleged losses arising out of German farm subsidies following a Council decision as prices had already fallen: *GAEC* v. *Council and Commission* (Case 253/84).

THE ROLE OF THE NATIONAL COURTS

14. Concurrent liability

The *Francovich* decision (Cases 6, 9/90: *see* Chapter 6) demonstrates the increasing emphasis placed by the ECJ on the pursuit of compensation in the national courts rather than the ECJ for failure to implement (or misimplementation of) EC law. In certain circumstances it may be possible to commence an alternative action in the ECJ under Article 215 (2). A line of decisions indicates that the applicant should exhaust the remedies of the national courts before bringing proceedings in the ECJ: *Kampffmeyer* (Cases 5 etc./66); *Haegemann Sprl* v. *Commission* (Case 96/71).

In *Krohn* v. *Commission* (Case 175/84) the ECJ held that where the national authority is primarily at fault (e.g. refusal to issue a licence) the action should be brought in the national courts. However, loss directly caused by an EC institution which cannot be attributed to a national body should be the subject of a claim in the ECJ.

Where a remedy is needed from the national courts and the ECJ, applicants should bring actions before both courts: *Roquette* v. *Commission* (Case 26/74). If no effective remedy exists at national level failure to bring an action before the national courts is not a bar to an action before the ECJ under Article 215(2): *Ludwigshafener Walzmühle Erling KG* v. *Council* (Cases 197 etc./80).

Progress test 9

1. What is the difference in jurisdiction between contractual and non-contractual liability?

2. What are the basic elements which must be proved to establish non-contractual liability under Article 215?

3. What is the 'Schoppenstedt' formula? How are the requirements applied?

4. What does the decision in *Adams* v. *Commission (No. 1)* demonstrate in relation to contributory negligence?

5. Are damages for economic loss recoverable?

6. In what circumstances should a claim be brought before the national courts and the ECJ respectively.

10

PRELIMINARY RULINGS UNDER ARTICLE 177

1. Introduction

The procedure for obtaining a preliminary ruling on the interpretation or validity of EC law is of immense significance. Most of the decisions of major importance by the ECJ have been made under Article 177 references. By this means uniformity in the interpretation of EC law throughout the Community has been achieved. The procedure provides a means by which a national court, in need of guidance on a point of interpretation or validity of EC law, may formulate a question or questions for clarification by the ECJ. At this stage, national proceedings are suspended until a ruling is given by the ECJ. The ECJ does *not* apply the law. It is the function of the national court, with the benefit of the ECJ ruling, to apply the law and reach a decision on the facts.

Note: The CFI has *no* jurisdiction under Article 177.

2. The procedure

Article 177(1) as amended by the TEU provides that the ECJ shall have jurisdiction to give preliminary rulings concerning:

(a) the interpretation of the EEC Treaty

(b) the validity and interpretation of acts of the institutions of the Community and of the European Central Bank (ECB)

(c) the interpretation of the statutes of bodies established by an act of the Council, where those statutes so provide.

Article 177(2 and 3) provides that where such a question is raised before any court or tribunal of the member state, that court or tribunal may, if it considers that a question is necessary to enable it to give judgment, request the ECJ to give a ruling on it.

Where any such question is raised in a case pending before a court or tribunal of a member state, against whose decisions there is no judicial remedy under national law, that court or tribunal shall bring the matter before the ECJ.

The jurisdiction of the ECJ on validity is limited to the acts of the institutions and the ECB. The ECJ may not declare such acts invalid under Article 177:

Foto-Frost (Case 314/85). To do so, it is necessary to invoke the Article 173 procedure: *see* Chapter 8.

> *Note:* The jurisdiction of the ECJ is restricted to questions of EC law. Thus, the ECJ may not interpret domestic law, nor may it rule on the validity of a particular national provision under EC law. When a question is phrased by the national court in terms of compatibility, the ECJ will rephrase the question as one requiring interpretation of a point of EC law.

3. What is a 'court of tribunal'?

Article 177 provides that 'any court or tribunal of a member state' has the power to make a reference. It does not matter how the body making the reference is named. Provided it exercises a judicial function (i.e. can take decisions which are legally binding on the rights and duties of individuals and exercises a compulsory jurisdiction), it is competent to make a reference and is subject to control by public authorities. The following were held by the ECJ to be a 'court or tribunal' for the purposes of Article 177:

Examples
(1) An appeal committee (in this case, the Dutch medical body which had refused Mr Broekmeulen registration as a GP): *Broekmeulen* (Case 246/80).
(2) A magistrate acting as both prosecutor and investigating judge: *Pretore di Salo* v. *Persons Unknown* (Case 14/86).
(3) An administrative tribunal in a French overseas territory: *Kaefer and Procacci* v. *France* (Cases C-100/89 and C-101/89).

A key factor appears to be the element of public control or participation, lacking in the following which were held by the ECJ *not* to constitute a court or tribunal:

Examples
(1) The Council of the Paris Bar (in an action arising out of a request for a declaration that a member of the Paris Bar denied access to a court in Germany was entitled to provide legal services under EC law): *Borker* (Case 138/80).
(2) An arbitrator appointed under a private contract (without consideration by the ECJ of the significance of excluding recourse to the courts): *Nordsee Deutsche Hochseefischerei GmbH* (Case 102/81).

4. Limitations on jurisdiction under Article 177

Two conditions limit the ECJ's jurisdiction under Article 177:

(a) The question must involve genuine issues of EC law, which have been raised before the national court, either by one of the parties or by the court itself: *Salonia* v. *Poidomani* (Case 126/80). The ECJ will not rule on a question which has been artificially fabricated by the parties in order to obtain an ECJ ruling: *Foglia* v. *Novella (No. 1)* (Case 104/79) and (*No. 2*) (Case 244/80). In the second of these cases the ECJ stated that its function under Article 177 was to assist in the administration of justice in the member states, not to give advisory opinions on general or hypothetical questions. |

> Note: In order to ensure the uniform interpretation of EC law, the ECJ has jurisdiction to give a preliminary ruling on the interpretation of a provision of EC law where the national law of a member state referred to the content of that provision in order to determine the rules applicable to a purely internal situation in that state: *Dzodzi* v. *Belgium* (Joined cases C-297/88 and C-197/89).

(b) The national court must consider that a ruling from the ECJ *necessary* to enable it to give judgment.

5. When is a reference necessary?

In general terms a reference will be necessary when a national court requires a ruling from the ECJ in order to give judgment. The ECJ provided guidelines in *CILFIT Srl* (Case 283/81), a reference from the Italian Supreme Court, as to when a reference is *not* 'necessary'. These guidelines were drawn up in relation to the mandatory jurisdiction of the national courts, but apply also to their discretionary jurisdiction.

The ECJ held that a reference is not necessary where:

(a) The question of EC law is irrelevant

(b) The question has already been decided by the ECJ

(c) The correct interpretation is so obvious as to leave no scope for doubt. (This question must be examined on the basis of the special features of EC law, in particular the need for a uniform interpretation despite the existence of texts in different languages and the use of concepts and terminology which differ from the national legislation.)

6. Necessity and the UK courts

In *Bulmer* v. *Bollinger* (CA 1974) Lord Denning drew up guidelines as to when a reference from the UK courts was 'necessary'. A reference would only be necessary if it were 'conclusive' to the judgment; it would not be necessary if the ECJ had already pronounced on the question or the matter were reasonably clear and free from doubt (cf. the French concept of *acte clair: see* below). These guidelines have been criticised, but they have influenced UK courts in deciding whether to refer, sometimes with unfortunate results: *R.* v. *Henn and Darby* (CA 1978). It is not always easy for a national court to know at an early stage in proceedings whether the EC point is conclusive. Such a limitation is unnecessarily restrictive.

In *Polydor Ltd* v. *Harlequin Record Shops Ltd* (CA 1980) Ormrod LJ interpreted 'necessary' as meaning 'reasonably necessary' and not 'unavoidable'.

7. Acte clair

Acte clair is a doctrine deriving from French administrative law according to which no question of interpretation is taken to arise from a provision whose meaning is clear. It was usually invoked in the context of international treaties. Where the treaty meaning was clear, there was no need for the Conseil d'Etat to refer any question for interpretation to the government.[1]

Limited endorsement of the principle of *acte clair* was given by the ECJ in *Da Costa en Schaake NV* (Cases 28–30/62) (national courts should refer every question for interpretation to the ECJ unless a previous ruling had been made on a materially identical question) and in *CILFIT*. The approach of the Conseil d'Etat was demonstrated in *Re Société des Petroles Shell-Berre* (1964) in which it held (*see* Steiner p. 331) that a question of interpretation arose under Article 177 only where the judge was not competent to determine the meaning of an act.

8. Courts for which referral is mandatory

While any court or tribunal *may* make a reference to the ECJ, Article 177(3) provides that, where a question of interpretation is raised before any court or tribunal of a member state against whose decisions there is no judicial remedy under national law, that court or tribunal *shall* bring the matter before the ECJ.

The coverage of Article 177(3) is not clear and has given rise to controversy. According to the narrow view, only courts which constitute the court of final resort such as the House of Lords and the Conseil d'Etat are within its scope. However, in many circumstances there may be no right of appeal from a decision of a lower court (e.g. the Court of Appeal when leave to appeal to the House of Lords is refused). In the UK there has been reluctance to accept the view that courts below the House of Lords are within the mandatory jurisdiction of Article 177: *see* for example *Bulmer* v. *Bollinger*.

The ECJ adopted a 'wide' view in *Costa* v. *ENEL* (Case 6/64), a referral from an Italian small claims court from which there was no right of appeal due to the low sum claimed, stating that national courts from whose decisions there is no judicial remedy (as in the present case) *must* refer the matter to the ECJ.

> Note: In *Magnavision NV* v. *General Optical Council* (No. 2) (1987) the Queen's Bench Divisional Court in the UK refused to make a reference to the ECJ to determine whether the Divisional Court, if it refused leave to appeal to the House of Lords, was a court of last resort under Article 177(3). Thus, this important question remains unanswered by the ECJ.

The *acte clair* principle is particularly important in relation to Article 177(3). A national court of last resort need not make a reference under Article 177 where one of the three criteria in *CILFIT* is satisfied: *see* **5** above.

9. Courts with a discretion to refer

Courts not covered by the requirement for mandatory references under Article 177(3) have a discretion to refer where they consider that a reference is *necessary*. In reaching a decision the national courts must exercise their discretion, again subject to the *CILFIT* criteria. Lord Denning's guidelines, *see* **6**, purport to direct UK courts as to the factors that should be taken into account, namely: timing ('Decide the facts before making the reference'), delay (A reference may take two years), cost, workload of the ECJ and the wishes of the parties.

The first of these points found approval in the ECJ decision in *Irish Creamery Milk Suppliers Association* v. *Ireland* (Cases 36 and 71/80). In *R. v. Henn and Darby* (1980), however, the House of Lords accepted that references would sometimes have to be made before all the facts were known, where important financial issues were at stake.

The remaining criteria (delay, cost, workload and the wishes of the parties) should be treated with caution. Making a reference may take less time than appealing to the highest court of appeal. *See*, for example, the references to the ECJ on Sunday trading which have mostly been made by magistrates courts: 5:20. The workload of the ECJ is a matter for the ECJ itself. This should be alleviated to some degree by the creation of the CFI. The parties' wishes may conflict; it is for the national court to decide whether a reference is necessary.

> *Note*: National courts may declare an EC act valid, but not invalid. If in doubt about validity, a reference is desirable. A national court may, however, grant an interim injunction where it considers that an act may be invalid under EC law: *Foto-Frost* v. *Hauptzollampt Lübeck Ost* (Case 314/85). *See* also *Zuckerfabrik Suderdithmarschen AG* v. *Hauptzollamt Itzehoe* (Joined Cases C-143/88 and C-92/89) in which the ECJ held (under Article 177) that the power of national courts to order the suspension of an administrative act of a national authority based on an EC measure whose validity is in doubt corresponded to the jurisdiction of the ECJ to suspend a contested act under Article 185 of the Treaty. As a result such a suspension could only be ordered under the same conditions as those applied by the ECJ in interim proceedings.

10. Effect of an Article 177 ruling

An Article 177 ruling by the ECJ binds the national court in the case in which the reference was made: *Milch-Fett-und Eierkontor* v. *HZA Saarbrucken* (Case 29/68) and any other national court considering the same point of EC law. It is, however, open to another national court to request a fresh interpretation: *Da Costa* (Joined Cases 28–30/62), though not on a question of validity: *ICI* v. *Italian Financial Administration* (Case 66/80).

Progress test 10

1. What are the features of a 'court or tribunal' within the meanings of Article 177?

2. In what circumstances is a reference to the ECJ necessary before a national court can give judgment? How has the word 'necessary' been interpreted in the UK courts?

3. Which courts are required to make a reference to the ECJ and which have a discretion to do so?

4. What is the legal significance of an Article 177 ruling?

Part Two

FREE MOVEMENT WITHIN THE SINGLE MARKET

11

CUSTOMS DUTIES AND DISCRIMINATORY INTERNAL TAXATION

INTRODUCTION

1. The free movement of goods

There are four factors, goods, persons, services and capital, which must be capable of moving freely within the EC if the single market is to be achieved. The purpose of the Treaty provisions on the free movement of goods is to create an internal market within which there are no tariff or non-tariff barriers to trade: Article 8A EC. Outside the EC, however, a common tariff is applied to imports. All quantitative restrictions and measures having equivalent effect must be eliminated. State aids to industry must be adjusted so that there is no discrimination between the way goods are obtained and sold. The European Economic Area Agreement extended the territory of the internal market from 1 January 1994 for the purpose of free movement of the factors of production to cover the whole of the EFTA territory excluding Switzerland.

2. Customs union (Articles 12–17)

Member states are required under Article 9 of the Treaty to form a customs union involving:

(a) the prohibition between member states of customs duties on imports and exports and of charges having an equivalent effect

(b) the adoption of a common customs tariff in relation to third countries (Article 9).

3. Common customs tariff (Articles 18–29)

Goods entering the EC from third countries face the common customs tariff (CCT), otherwise known as the common external tariff (CET). The CCT is governed by Articles 18 to 29 of the EEC Treaty. It is published by the Commission and regularly updated. Under Article 28 the Council may, by a qualified majority on a Commission proposal, modify or suspend duties. If the Commission finds that a member state is traditionally dependent on imports of a particular product from a third country because its own production is inadequate the Council is empowered under Article 25 by a qualified majority to reduce the rate of duty or to allow the goods to enter duty free.

4. 'Goods'

The term 'goods' is not defined in the Treaty and is used interchangeably with 'products'. However, the terms were defined by the Court of Justice in *Commission* v. *Italy (Re Export Tax on Art Treasures)* (Case 7/68), Article 169 proceedings, as meaning anything capable of money valuation and of being the object of commercial transactions. The term 'goods' was held to cover goods supplied in a contract for work and materials as well as goods in a contract of sale (*Ireland Re Dundalk Water Supply* (Case 45/87), Article 169 proceedings). In *R.* v. *Thompson* (Case 7/78), an Article 177 reference, the term was held to cover gold and silver collectors' coins provided the coins were not in circulation as legal tender.

5. Origin of goods (Articles 9–11)

In a customs union the abolition of duties is not limited to goods originating in the contracting states. It also covers goods coming from third countries which are in free circulation in the member states: Article 9(2). The application of a common tariff to third countries prevents goods produced outside the EC from entering the internal market at a lower tariff than EC produced goods.

PROHIBITION OF CUSTOMS DUTIES ON IMPORTS AND EXPORTS WITHIN THE EC AND OF ALL CHARGES OF EQUIVALENT EFFECT (ARTICLES 12–17)

6. The prohibition provisions

Article 12 is a 'standstill' provision prohibiting member states from introducing any new customs duties or charges having equivalent effect. Articles 13–15 provide for the abolition of duties on imports by the end of the transitional period. Articles 9–15 apply to customs duties of a fiscal nature: Article 17. Article 16 provides for the abolition of duties on exports.

7. The 'standstill' provision

Under Article 12 member states must refrain from introducing any new customs duties on imports and exports and from increasing existing duties. Article 12 applies equally to agricultural goods (*Commission* v. *Luxembourg and Belgium* (Cases 90 and 91/63)). It is also directly applicable (*Van Gend en Loos* (Case 26/62)). In *Van Gend en Loos* the product in question, glue, had been reclassified under Dutch law, as a result of which it attracted a high rate of duty. Such a reclassification was held by the ECJ to contravene Article 12.

Note: Exception to the rules in Articles 12–17 are not permitted (cf. Articles 34 and 36 which permit derogation from Article 30): see *Commission* v. *Italy (re Export Tax on Art Treasures)* (Case 7/68) in which the ECJ held that Article 36 could not be invoked to justify an illegal tax (levied by the Italian government to protect the Italian artistic heritage).

8. 'Charges having equivalent effect'

(a) *Abolition of charges*. Article 13(2) provides for the abolition of charges having an effect equivalent to import duties. Such charges must be interpreted in the spirit of the Treaty, particularly the provisions on free movement of goods.

In the 'Statistical Levy' case (*Commission* v. *Italy*) (Case 24/68) the Italian government had levied a charge for the compilation of statistical data in trade patterns. The ECJ held that the advantage to individual traders was too uncertain to be an identifiable benefit. As a result there had been a breach of Articles 9–16. The ECJ declared that:

> . . . any pecuniary charge . . . which is imposed unilaterally on domestic or foreign goods by reason of the fact that they cross a frontier and which is not a customs duty in the strict sense constitutes a charge having equivalent effect within the meaning of Articles 9, 12, 13 and 16 of the Treaty, even if it is not imposed for the benefit of the State, is not discriminatory or protective in effect and if the product on which the charge is imposed is not in competition with any domestic product.

(b) *Disguised charges.* Charges having equivalent effect come in many forms and may be disguised as a tax or levy. *Social Fonds voor de Diamantarbeiders* (Cases 2 and 3/69), an Article 177 reference, concerned a Belgian levy on imported diamonds. The levy was not protectionist as Belgium did not produce diamonds, but was intended to provide social security benefits for diamond workers. The ECJ ruled that customs duties on goods between member states are prohibited independently of their purpose and destination. The imposition of any charge on goods crossing a frontier amounts to an obstacle to the free movement of goods.

A genuine tax, however, is permissible provided it complies with Article 95. A charge levied as a payment for services is permissible but is limited in scope. A mandatory inspection charge under a common EC scheme may be recovered: *Bauhuis* v. *Netherlands* (Case 46/76) as may a mandatory charge under international law: *Bakker Hillegon* (Case C-111/89), but not an inspection merely *permitted* under EC law: *Commission* v. *Belgium (Re Health Inspection Service)* (Case 314/82). However, a storage charge imposed by Belgium on imported goods temporarily stored for customs clearance under an EC transit scheme was held to be illegal: *Commission* v. *Belgium* (Case 132/82). There will be no breach of Articles 12–17 unless all three conditions are fulfilled, see: *Fratelli Cucchi* v. *Avez SpA* (below). However, there may be a breach of Article 95 (discriminatory taxation) or of Articles 92 (state aids): *Commission* v. *Italy Re Reimbursement of Sugar Storage Costs* (Case 73/79).

Note: Sums paid under an illegal charge are recoverable, since Articles 9 and 12–17 are directly effective. National law must not be allowed to frustrate recovery: *Amministrazione della Finanze dello Stato* v. *San Giorgio* (Case 199/82).

(c) *Non-discriminatory charges.* A non-discriminatory charge taxed at the same rate regardless of source should be reviewed in the light of Article 95. However, if the proceeds of the charge are applied to the exclusive benefit of the domestic product, there may still be a breach of Articles 12–17: *see Capalonga* v. *Azienda Articolo Maya* (Case 70/72), in which Italy introduced a charge on both imported and domestically produced egg boxes to finance the domestic production of paper and cardboard. The ECJ held that the charge was discriminatory.

This ruling was modified by the ECJ in two subsequent cases, *Fratelli Cucchi* v. *Avez SpA* (Case 77/76) and *Interzuccheri* v. *Ditta Rezzano e Cassava* (Case 195/76) which concerned the legality of a levy on imported and domestically produced sugar, intended for the exclusive benefit of national sugar refineries and sugar beet producers. In both cases the ECJ ruled that such a charge would be of equivalent effect to a customs duty if:

(*i*) it has the sole purpose of providing financial support for the specific advantage of the domestic product

(*ii*) the taxed product and the domestic product benefiting from it are the same

(*iii*) the charges imposed on the domestic product are made good in full.

PROHIBITION OF DISCRIMINATORY TAXATION (ARTICLE 95)

9. A 'genuine tax'

The importance of the distinction between a genuine tax and a charge having equivalent effect has already been considered: *see* **8** above. A 'genuine tax' was defined by the ECJ in *Commission* v. *France (Re Levy on Reprographic Machines)* (Case 90/79) as a measure relating to a system of internal dues applied systematically to categories of products in accordance with objective criteria irrespective of the origin of the products. Such taxes are governed by Article 95 which provides:

No member state shall impose, directly or indirectly, on the products of the other member states any internal taxation or any in excess of that imposed directly or indirectly on similar domestic products.

Furthermore, no member state shall impose on the products of other member states any internal taxation of such nature as to afford indirect protection to other products.

10. The purpose of Article 95

Article 95 thus allows member states the freedom to establish the taxation system for each product provided there is no discrimination against imported products or indirect protection of domestic products. The purpose of Article 95 is to abolish discrimination against imported products, not to accord them tax privileges: *Kupferberg* (Case 253/83). Thus, internal taxation may be imposed on imported products where the charge relates to the whole class of products, irrespective of origin, even in the absence of a domestically produced counterpart: *Commission* v. *France* (Case 90/79).

Note: Article 95 does not prohibit the imposition of a higher rate of tax on domestic than on imported products: *Grandes Distillerie Peureux* v. *Directeur des Services Fisceaux* (Case 86/78).

11. Assessment of taxation

In *Molkerei-Zentrale* v. *Hauptzollamt Paderborn* (Case 28/67), the ECJ ruled that the words 'directly or indirectly' must be construed broadly to include all taxation actually and specifically imposed on the domestic products at earlier stages of the manufacturing process.

12. 'Similar' products

To be covered by Article 95 it is not necessary that products are identical. It is enough if they are 'similar', an expression which the ECJ has held must be widely interpreted. Most cases alleging discrimination have arisen in the context of the taxation of alcoholic drinks.

Examples
  (1) A comparison was made between fruit liqueur wines and whisky. The ECJ held that it was not enough that both products contained alcohol. To be 'similar', alcohol would have to be present in more or less equal quantities. As whisky contained twice as much alcohol as fruit liqueur wines it was not similar, within the meaning of Article 95(2): *John Walker* (Case 243/83).
  (2) In the UK wine is more highly taxed and less widely drunk than beer. Allowing for changing habits and the growing popularity of wine, the ECJ held that it was possible to compare beer with certain categories of lighter, cheaper wines: *Commission* v. *UK (Re Excise Duties on Wine)* (Case 170/78), Article 177 proceedings.

It is, however, permissible to tax 'similar' products differently where the difference is based on objective criteria to achieve acceptable economic objectives: *see Commission* v. *France* (Case 196/85) in which 'traditional' natural sweet wines were taxed at a lower rate than ordinary wine. The ECJ accepted as justified the purpose of the differential (to provide economic assistance to rural areas dependent on wine production). There was no contravention of EC law without protectionist or discriminatory motives.

13. Indirect discrimination against imports

Internal taxation contravenes Article 95(2) if it discriminates against imports. Unlike Article 95(1), Article 95(2) does not provide for a direct comparison between domestic and imported products. Indirect protection will occur where the imported products are taxed more heavily than their domestic competitors: *Fink Frucht GmbH* (Case 27/67). *See also Commission* v. *UK* (Case 170/78) *above,* in which the ECJ held that whichever criteria for comparison were adopted, the tax system benefited domestic production.

Particular risk of indirect discrimination arises from the use of a sliding scale of taxation which distinguishes between imports and exports.

Examples

(1) The German government taxed small brewers, normally German, on a scale which benefited them to the detriment of larger brewers, normally importers, who were charged at a fixed rate. The ECJ held that the possibility of discrimination under such a system amounted to a breach of Article 95: *Bobie* v. *HZA Aachen-Nord* (Case 127/75).

(2) The French government applied road tax on a sliding scale with a significantly higher rate payable on cars exceeding 16 c-v (horsepower) rating. No cars exceeding 16 c-v were made in France. A French taxpayer who imported a 36 c-v Mercedes from Germany sought repayment in the French courts of the tax differential. The ECJ held that such a system of taxation amounted to indirect discrimination based on nationality contrary to Article 95: *Humblot* v. *Directeur des Services Fiscaux* (Case 112/84).

(3) In an attempt to remedy the discrimination found in *Humblot* the French government amended the taxation system to introduce 9 new categories under the sliding scale for tax purposes. The rate of taxation increased sharply at 16 c-v. The ECJ found that the discrimination had merely been modified but not removed: *Feldain* v. *Directeur des Services Fiscaux* (Case 433/85).

Progress test 11

1. Explain the operation of the common customs tariff both in relation to goods produced within the EC and by third countries.

2. What is a charge having equivalent effect? In what form does such a charge often appear?

3. What is the underlying purpose of Article 95 in relation to genuine taxes?

4. What is the meaning of 'similar' products under Article 95? When is it permissible to tax similar products at a differential rate?

5. In which circumstances will an internal tax contravene Article 95?

12

QUANTITATIVE RESTRICTIONS AND MEASURES HAVING EQUIVALENT EFFECT

INTRODUCTION

1. Non-tariff barriers and the need for elimination of quantitative restrictions and measures having equivalent effect

While the EC was successful in removing tariff barriers between states as well as the more obvious non-tariff barriers such as quotas many other obstacles to interstate trade remained. A quantitative restriction or quota is a measure which restricts the import of a product by amount or by value. Measures having equivalent effect are usually administrative measures which, like quotas, are capable of restricting the free movement of goods to an even greater extent than tariff barriers.

2. The principal Treaty provisions

The principal provisions are:

(a). Article 30 prohibiting quantitative restrictions, and all measures having equivalent effect, on imports

(b) Article 34 prohibiting quantitative restrictions, and all measures having equivalent effect, on exports

(c) Articles 31–33 providing for the gradual abolition of import restrictions during the transitional period

(d) Article 36 providing that the prohibitions in Articles 30–34 will not apply to import and export restrictions justified on various specific grounds.

3. 'Measures taken by member states'

While these Articles are addressed to measures taken by member states, the expression has been interpreted widely to cover the activities of any public or semi-public body, such as measures adopted by professional bodies on which national legislation has conferred regulatory powers: *R.* v. *Royal Pharmaceutical Society of Great Britain* (Cases 266 and 267/87). *See also Apple and Pear Development Council* (Case 222/82) in which the ECJ held that a body established and funded by the government was covered. In *Commission* v. *Ireland* (Case 249/81) the ECJ held that a member state could not avoid liability under Article 30 by relying on the fact that the campaign 'Buy Irish' was conducted by a private undertaking. No binding decisions were involved but the Irish Goods Council was capable of influencing traders through its promotional activities.

PROHIBITION OF QUANTITATIVE RESTRICTIONS ON IMPORTS AND OF MEASURES HAVING EQUIVALENT EFFECT (ARTICLE 30)

4. The prohibition

The prohibition covers both quantitative restrictions and measures equivalent to quantitative restrictions.

(a) *Quantitative restrictions.* The ECJ interpreted 'quantitative restrictions' in *Geddo* v. *Ente Nazionale Risi* (Case 2/73) as measures which amount to a total or partial restraint on imports, exports or goods in transit. Examples include a quota system: *Salgoil SpA* v. *Italian Minister of Trade* (Case 13/68), and a ban: *Commission* v. *Italy (Re Ban on Port Imports)* (Case 7/61), and *R.* v. *Henn and Darby* (Case 34/79) involving a ban on pornographic materials. However, a national prohibition on the sale of sex articles from unlicensed premises, applied without distinction to domestic and imported products, is not a quantitative restriction: *Quietlynn* v. *Southend Borough Council* (Case C-23/89).

(b) *Measures having equivalent effect to quantitative restrictions on imports.* This expression has been more widely interpreted than quantitative restrictions (see Steiner p. 95). It may be applied to domestic goods as well as imports and exports. It covers regulatory measures such as standards on size, quality and weight as well as inspection or certification requirements: *Commission* v. *Ireland* (Case 249/81).

5. Distinctly and indistinctly applicable measures

Directive 70/50 was issued to guide member states by providing a non-exhaustive list of measures equivalent to quantitative restrictions. Measures are divided, under the Directive into:

(a) Measures other than those applicable equally to domestic or imported products (i.e. distinctly applicable measures) which hinder imports which could otherwise take place, including those 'which make importation more difficult than the disposal of domestic production': Article 2(1).

(b) Measures which are equally applicable to domestic and imported products (i.e. indistinctly applicable measures): Article 3. These measures only contravene

Article 30 'where the restrictive effect of such measures on the free movement of goods exceeds the effect intrinsic to trade rules': Article 3.

Note: Directive 70/50, a Commission directive, has been subject to many further decisions by the ECJ.

6. The '*Dassonville* Formula'

In *Procureur du Roi* v. *Dassonville* (Case 8/74) the ECJ produced its own definition of measures having equivalent effect. Known as the '*Dassonville* Formula', the definition states:

All trading rules enacted by member states which are capable of hindering directly or indirectly, actually or potentially, intra-Community trade are to be considered as measures having an effect equivalent to quantitative restrictions.

In *Dassonville* the defendants had imported into Belgium a consignment of Scotch whisky purchased from French distributors without the certificate of origin required by Belgian law. The defendants argued that the requirement contravened Article 30. In an Article 177 reference arising out of criminal proceedings in Belgium against the importers, the ECJ ruled that a requirement such as that laid down by Belgium law constituted a measure having equivalent effect in favouring direct imports from the country of origin over imports from another member state where the goods were in free circulation.

7. ECJ decisions after *Dassonville*

The definition in *Dassonville* has been confirmed and applied in numerous subsequent decisions: *see*, for example, *Tasca* (Case 65/75), *Van Tiggele* (Case 82/87) below, *SADAM* (Cases 88–90/75) and *Laboratoires de Pharmacie de Legia* (Cases 87 and 88/85). The prohibition in Article 30 was held in *Ianelli & Volpi* (Case 74/76) to be directly effective.

Examples
(1) In *Tasca* the defendant was charged with selling sugar above the national maximum price in Italy. HELD (ECJ): Fixing a maximum price is not a measure equivalent to a quantitative restriction unless it is fixed at such a level that it makes the sale of imported goods more difficult: *Tasca* (Case 65/75).
(2) In *Van Tiggele* the defendant was charged with selling gin below the national minimum price in Holland. HELD: A minimum price may contravene Articles 30–34 by preventing imports from being sold at a price below the fixed price: *Van Tiggele* (Case 82/77).

Note: The ECJ has consistently rejected the argument that although a measure contravenes Articles 30 to 34 it is administered with sufficient flexibility to allow exceptions, stating that freedom of movement is a right which may not be made dependent upon the discretion of a national authority: *Kelderman* (Case 130/80).

It is not necessary to show that a measure has an appreciable effect on trade between member states. It is sufficient to show that the measure is capable of producing such effect: *Prantl* (Case 16/83), even where the hindrance is slight: *Van der Haar* (Case 177/82).

A measure which is incapable of hindering trade between member states will not contravene Articles 30–34 even where the sale of domestic goods is affected. The following measures were held by the ECJ not to contravene Article 7 (the principle of non-discrimination, now Article 6 EC):

Examples
(1) A Belgian law, intended to improve working conditions, banned the production and delivery of bread during the night. Competing bakers in adjoining member states were not similarly controlled: *Oebel* (Case 155/80).
(2) A Dutch law regulated the permitted ingredients in cheese produced in the Netherlands but not outside: *Jongeneel Kaas BV* v. *Netherlands* (Case 237/82). (*See* Steiner pp. 96–97.)

8. 'Cassis de Dijon'

The next major development came in the *'Cassis de Dijon'* decision.

'Cassis de Dijon' (*Rewe-Zentral AG* v. *Bundesmonopolverwaltung für Branntwein*) (Case 120/78): German law laid down a minimum alcohol content of 25 per cent for spirits including cassis, a blackcurrant-flavoured liqueur, a requirement which was satisfied by cassis produced in Germany but not in France where the alcohol level was only 15 to 20 per cent. The effect of the measure, although indistinctly applicable, was to exclude French cassis from the German market. The measure was challenged by German importers in the German court which made an Article 177 reference to the ECJ. The ECJ applied the *Dassonville* formula and held that German law contravened Article 30. The ECJ rejected German claims relating to public health (that a higher alcohol level would prevent increased consumption), the fairness of commercial transactions (that weak imported cassis would have an unfair commercial advantage over the more expensive German product) and protection of the consumer.

9. The 'Cassis de Dijon' principle

In *Cassis* the ECJ ruled that:

Obstacles to movement within the EC arising from disparities between national laws relating to the marketing of the product in question must be accepted in so far as those provisions may be recognized as being necessary in order to satisfy the mandatory requirements relating in particular to the effectiveness of fiscal supervision, the protection of public health, the fairness of commercial transactions and the defence of the consumer.

This principle whereby a restriction may be upheld where certain conditions are satisfied is sometimes known as the 'the rule of reason'.

The *Cassis* decision is important because it displaced the previous assumption that Article 30 did not apply to a national measure unless it could be shown that the measure discriminated between imports and domestic products or between different forms of intra-Community trade. After *Cassis* the position has been seen by some commentators (Steiner Chap. 8 and Weatherill and Beaumont Chap. 17) (subject to the later ruling in *Keck*: **8** below) as follows:

(a) *Indistinctly applicable measures:* The rule of reason may be applied to establish a breach of Article 30. Where a measure is necessary to protect a mandatory requirement there will be no breach of Article 30.

(b) *Distinctly applicable measures:* Distinctly applicable measures will normally contravene Article 30 but may be justified under Article 36.

However in many cases the ECJ has apparently attached little significance to the distinction between distinctly and indistinctly applicable measures (*see* Charlesworth and Cullen p. 228 and Wyatt and Dashwood chapter 8).

> *Note:* The measure in *Cassis*, although mandatory, failed because the ECJ found that it was not *necessary*. The objectives could have been achieved by other means such as labelling. It follows that 'necessary' means *no more than is necessary* and is subject to the principle of proportionality.

10. Decisions since *Cassis*

The following national rules have been held by the ECJ to be mandatory requirements under the *Cassis* formulation:

Examples
   (1) Improvement of working conditions by limiting night working: *Oebel* (Case 155/80).
   (2) Protection of the environment: *Commission* v. *Denmark (Re Disposable Beer Cans)* (Case 302/86).

> *Notes:* (1) A justification based on purely economic grounds was held by the ECJ not to be a mandatory requirement: *Duphar BV* v. *Netherlands* (Case 238/82).
> (2) A French rule designed to protect the cinema industry by prohibiting the distribution of video-cassettes within one year of release of the film in question was not expressly held to be a mandatory requirement. Nevertheless, the ECJ held that the rule was justifiable and did not contravene Article 30: *Cinethèque SA* (Cases 60 and 61/84).

The ECJ has held that certain other rules contravene the *Cassis* formulation (subject to justification under Article 36):

Examples
   (1) Imposition of a labelling requirement: *Fietje* (Case 27/80).
   (2) Requirement that silver goods be hallmarked: *Robertson* (Case 220/81).
   (3) Prohibition on retail sale of certain products unless marked with their country of origin: *Commission* v. *United Kingdom* (Case 207/83).

11. Modification of the rule in *Cassis*

The approach of the ECJ was confirmed in *Gilli* v. *Andres* (Case 788/79), in which a national measure prohibited the selling of vinegar containing acetic acid unless produced by the acetic fermentation of wine. However, the ECJ suggested a modification to the *Cassis* principle, namely that the principle applied only where national rules do not discriminate in application between domestic and imported goods. The ECJ considered that such legislation contravened Article 30 because it discriminated against goods which did not satisfy the national requirement for vinegar.

12. The principle of mutual recognition

To clarify the implications of the *Cassis* decision the Commission issued a statement in 1980 recognising the need for mutual recognition. They stated: 'There is no valid reason why goods which have been lawfully produced and marketed in one of the member states should not be introduced into any other member state.'

This means that goods which have been lawfully marketed in one member state will comply with the mandatory requirements of the state into which they are being imported unless it can be shown that the measure is necessary. The ECJ adopts a rigorous approach to determining what is 'necessary' and will not allow any measure which is disproportionate.

> *Note*: The principle of mutual recognition has operated as the cornerstone of the Commission's internal market programme through the harmonisation of identified sectors of the market. It has been applied outside the free movement of goods, for example to recognition of professional qualifications.

13. Failure to establish 'necessity'

In a number of instances, the governments in question have failed to show that the measure was necessary.

Examples
(1) P was charged with breach of a German law intended to prevent unfair competition. He had imported Italian wine in a traditional Italian bulbous bottle of similar shape and design to a traditional German quality wine. HELD: As long as the imported wine conformed with fair and traditional practice in its state of origin, its exclusion from Germany could not be justified: *Prantl* (Case 16/83).
(2) In the Netherlands the name 'jenever' was restricted to gin with a minimum 35 per cent alcohol level. HELD: The name could not be reserved for one national variety provided the import (Belgian 'jenever' with a 30 per cent alcohol level) had been lawfully produced and marketed in the exporting state: *Miro BV* (Case 182/84).

Other prohibited restrictions include Dutch requirements on the permitted ingredients in bread: *Kelderman* (Case 130/80), Italian requirements on pasta: *Drei Glocken* v. *USL* (Case 407/85).

14. Justification in the interests of consumers

A further criterion was introduced in *Duphar BV* v. *Netherlands* (Case 238/82) involving a list drawn in a Dutch regulation of approved drugs, to be paid for out of public funds. Duphar challenged its exclusion from the list in the Dutch courts. The ECJ, in an Article 177 reference, ruled out economic justification but accepted that such a measure may be necessary in the interests of consumers provided the choice of drugs on the list did not discriminate against imports. The ECJ stated that the list must be drawn up according to objective criteria, without reference to the origin of products, both requirements being verifiable by the importer. *See also Oosthoek's Uitgeversmaatschappij BV* (Case 286/81) in which the ECJ upheld national consumer protection measures which restricted the giving of free gifts as a sales promotion, despite the fact that such legislation could impede inter-member trade. In *GM INNO-BM* v. *Confédération du Commerce Luxembourgois* (Case C-362/89) a Belgian company had distributed leaflets advertising cut-price products. The leaflets were lawful in Belgium but not in Luxembourg where they were seized and the supermarket prosecuted. The company invoked Article 30 as a defence. In an Article 177 reference the ECJ ruled that the ban was unlawful under Article 30, not being justifiable as a consumer protection measure. The Court considered the ban prejudicial to small importers who were denied a particularly effective means of advertising.

15. Article 30 as a defence

As the cases in **13** and **14** above show, Article 30 has frequently been invoked as a defence in charges involving regulatory offences before the national courts. *See also Buet* v. *Ministre Public* (Case 382/87) in which an unsuccessful challenge was brought against French legislation prohibiting the door-to-door selling of educational materials. The ECJ held the measure to be justified.

The most controversial use of the Article 30 defence in recent years has probably been in relation to prosecutions in England and Wales for breaches of the law on Sunday trading, prior to the limited liberalisation of the law by the Sunday Trading Act 1994. The first ruling from the ECJ on the subject was in *Torfaen BC* v. *B&Q plc* (Case 145/88).

> *Torfaen Borough Council* v. *B&Q plc* (Case 145/88). A DIY retail company was charged with trading on a Sunday contrary to s. 47 of the Shops Act 1950. The company argued that the measure was unlawful under Article 30. HELD (ECJ, Article 177): Such measures constitute a legitimate part of social and economic policy intended to accord with national or regional socio-cultural characteristics and do not contravene Article 30 provided their restrictive effect did not exceed the effects intrinsic to rules of that kind.

In other words, the Court stated in *Torfaen* that Sunday trading is a legitimate area for legislation by member states provided the measures comply with the principle of proportionality. This emphasis on proportionality has been upheld by the ECJ in other cases on Sunday trading such as *Stoke-on-Trent City Council* v. *B&Q plc* (Case C-169/91) and on bans on Sunday employment in France and Belgium: *Union Départmentale des Syndicats CGT* v. *Sidef Conforama* (Case C-312/89) and *Criminal Proceedings* v. *Marchandise* (Case C-332/89). The ECJ held that the restrictive effects on trade which might stem from national rules in shop opening hours were not disproportionate to those rules (to arrange working hours to accord with national or regional socio-cultural characteristics).

16. Recent developments in limiting the application of Article 30

There has been concern that Article 30 has been invoked too frequently in attempts to undermine national legislation which has little or no relevance to imports. In *Keck and Mithouard* (Joined Cases C-267 and C-268/91) the ECJ has signalled its determination to identify the limits of Article 30, interpreted by some commentators (*see* e.g. Steiner p. 103) as possible evidence of the ECJ's growing commitment to subsidiarity.

> *Keck and Mithouard* (Joined Cases C-267 and 268/91). K. and M. resold goods at a loss contrary to French law. They argued that the law infringed Article 30 as it restricted the volume of imported goods. After expressing the need to reappraise its previous jurisprudence under Article 30 the ECJ ruled that: 'The application to products from other member states of national provisions restricting or prohibiting certain selling arrangements is not such as to hinder directly or indirectly, actually or potentially, trade between member states, provided that the provisions apply to all affected traders operating within the national territory and provided that they affect in the same manner, in law and in fact, the marketing of domestic products and those from other member states.'

Thus the current legal position under Article 30 clearly allows member states to determine their own selling arrangements where these have no effect on imports, denying traders and importers the right to challenge such legislation under Article 30. How the decision will be applied more widely awaits clarification by the ECJ. Meanwhile the Commission has stated that in the *Keck* decision 'the Court has completed its case law' (*see* Weatherill p. 255).

PROHIBITION BETWEEN MEMBER STATES OF QUANTITATIVE RESTRICTIONS ON EXPORTS AND OF MEASURES OF EQUIVALENT EFFECT

17. The prohibition (Article 34)

The principles relating to imports under Article 30 also apply to exports under Article 34 except that indistinctly applicable measures will not contravene Article 34 unless they discriminate against exports. Thus measures will only breach Article 34 if they have as their object or effect the restriction of export patterns, providing an advantage to the home product or market to the disadvantage of the EC import: *P.B. Groenveld BV* (Case 15/79).

In *Groenveld* manufacturers of meat products banned the possession of horsemeat to prevent its export to countries where such trade was prohibited. The ECJ held that the measure did not contravene Article 34, contrary to the opinion of Advocate-General Capotorti. It is clear from the Court's decision that the *Dassonville* test does not apply to exports where the measures in question are indistinctly applicable.

Examples

(1) Restrictions on night working in bakeries were found not to contravene Article 34: *Oebel* (Case 155/80).

(2) Prohibition on free gifts as sales promotion was upheld: *Oosthoek's* (Case 286/81).

The *Dassonville* test will, however, be applied to distinctly applicable measures against exports which will usually contravene Article 34.

Examples

(1) Watches for export were required under French law to undergo a quality inspection in order to obtain an export licence. HELD (ECJ, Article 177): Such a requirement contravened Article 34 as it was not imposed on watches for the home market: *Bouhelier* (Case 53/76).

(2) Indistinctly applicable Dutch rules on the content and quality of Dutch cheeses, while not overtly protectionist, gave an advantage to importers not bound by the same standards. HELD (ECJ, Article 177): There was no breach of Article 34 as the rules were not intended to give advantage to domestic production: *Jongeneel Kaas BV* (Case 237/82).

DEROGATION FROM ARTICLES 30–34

18. The main principle for derogation (Article 36)

Article 36, the main principle for derogation, provides:

The provisions of Articles 30 to 34 shall not preclude prohibitions or restrictions on imports, exports or goods in transit justified on grounds of public morality, public policy or public security; the protection of health and life of humans, animals or plants; the protection of national treasures possessing artistic, historic or archaeological value; or the protection of industrial and commercial property. Such prohibitions or restrictions shall not, however, constitute a means of arbitrary discrimination or a disguised restriction on trade between member states.

19. The grounds of derogation

As an exception to one of the basic freedoms of the common market, Article 36 must be interpreted strictly. The list of exceptions is exhaustive: *Commission v. Italy* (Case 95/81). The following have been held by the ECJ not to justify derogation since they are not listed in Article 36.

Examples

(1) Consumer protection or the fairness of consumer transactions: *Commission* v. *Ireland* (Case 113/80), in which the Irish government unsuccessfully sought to justify its origin-marking rules as consumer protection measures.

(2) Protection of cultural diversity: *Association des Centres Distributeurs Edward Leclerc* v. *'Au Blé Vert' Sarl* (Case 229/83).

(3) Economic policy: *Duphar* (Case 238/82).

20. Justification and arbitrary discrimination

Member states are able to derogate from the free movement of goods to the extent that a measure is justified to achieve the objectives in Article 36. 'Justified' is to be interpreted as meaning 'necessary': *Leendert van Bennekom* (Case 227/82), with the onus of demonstrating necessity resting on the national authorities.

Thus, Article 36 may only be invoked subject to the principle of proportionality. Article 36 may not be relied upon to facilitate administrative tasks or to reduce public expenditure, unless alternative arrangements would place an excessive burden on the authorities: *Officier van Just* v. *De Peijper* (Case 104/75).

21. Arbitrary discrimination

Measures must not only be necessary. They must not amount to a means of arbitrary discrimination or a disguised restriction on inter-member trade, e.g. by providing an advantage to the marketing of one state (including the domestic state) over the other state.

22. Public morality

There have been three Article 177 references to the ECJ from UK courts in which the public morality ground was raised: *R. v. Henn and Darby* (Case 34/79), *Conegate Ltd* v. *Customs and Excise Commissioners* (Case 121/85) and *Quietlynn* v. *Southend Borough Council* (Case C-23/89).

> *R v. Henn and Darby* (Case 34/79). This case arose out of a prosecution under customs legislation of importers who had attempted to bring pornographic materials from the Netherlands into the UK. The customs legislation banned material which was 'indecent or obscene' whereas domestic legislation prohibited material only where it was likely to 'deprave or corrupt', a distinction apparently discriminating against imported goods since indecency is a less rigorous concept than obscenity. A reference to the ECJ was made on appeal to the House of Lords.
>
> HELD: **(a)** There was a breach of Article 30, but the breach was justified under Article 36. A member state is permitted under Article 36 to prohibit imports from another member state of articles which are of an obscene or indecent nature in accordance with its domestic laws. **(b)** If a prohibition on the importation of goods is justifiable on the ground of public morality and is imposed for that purpose, enforcement of the prohibition cannot constitute a means of arbitrary discrimination or a disguised restriction on trade contrary to Article 36 unless there is a lawful trade in the same goods within the member states concerned.
>
> *Conegate Ltd* v. *Customs and Excise Commissioners* (Case 121/85). Customs and Excise seized a number of inflatable rubber 'love dolls' on the ground that they were indecent and obscene. The importers claimed that the seizure of the goods contravened Article 30, the sale of such objects being restricted but

not banned in the UK. HELD: The seizure was not justified, in the absence of a general prohibition on the manufacture and marketing of the goods in the UK and of effective measures to restrict domestic distribution.

Note: In *R. v. Bow Street Magistrates, ex parte Noncyp Ltd* (1989) the Court of Appeal decided *not* to refer to the ECJ the question of whether seizure of a book deemed to be obscene but published in the public interest was permitted by Article 36. The CA held that such books remained 'obscene' and liable to forfeiture under Article 36 in the absence of lawful UK trade.

Quietlynn v. Southend Borough Council (Case C-23/89). HELD (in an Article 177 reference from the Crown Court arising out of a prosecution under UK licensing legislation): Article 30 should be construed as meaning that national provisions prohibiting the sale of lawful sex articles from unlicensed sex establishments did not constitute a measure having equivalent effect to a quantitative restriction on imports.

23. Public policy

To date public policy has succeeded on one occasion only as a derogation under Article 36. In *R v. Thompson and others* (Case 7/78) the ECJ held that silver alloy coins minted before 1947 were not legal tender and thus not a 'means of payment'. They should therefore be regarded as 'goods'. Restrictions on the exportation of such coins to prevent their being melted down were found to be justified on grounds of public policy.

It has been strictly construed by the ECJ which has ruled that it may *not* be invoked: **(a)** to serve economic ends: *Cullet v. Centre Leclerc* (Case 231/83); **(b)** to restrict criminal behaviour: *Prantl* (Case 16/83); **(c)** to protect consumers: *Kohl* (Case 177/83).

24. Public security

Public security was successfully invoked by the Irish government in *Campus Oil* to justify an order instructing petrol importers to purchase up to 35 per cent of their requirements from INPC (the Irish National Petroleum Co.) at government-fixed prices. The ECJ stated that although petroleum products were of fundamental national importance, they were not automatically exempt from Article 30 and ruled that the measure, being clearly protectionist, contravened Article 30. While rejecting the validity of claims based on public policy or purely economic objectives, the ECJ held that the measure was, however, justified on grounds of public security, to maintain the continuity of essential oil supplies in times of crisis.

25. Protection of the health and life of humans, animals and plants

Discriminatory measures invoking this ground include import bans, import licences, health inspections and prior authorisation requirements. Import bans are hard to justify under Article 36 as they are usually unnecessary to protect health: *see Commission v. Germany (Meat Preparations)* (Case 153/78). There must be a real, not a slight, health risk: *Commission v. UK (French Turkeys)* (Case 40/82) in which a licensing system had been established by the UK government to exclude poultry imported from countries adopting a policy of vaccination rather than slaughter in response to Newcastle disease, a contagious poultry disease. The ECJ held that such a ban could not be justified on grounds of animal health. The ban, the Court ruled, did not form part of a seriously considered health policy but operated as a disguised restriction on inter-member trade.

A requirement to obtain an import or export licence constitutes a measure having equivalent effect: *Commission v. UK (UHT Milk)* (Case 124/81). Here the ECJ accepted the UK argument that an import licence system was necessary to regulate the heat treatment of imported milk and to trace the origins of infected milk, but held that the system which involved retreating and repackaging imported milk was not justified since milk in all the member states was subject to equivalent controls.

Note: In *Commission v. Ireland (Re Protection of Animal Health)* (Case 74/82), a case involving similar licensing requirements was accepted as justified by the ECJ because British poultry did not match the high standards of Irish poultry. This decision emphasises the need to examine each case on its merits to see whether the disadvantages of control are greater than the danger and risks to animal health.

Examples

(1) A plant health inspection to control a plant pest applied to imported but not domestically produced apples was found by the ECJ to be justified as only imported apples posed a threat: *Rewe-Zentralfinanz GmbH* (Case 4/75).

(2) The rules of a national pharmaceutical society prohibiting the substitution by pharmacists of equivalent drugs instead of proprietary prescribed brands was found to be discriminatory against imports. However, the ECJ accepted that the prohibition was necessary to avoid anxiety caused by product substitution and to maintain confidence: *Royal Pharmaceutical Society of Great Britain* (Cases 266 and 267/87).

Health inspections carried out at national frontiers may also constitute a measure having equivalent effect. Such inspections may in certain cases be an appropriate way to protect the health and life of humans, animals and plants. However, they are only justified if they are reasonably proportionate to the aim pursued and health protection may not be achieved by less restrictive means. In *Commission v. France (Re Italian Tables Wines)* (Case 42/82) the ECJ found that excessive delays in the customs clearance of wine imported from Italy into France caused by analyses of goods sampled for checks were disproportionate and discriminatory. 'Random' checks on three out of four consignments were seen by the ECJ to be systematic. (Random but not systematic checks are permitted.)

The requirement to produce a health or other certificate contravenes Article 30: *Denkavit Futtermittel v. Land-Nordrhein-Westfalen* (Case 73/84), but is frequently justified under Article 36 being less restrictive in effect than licences or inspections.

A national system of prior authorisation for marketing food imported from other member states contravenes Article 30: *Simmenthal* (Case 35/76). However, justification under Article 36 is likely, with member states exercising considerable discretion, in the absence of harmonisation, in the degree of protection to be accorded to the health and life of humans, animals and plants. National authorisation schemes have been upheld on pesticides, fungicides, bacteria and additives. Factors which may be taken into account include the harmful effect of the substance, the eating habits of the importing country and national storage habits: *Officer van Justitie* v. *Koninklijeke Kaasfabriek* (Case 53/80).

> *Commission* v. *Germany (The German beer case)* (Case 178/84). The German government banned all additives in beer, not merely a particular additive which could have been justified by German drinking habits. The ECJ held the ban to be disproportionate. It was not justified to satisfy mandatory health or consumer protection requirements.

26. Protection of national treasures possessing artistic, historic or archaeological value

These grounds have not yet been invoked to justify a derogation under Article 36. Italy was unsuccessful in its attempt to rely on Article 36 to justify a special tax on the exportation of works of art in *Commission* v. *Italy (Re Export Tax on Art Treasures)* (Case 7/68). While the caselaw of the ECJ remains undeveloped in this area two measures have been adopted as part of the internal market programme. Regulation 3911/92 on exports of cultural goods seeks to impose uniform controls at borders on the export of protected goods. Categories of protected goods are listed in the Annex to the Regulation and in Directive 93/7 which also provides that member states retain the right to define their national treasures unlawfully removed from states and for co-operation between national authorities. (What will the future hold for the Elgin Marbles, brought to Britain from Greece in the early Nineteenth Century?)

27. Protection of industrial and commercial property

The protection of industrial and commercial property is one of the exceptions listed in Article 36 for derogation from Articles 30 to 34. This area is considered separately in Chapter 22.

28. Internal market measures

After amendment by the SEA, harmonisation under Article 100A(4) to complete the internal market has created a new procedure. Member states applying national provisions relating to major needs specified in Article 36 or to protection of the environment or working environment must notify the Commission who may confirm the provisions if they do not constitute a means of arbitrary or disguised restriction on inter-member trade. Improper use of these powers entitles the Commission or another member state to bring an action in the ECJ.

29. Derogation outside Article 36

Derogation from Article 30, not permitted under Article 34, is provided in the form of measures to meet:

(a) Short-term economic difficulties: Article 103

(b) Balance of payment difficulties: Articles 107, 108 and 109

(c) Deflections of trade capable of obstructing EC commercial policy, or economic difficulties in any member state arising out of the implementation of the common commercial policy: Article 115 (*see Donckerwolcke* v. *Procureur de la République* (Case 41/76)).

Such measures may be taken by the Commission or the Council on a proposal from the Commission and are subject to the principle of proportionality. See also *Tezi Textiel* v. *Commission* (Case 59/84) in which the ECJ insisted on a strict interpretation of Article 115 as a departure from the purpose of the common market.

Derogation may also take place in the interests of national security under Articles 223 and 224. Article 224 enables a state to take the measures it considers necessary to protect national security by producing arms provided competition within the EC in non-military products is not affected. Article 225 provides for a consultation procedure to counteract measures taken by another member state in wartime, threat of war or serious internal disturbances, or to carry out peacekeeping or international security. Improper use may lead to action by the Commission before the ECJ under Article 225.

A case is currently pending before the ECJ in relation to the closure by Greece of its frontier with the former Yugoslavian Republic of Macedonia: *Commission* v. *Greece* (Case C-120/94). The ECJ refused the Commission's application for interim relief (Case C-120/94R) due to uncertainty over the interpretation of Articles 223–225.

Progress test 12

1. What is meant by the expressions 'quantitative restrictions' and 'measures taken by member states'?

2. How does Directive 70/50 clarify the prohibition on quantitative restrictions on imports and measures having equivalent effect? What further clarification was provided in *Procureur du Roi* v. *Dassonville* (Case 8/74)?

3. In which circumstances may barriers to the movement of goods resulting from different standards of national legislation be compatible with Article 30?

4. Antonio, an Italian vintner, has reduced the prices on some of his stock as a 'loss leader.' In consequence he has been charged with reselling wine at a loss, contrary to Italian law. Advise Antonio whether the charge is valid under Italian law.

5. How does the prohibition of quantitative restrictions on exports and of measures having equivalent effect under Article 34 differ from the prohibition in relation to imports under Article 30?

6. Does a restriction on the importation of pornographic materials from one member state into another contravene Article 30? Does it make any difference whether or not there is a lawful trade in such materials in the state into which the materials are imported?

7. Following discovery of a new disease in pigs which, it is suspected, may have an adverse effect on the health of consumers of pork, the UK government has imposed a licensing system on pork importers. Michael, an importer, complains that the requirements are so stringent that they are impossible to satisfy. Advise Michael.

13

STATE MONOPOLIES OF A COMMERCIAL CHARACTER

1. Adjustment of state monopolies

Article 37, the final article in the chapter on the elimination of quantitative restrictions, complements the obligations in Articles 30 and 34. Article 37 provides that member states must adjust any state monopolies of a commercial character by the end of the transitional period to ensure that no discrimination exists between nationals of member states affecting conditions under which goods are procured and marketed. Article 37(2) also provides for a 'standstill' on the introduction of any new measures contrary to Article 37(1). Article 37(1) is directly effective from the end of the transitional period: *Pubblico Ministero* v. *Flavia Manghera* (Case 59/75), Article 37(2) from the entry into force of the Treaty: *Costa* v. *ENEL* (Case 6/64).

2. Need for control of state monopolies

Without regulation state monopolies would be able to obstruct the free movement of goods.

Example
The French tobacco monopoly was examined in 1962 by the Commission which issued a recommendation identifying three types of discrimination for elimination:

    (a) Limitation of exports by the use of discretion

    (b) Discrimination in pricing between imports and domestic products in favour of domestic products

    (c) Discrimination in the conditions of distribution and advertising.

Specific recommendations were made to deal with these issues.

The Commission made similar recommendations following analyses in 1962 of the French match monopoly, the Italian match monopoly and the French potash monopoly.

Note: The Commission's power under Article 37(6) is limited to the making of recommendations (cf. Article 33(7) which empowers the Commission to issue directives in relation to the abolition of measures equivalent to quotas).

3. Meaning of 'monopoly'

To be considered a state 'monopoly' the organisation in question need not enjoy exclusive control over the market in particular goods. It will be covered if the object of the organisation is to enter into transactions involving a commercial product which is capable of being traded between member states, and to play an effective part in such trade: *Costa* v. *ENEL* (Case 6/64).

4. Purpose of Article 37

Article 37 does not prohibit the existence of monopolies. Its purpose is to prevent the discriminatory use of monopolies, with resultant obstruction to the free movement of goods and distortion of completion. (A parallel may be drawn with Article 86 which does not prohibit the holding of a dominant position, merely the abuse of dominance.)

5. State monopolies in the provision of services

State monopolies in the provision of services are not prohibited by Article 37: *Italy* v. *Sacchi* (Case 155/73). But *see Société d'Insemination Artificielle* (Case 271/81) in which the ECJ recognised that a monopoly over the provision of services may indirectly influence trade in goods. State monopolies in relation to services may contravene other Treaty provisions: Article 7 (non-discrimination), Articles 59–66 (services) and Article 86 (competition).

6. Relationship between Article 37 and other Treaty provisions

In *Rewe-Zentrale des Lebensmittel-Grosshandels* (Case 45/75) the ECJ considered a monopoly equalisation charge imposed under the German alcohol monopoly. Having considered the charge first under Article 37 and then under Article 95 the Court held that compatibility with Article 95 did not preclude the application of other Treaty provisions and interpreted Article 37(1) in the same terms as Article 95.

7. A later view

In *Hansen* (Case 148/77), a case arising out of differential rates of tax applied by the German Federal Monopoly Administration, the ECJ decided that it was preferable to consider the issue from the perspective of Article 95 rather than Article 37 (cf. *Rewe-Zentrale above* in which Article 37 was considered first).

The emphasis on Article 95 rather than Article 37 is borne out by the later decisions in *Cassis* (Case 120/78) and the first *Grandes Distilleries* case (Case 120/78) concerning the French alcohol monopoly. The ECJ held that at the end of the transitional period internal taxes were subject exclusively to Article 95. Article 37 was held to apply only to activities intrinsically connected with the specific business of the monopoly. These activities must be capable of affecting trade between member states. In the second of the *Grandes Distilleries* cases (Case 119/78) the ECJ held that Article 37 required the adjustment but not the abolition of state monopolies. However, the distinction between alcohol produced domestically from national raw materials and alcohol produced domestically from raw materials from other member states contravened Articles 30 and 37.

8. Conclusion

Thus, it now appears that internal charges after the transitional period are regulated by Article 95 not by Article 37, whereas Article 37 may still be applied in conjunction with the other provisions on the elimination of quantitative restrictions, customs duties and charges having equivalent effect.

Progress test 13

1. What is a 'state monopoly' in goods and when is such a monopoly prohibited?

2. How does the EEC Treaty differentiate between state monopolies in goods and in the provisions of services?

3. In which way, following the end of the transitional period, has the scope of Article 37 been limited in relation to state monopolies?

14

THE FREE MOVEMENT OF WORKERS

1. Introduction

The free movement of persons and services are two of the essential elements of the internal market. Article 3(c) of the Treaty requires 'the abolition, as between member states, of obstacles to freedom of movement of persons'. More detailed provision for workers is made in Articles 48 to 51, for the right of establishment in Articles 52 to 58 and for the freedom to provide services in Articles 59 to 66. There is no Treaty definition of the word 'worker'. It is unhelpful to attach too much significance to the distinction between workers and the self-employed since both are governed by the same principles on entry and residence, prohibition of discrimination and derogations.

2. An individual right

While the free movement of persons prior to amendment of the EEC Treaty by the TEU may be seen as an essentially economic concept, the ECJ has emphasised its social nature as an individual right. Family members benefit from most of the rights accorded to EC workers and the self-employed. The social nature of individual rights has recently been extended to cover the rights of residence of non-workers under three directives: Directives 90/364, 365 and 93/96: *see* 15:**38–40**. The new category of Union citizenship will entitle EU nationals to move and reside throughout the EU without reference to economic status or dependency when it has been fully implemented.

3. Derogations and exceptions

The free movement of workers and the self-employed are subject to derogations under Article 48(3) and Directive 64/221 on grounds of public policy, public security and public health: *see* below. Employment in the public service (Article 48(4)) and activities connected with the exercise of state authority (Article 55) are excluded from the right of free movement.

4. Non-discrimination

Underlying much of the case law of the ECJ on persons is Article 7 EEC, now Article 6 EC, prohibiting any discrimination on grounds of nationality. This provision, however, only applies within the scope of the Treaty, i.e. in relation to economic activity: *see Walrave and Koch* v. *Association Union Cycliste Internationale* (Case 36/74) in which Article 7 was held by the ECJ to cover sport only in so far as it constitutes an economic activity. Thus the discriminatory rules of a cycling association on 'pacemaker' cyclists were not covered.

5. Treaty provision

The essential Treaty provision is contained in Article 48 under which freedom of movement of workers must be secured by the end of the transitional period. This freedom requires the abolition of any discrimination based on nationality between workers of the member states in relation to employment, remuneration and other conditions of work and employment. Under Article 48(3) freedom of movement entails the right, subject to limitations justified on grounds of public policy, public health or public security:

(a) to accept offers of employment actually made

(b) to move freely within the territory of member states for this purpose

(c) to stay in a member state for the purpose of employment under the same provisions laid down by law, regulation or administrative action governing employment of nationals of that state

(d) to remain in the territory of a member state after employment in that state, subject to conditions to be contained in secondary legislation.

6. Secondary legislation

The principal secondary legislation issued to implement Articles 48 and 49 are:

(a) Directive 68/360: rights of entry and residence

(b) Regulation 1612/68: access to, and conditions of, employment

(c) Regulation 1251/70: the right to remain in the territory of a member state after employment there

(d) Directive 64/221: the right of member states to derogate from free movement provisions on grounds of public policy, public security or public health.

SCOPE OF ARTICLE 48

7. 'Workers'

The Treaty does not define the word 'worker'. The only definition in the secondary legislation is in Regulation 1408/71 (in the context of social security: *see* **14**) which defines 'worker' by considering whether the individual is insured against one of several risks in relation to salaried workers or is covered by the Regulation itself.

The ECJ has interpreted Article 48 liberally in a number of Article 177 references. The essential characteristic of a worker was stated by the ECJ in *Lawrie-Blum* v. *Land Baden-Württemberg* (Case 66/85) to be the performance of services for and under the direction of another in return for remuneration during a certain period of time. The concept of 'worker' is an EC one and may not be determined by the laws of member states: *Levin* v. *Staatsecretaris van Justitie* (Case 53/81).

The term 'worker' has been construed by the ECJ to include the following:

Examples

(1) A worker who had lost his job but was capable of finding another: *Hoekstra (née Unger)* v. *BBDA* (Case 75/63).
(2) A part-time worker, provided the work was 'real' work of an economic nature and not nominal or minimal: *Levin* (Case 53/81).
(3) A part-time music teacher (from Germany) receiving supplementary benefit (in the Netherlands) to bring his income up to subsistence level: *Kempf* v. *Staatsecretaris van Justitie* (Case 139/85).
(4) A member of a religious community paid 'keep' and pocket-money but not formal wages where commercial activity was a genuine and inherent part of membership: *Steymann* v. *Staatsecretaris van Justitie* (Case 196/87) (cf. *Bettray* (Case 344/87) *below*).
(5) A Portuguese national employed prior to Portuguese accession on board ship of another member state, provided the employment relationship had a sufficiently close link with the territory of that state: *Lopes da Veiga* v. *Staatsecretaris van Justitie* (Case 9/88).
(6) An EC national employed by an international organisation in a member state other than his state of origin, even if the rules of entry and residence are governed by an international agreement between the organisation and the host state: *GBC Echternach* v. *Netherlands Minister for Education and Science* (Case 389/87).

Note: (1) In *Bettray* v. *Staatsecretaris van Justitie* (Case 344/87) the ECJ held that paid activities carried out as a part of a state-run drug rehabilitation scheme did not (unlike *Steymann*) amount to real and genuine economic activity. It follows that, to enable someone to qualify as a 'worker', the activities performed must serve some economic purpose. (2) A self-employed person working in another member state is not a 'worker' under Article 48, but is covered by Articles 52–59: *Middleburgh* v. *Chief Adjudication Officer* (C-15/90).

8. Family rights

Families are defined as a worker's spouse and descendants who are under 21 years of age or dependant and dependant relatives in the ascendant line of the worker and his spouse: Article 10(1), Regulation 1612/68. Article 10(2) of the Regulation merely requires that member states shall facilitate the admission of other family members. Both Articles 10(1) and 10(2) are subject to Article 10(3), namely that the worker has available for the family housing considered normal for national workers in the area where the worker is employed. This housing requirement only applies when the worker first arrives: *Commission* v. *Germany* (Case 249/86).

In *Surinder Singh* (Case C-370/90) the ECJ held that Article 10(1) covers family members where a worker who has worked outside his home state returns to the home state.

9. Rights of spouses and cohabitees

In *Netherlands State* v. *Reed* (Case 59/85) the ECJ considered the status of a cohabitee in a member state which granted residence rights to aliens in a stable relationship with one of its own nationals. Ms Reed was cohabiting with a British national working in Holland. It was held that as her cohabitee was an EC worker, he should, pursuant to the principle of non-discrimination under Articles 7 and 48, be accorded the same treatment as a Dutch national. Ms Reed's rights to remain derived from being a cohabitee, not a spouse.

In *Diatta* v. *Land Berlin* (Case 267/83) a Senegalese woman was living separately from her husband, a worker in Germany. The ECJ held that separation does not dissolve the marital relationship. Thus, the spouse did not lose her right to reside in Germany. The effect of divorce on the legal position was not raised. See also *Surinder Singh* (Case C-370/90).

In *R* v. *Secretary of State for the Home Department (ex parte Sandhu)* (1985, HL) S, an Indian, married a German woman, settling in the UK where a son was born. Following the breakdown of the marriage his wife and son went to live in Germany where S visited them. Despite having been in regular employment in the UK, S was refused entry to the UK on his return from Germany on the ground that his residence rights had terminated when his wife left the UK. The immigration decision was eventually upheld by the House of Lords which refused to make a reference to the ECJ upon the basis that the issue was already covered by the *Diatta* decision. In fact, *Diatta* involved different issues. (*See* Steiner p. 212, and Weatherill and Beaumont pp. 489–90.)

10. Dependants and descendants

The ECJ has not yet considered the rights of a dependant spouse's relatives who risk losing residence rights on the marriage breakdown of the person on whom they depend. Steiner (p. 213) considers that it is likely that the ECJ would interpret 'dependants' and 'descendants' liberally to cover children who had been treated as children of the family without being descendants.

RIGHTS OF ENTRY AND RESIDENCE AND THE RIGHT TO REMAIN

11. Rights of entry and residence

These rights provided by Directive 68/360 are directly effective and entitle the worker and his family (in accordance with Article 10(1) of Regulation 1612/68):

(a) to leave their home state to enable the worker to pursue activities as an employed person in another member state: Article 2

(b) to enter the territory of another member state on production of a valid identity card or passport: Article 3(1). Member states may only demand entry visas for family members who are not EU nationals: Article 3(2)

(c) to obtain a residence permit on production of the document of entry and confirmation of engagement from the employer or a certificate of employment (for workers), of the document of entry and a document proving relationship to the worker certified by the country of origin (for families) plus a document certifying dependence on the worker or residence under his roof (for dependants): Articles 4(3) (a) to (e).

12. Residence permits

Workers and their families are entitled to automatically renewable residence permits valid in the member state issuing the permit for five years: Article 6. A residence permit may not be withdrawn because a worker is temporarily unable to work through illness or accident, or through involuntary unemployment: Article 7(1). Involuntary unemployment for more than 12 months may lead to a limitation of not less than 12 months on first renewal: Article 7(2).

13. Right to enter in search of work

Directive 68/360 has been held by the ECJ to cover the right to enter in search of work: *Procureur du Roi* v. *Royer* (Case 48/75). No period is specified but the ECJ has held that a period of 6 months is sufficient: *R.* v. *Immigration Appeal Tribunal ex parte Antonissen* (Case C-292/89). The decision in *Antonissen* arose out of UK law under which nationals of other member states could be required to leave if unsuccessful in finding work within 6 months. It should be noted that the ECJ did *not* stipulate that 6 months is the maximum period. In theory a longer period may be available (even in the UK) where there is genuine opportunity of employment.

The right to enter in search of work is confined to EC nationals. In *Morson* v. *The Netherlands* (Cases 35 and 36/82) the ECJ held that Article 48 does not cover nationals working in their home state.

14. Non-compliance with administrative formalities

Once in employment, the ECJ has held that residence rights derive from the Treaty, not from secondary legislation or administrative formalities: *Royer*. Lack of a residence permit does not entitle a member state to refuse entry or to deport: *R.* v. *Pieck* (Case 157/79). While failure to comply with administrative formalities may be penalised, it may never be a ground for deportation: *Watson and Belmann* (Case 118/75). Member states are, however, entitled to take reasonable measures to regulate the movement of aliens: *Watson and Belmann*. A requirement that aliens make a declaration of residence within three days of entry was found to be unreasonable: *Messner* (Case 265/88).

15. Unemployment

A valid residence permit may not be withdrawn through involuntary unemployment: Article 7(1) of Directive 68/360, but voluntary unemployment implies no such right: *Giangregorio* v. *Secretary of State for the Home Department* (1983, Immigration Appeals Tribunal).

16. Temporary and seasonal workers

Under Article 6(3) temporary workers working from 3 to 12 months in another member state are entitled to a temporary residence permit for the duration of the work, but those working for less than three months or seasonally may reside in the member state during employment but are not entitled to a residence permit.

The rights of entry and residence are subject to the public policy, public health, public security proviso under Article 10.

Note: The BENELUX states (Belgium, the Netherlands and Luxembourg) signed an agreement with France and Germany in 1985 at Schengen in Luxembourg. As a result, border formalities were relaxed on EC nationals moving between participating states. In 1992 Italy, Greece, Portugal and Spain agreed to join the scheme. The UK, Ireland and Denmark remain outside due to concern about terrorism, drug trafficking and other issues. It follows that Article 8A of the SEA to co-operate on police matters has not been fully adopted outside the Schengen agreement. Removal of *all* barriers to the free movement of individuals would, in the opinion of one commentator (Weatherill p. 499) make more likely a system of compulsory identity cards for the UK citizen.

EQUALITY OF TREATMENT

17. Introduction

Article 48(2) of the Treaty provides for the abolition of any discrimination based on nationality between workers of the member states in employment, remuneration and other conditions of work and employment. Regulation 1612/68 implements Articles 48(2) and 3 (a) and (b). The Regulation requires equality of treatment in all matters relating to the actual pursuit of activities of employed persons and the elimination of obstacles to the mobility of workers, particularly the right to be joined by family members and integration of the family into the host country: Fifth Recital. It is divided into three titles:

(a) Title I: eligibility for employment

(b) Title II: employment and equality of treatment

(c) Title III: worker's families.

18. Eligibility for employment

Under Regulation 1612/68 EC nationals are guaranteed the right to take up and pursue employment in the territory of another member state under the same conditions as nationals of that state: Article 1. Member states are prohibited from discriminating, either overtly or covertly, against non-nationals by limiting applications and offers of employment: Article 3(a), by prescribing special recruitment procedures or limiting advertising or in any other way hindering recruitment of non-nationals: Article 3(2).

Restriction by number or percentage of foreign nationals employed in any particular activity or area is also forbidden: Article 4. *See Commission* v. *France (Re French Merchant Seamen)* (Case 167/73) in which a ratio of three French to one non-French crew laid down in the Code du Travail Maritime 1926 was held by the ECJ under Article 169 to contravene Article 4, even though the French government had given oral instructions not to apply the ratio.

Non-nationals must be offered the same assistance as nationals in seeking employment: Article 5. Engagement or recruitment of non-nationals must not depend on discriminatory medical, vocational or other recruitment criteria: Article 6(1). Vocational tests when expressly requested on making a job offer to a non-national are permitted: Article 6(2). States are also permitted to impose on non-nationals conditions relating to linguistic knowledge required by the nature of the post: Article 3(1) – *see Groener* v. *Minister for Education* (Case 397/87). In this case the ECJ held that a requirement that teachers in vocational schools in Ireland should be proficient in the Irish language was permissible under Article 3(1) in the light of national policy on the promotion of the Irish language.

19. Equality in employment

(a) *Conditions of employment.* Equality in employment is expressly granted to workers by Article 7(1) of Regulation 1612/68 which provides that an EC worker may not, in the territory of another member state, be treated differently from national workers on account of his nationality in relation to conditions of employment and work, and in particular in relation to remuneration, dismissal and reinstatement or re-employment on becoming unemployed.

Examples

(1) Legislation which recognised periods of national service in the home state but not in another member state for calculating seniority was held to be unlawful: *Ugliola* (Case 15/69).

(2) A decision to increased separation allowances only to those living away from home in the state in question was held capable of breaching Article 7(1): *Sotgiu* v. *Deutsche Bundespost* (Case 152/73).

(b) *Entitlement to social and tax advantages.* Under Article 7(2) non-national EC workers are entitled to 'the same social and tax advantages as national workers'. The ECJ has interpreted 'social and tax advantages' widely.

Fiorini v. *SNCF* (Case 32/75). An Italian widow living in France claimed the special fare reduction card issued to the parents of large families. During his lifetime the Italian husband had claimed the card. HELD (ECJ, Article 177): Article 7(2) covers all social and tax advantages, whether or not deriving from contracts of employment. Since the family had the right to remain in France under Regulation 1251/70, they were entitled to equal 'social advantage' under Article 7(2).

Fiorini was followed in *Even* (Case 207/78) in which the ECJ held that Article 7(2) applies to any benefit whether or not linked to a contract of employment, payable by virtue of an individual's status as a worker or by virtue of residence on national territory. The *Even* ruling has been applied in a number of subsequent cases, with the following held to be a 'social advantage':

Examples

(1) An interest-free discretionary loan payable to German nationals living in Germany to increase the birth rate was granted to an Italian couple resident in Germany on the basis of the claimant's status as a worker or a resident: *Reina* (Case 65/81).

(2) An allowance to handicapped adults: *Inzirillo* (Case 63/76).

(3) An old-age benefit system for those not entitled to a pension under the national social security system: *Frascogna* (Case 157/84).

(4) A special unemployment benefit for young people: *Deak* (Case 94/84).

(5) Claims in Belgium to qualify for a minimum income allowance (the 'minimex') by members of the family of a worker: *Hoecks* (Case 249/83), and the family of an unemployed worker: *Scrivner* (Case 122/84).

(6) A guarantee minimum income paid for old persons, paid to an Italian widow living with her retired son in Belgium: *Castelli* v. *ONPTS* (Case 261/83).

(7) A scholarship to study abroad under a reciprocal scheme between Belgium and Germany, paid to the child of an Italian worker in Belgium: *Matteucci* v. *Communauté Française de Belgique* (Case 235/87).

(8) A fare reduction offered to large families: *Fiorini* v. *SNCF* (Case 32/75). But see *Backman* (Case C-204/90), in which the ECJ held that while in principle national legislation making pension contributions in the home territory tax-deductible contravened Article 48, it could be justified where the resulting pensions were liable to be taxed.

In *Brown* (Case 197/86) the applicant had a place at Cambridge to study engineering and in *Lair* (Case 39/86) the place was for languages at the University of Hanover. Brown, who held dual UK/French nationality and had worked for a UK engineering company for eight months before university under sponsorship from the company, sought the UK government maintenance grant. Lair sought a similar grant from the German government after working for five years in Germany with periods of involuntary unemployment. The refusal of a grant in both cases led to challenge under Article 7(2) and (3) of Regulation 1612/68. Judgments in the two cases were delivered on the same day. It was held by the Court that while neither course constituted vocational training a grant for university education was a social advantage. The word 'worker', the Court stated, must have an EC meaning. While Brown was regarded as a worker, he had acquired that status purely as a consequence of his university place. A migrant worker such as Lair, however, was entitled to equal treatment if involuntarily unemployed and legitimately resident. A worker who gave up a job to pursue further training in the host state was only eligible for a grant when there was a link between the work and the subject studied.

20. Rights relative to trade union activities, sport and housing

Migrant workers are entitled to equality of treatment in trade union member-ship: Article 8. They may be excluded from the management of bodies governed by public law but may sit as workers' representatives in such bodies.

Professional and semi-professional sporting activities are regulated by the EC Treaty in so far as they constitute economic activity: *Dona* v. *Mantero* (Case 13/76). Exclusion of a non-EU national on non-economic grounds from a national team would not appear to contravene Article 48 (*see* Green, Hartley, Usher p. 148).

Migrant workers enjoy the same rights and benefits in matters of housing including ownership as nationals of the host state: Article 9. Restrictions on foreigners' rights to acquire property were held by the ECJ to be unlawful: *Commission* v. *Greece* (Case 305/87).

21. Workers' families

Members of a worker's family are defined as:

(a) his spouse and their descendants who are under the age of 21 years or who are dependants

(b) dependant relatives in the ascending line of the worker and his spouse.

22. Rights of residence of families

The family members of a migrant worker provided he is an EC national are entitled to install themselves with the migrant worker irrespective of their nationality: Article 10(1). States must facilitate the admission of other family members who are dependant or who were living under the worker's roof in the home state: Article 10(2).

> *Lebon* (Case 316/85). The adult dependant child of a retired French railway worker living in Belgium claimed the 'minimex'. HELD (ECJ): **(a)** Dependency resultsfrom a factual situation, not from objective factors indicating a need for support; **(b)** claiming a social welfare benefit does not terminate depen-dency; **(c)** a worker's children over 21 years cease to be 'members of the family' unless they are still dependant, thus losing their status as favoured EC citizens until becoming workers themselves.

> *Commission* v. *Germany* (Case 249/86). The requirement under Article 10(3) that a worker must have housing considered to be normal for workers in the region of employment in order that the family may install themselves need not be satisfied throughout the duration of employment. It is enough if housing conditions are adequate at the outset of employment.

23. Rights of families to employment

Article 11 provides that where a national of a member state is employed or self-employed in another member state, his spouse and children who are under 21 years or dependent on him have the right to take up any activity as an employed person in that same state even if they are not EC nationals.

> *Gül* (Case 131/85) (ECJ, Article 177). The Turkish-Cypriot husband of a British hairdresser working in Germany had been refused authorisation to practise medicine in Germany, having qualified as a doctor in Turkey and taken further qualifications in anaesthetics in Germany. HELD: The spouse of a migrant worker was entitled to practise a profession under Article 11 where the spouse's qualifications were recognised as equivalent (as Gül's had been) provided he observed the specific rules of the occupation.

24. Children's access to educational training

Article 12 of Regulation 1612/68 provides that children of migrant workers shall be admitted to the host state's general educational, apprenticeship and vocational training courses under the same conditions as the nationals of the host state.

> *Michel S* v. *Fonds national de reclassement social des handicappés* (Case 76/72). S, the mentally handicapped son of an Italian who had been employed, before his death, in Belgium, was refused benefit from a fund set up to assist people whose employment prospects were seriously affected by handicap. HELD: Article 12 entitled the handicapped child of a foreign worker to take advantage of rehabilitation benefits on the same basis as nationals of the host state.

> *Casagrande* v. *Landeshauptstadt München* (Case 9/74). The son of a deceased Italian who had worked in Germany was refused an educational grant. HELD: Article 12 entitles migrant workers not only to admission to courses but also to general measures of support such as grants and loans.

This financial support was held to include study abroad on the same basis as nationals of the host state: *Di Leo* v. *Land Berlin* (Case C-308/89).

In *Commission* v. *Belgium* (Case 42/87) in which the ECJ stated that the children of migrant workers (including workers who have retired or died in the state) are entitled to equal treatment in access to all forms of state education. But *see Belgian State* v. *Humbel and Edel* (Case 263/86) in which the ECJ ruled that Article 12 did not preclude a member state from charging a fee for admission to ordinary schooling (if classified as non-vocational) within its territory to the children of migrant workers residing in another member state, where no such fee was charged to the nationals of that other member state. Two further decisions extended the scope of entitlement: *Echternach and Moritz* and *Forcheri*.

> *GBC Echternach and A. Moritz* v. *Netherlands Minister for Education* (Cases 389 and 390/87). The child of a German migrant worker who had returned to Germany after working in the Netherlands sought an educational allowance

from the Dutch authorities to study there because the German authorities refused to recognise his Dutch diploma. HELD (ECJ, Article 177): Taking into account the need for integration of migrant workers in the host state and for continuity in education, a child did not lose his status as a 'child of the family' under Regulation 1612/68 on his parent's return to the country of origin. Such a child is entitled to continue his education in the host state where his parent (the worker) has returned to his country of origin if the educational systems are incompatible.

Forcheri v. *Belgian State* (Case 152/82). Mrs Forcheri, the wife of an Italian EC official, obtained a place on a social work training course in Brussels but was told that she would be required to pay the 'minerval', a fee payable by non-Belgian nationals. HELD (ECJ, Article 177): the requirement of the national of another member state lawfully established in the host state to pay a fee not required of the state's own nationals constituted discrimination on grounds of nationality contrary to Article 7, EEC Treaty. (This right may be seen to arise out of Mrs Forcheri's position as the spouse of a worker under the Treaty and not under Article 12 of Regulation 1612/68, since she was not a worker.)

Note: After *Lebon* (Case 316/85) payment of fees at the lower rate may be seen as a social advantage under Article 7(2) of Regulation 1612/68, available as an indirect benefit to members of workers' families. (*See* Steiner p. 255.)

RIGHTS TO REMAIN IN THE TERRITORY OF A MEMBER STATE AFTER HAVING BEEN EMPLOYED IN THAT MEMBER STATE

25. The right to remain

The right to remain is provided in Regulation 1251/70 which implements Article 48(3)(d) of the Treaty. The right to remain is stated in the preamble to the Regulation to be the corollary to the right of residence of workers and may also be exercised by members of the worker's family, even after the death of the worker. There are also special provisions for frontier workers.

26. Holders of the right to remain

Under Article 2(1) of the Regulation, the right to remain permanently in the territory of a member state is held by retired workers, workers suffering from an incapacity and frontier workers under the following conditions:

(a) *Retired workers:* a worker who reaches the statutory age for entitlement to an old-age pension, provided he has been employed in that state for at least the previous 12 months and has been continuously resident there for more than three years.

(b) *Incapacitated workers:* a worker who ceases to work as an employed person in the territory of a member state as a result of permanent incapacity to work, provided he haseen permanently resident in that state for more than two years (*Note*: no condition as to length of residence is imposed if incapacity is caused by an accident at work or an occupational disease entitling him to a state pension).

(c) *Frontier workers:* a worker who is employed in the territory of another member state while retaining his residence in the territory of the home state, provided that he has been continuously employed for three years and returns to his state of residence daily or at least once a week.

Time spent working in another member state counts as working in the state of residence for retirement and incapacity purposes. Retiring or incapacitated workers are not bound to fill the residence and employment requirements if married to a national of the state in question or if that nationality has been lost as a result of marriage to the worker: Article 2(2). Qualifying workers have two years in which to decide whether to exercise the right to remain. During this period, they may freely leave the territory without jeopardising their right to return: Article 5.

27. Rights of members of the family to remain

Under Article 3 of Regulation 1251/70, the members of a worker's family are entitled to permanent residence if the worker himself is entitled to remain. If a retired or incapacitated worker with a residence entitlement dies, his family may remain permanently after his death. If, however, the worker dies during his working life before acquiring the right to residence, his family are entitled to remain provided that:

(a) the worker, at the date of death, had been continuously resident in that state for at least two years; or

(b) his death was caused by an accident at work or an occupational disease; or

(c) the surviving spouse is a national of the state of residence or has lost the nationality of that state by marriage to a worker: Article 3(2).

28. Residence permits

Qualifying individuals exercising their rights to remain are entitled to a residence permit, valid for at least five years throughout the member state's territory and automatically renewable: Article 6.

29. Equality of treatment

The beneficiaries of Regulation 1251/70 are entitled to equal treatment as provided by Article 7(2) of Regulation 1612/68. This means that they may claim all social and tax advantages on the same basis as nationals: *see Fiorini* (Case 32/75) in which the ECJ allowed a claim based on Article 7(2) by the survivors of a worker.

EMPLOYMENT IN THE PUBLIC SERVICE

30. Exclusion of public service employment

Article 48(4) of the EEC Treaty permits member states to deny or restrict access to workers employed in the public service on the basis of nationality. This exclusion has been narrowly interpreted by the ECJ (Steiner pp. 227–229 for a useful summary) and was unsuccessfully invoked in the following cases:

Examples

(1) An Article 177 reference arose out of a claim that post office rules granting allowances to workers living apart from their families in Germany discriminated against non-nationals by denying the allowance to workers resident abroad at the time of recruitment. It was held that Article 48(4) does not apply to all employment in the public service, only to certain activities connected with the exercise of official authority. Further, the exception applies only to access not to conditions of employment: *Sotgiu v. Deutsche Bundespost* (Case 152/73).

(2) A Belgian law reserving posts in the public service for Belgian nationals (including such posts as nurses, plumbers and architects employed in central and local government) was held in an Article 169 action to contravene Article 48. The exception was intended to apply only to the exercise of public authority in order to safeguard the general interests of the state. The exercising of authority at junior level was not covered: *Commission v. Belgium (Re Public Employees)* (Case 149/79).

(3) A reservation under French law reserving the appointment of nurses in public hospitals for French nationals was also held to contravene Article 48: *Commission v. France (Re French Nurses)* (Case 307/84).

(4) A German training scheme organised within the civil service could not be restricted to German nationals: *Lawrie-Blum* (Case 66/85).

(5) Teachers in state universities are not covered, since they are not charged with the exercise of powers conferred by public law and are not responsible for safeguarding the interests of the state: *Allué & Coonan v. Università degli studi di Venezia* (Case 33/88).

(6) Employment as a secondary school teacher was not covered: *Bleis v. Ministère de l'Education* (Case C-4/91).

The implication of these decisions is that only high level posts in which the post-holder owes a particular allegiance to the state may be covered (e.g. the armed forces, police, judiciary and high-ranking civil servants). This view is reinforced by the Notice in 1988 (OJ No. 72/2) in which the Commission announced its intention to review certain sectors of employment which it considered were only rarely to be covered by the exception in Article 48(4). These sectors comprise:

(a) public health services

(b) teaching in state educational establishments

(c) research for non-military purposes in public establishments

(d) public bodies responsible for administering commercial services.

LIMITATIONS JUSTIFIED ON GROUNDS OF PUBLIC POLICY, PUBLIC SECURITY OR PUBLIC HEALTH

31. Scope of the limitation

The free movement of persons may be limited on grounds of public policy, public health and public security. In the case of workers, the proviso is contained in Article 48(3). A similar proviso for the self-employed is made in Article 56. Directive 64/221 was issued to implement these exceptions and to set out the general principles governing the circumstances in which restrictive measures may be taken to refuse entry or residence to non-nationals. The directive also applies to persons receiving services, to those exercising the right of residence under Directives 90/364 and 365 and 93/96, and to EC nationals and their families exercising the right to remain under Regulation 1251/70. Directive 64/221 is directly effective and has given rise to a number of challenges before the courts.

32. The proviso

The directive relates to all measures taken by member states concerning entry into their territory, issue or renewal of residence permits or expulsion from their territory on grounds of public policy, public security or public health. Measures must not be taken on economic grounds: Article 2.

33. 'Measures'

'Measures' were defined in R. v. *Bouchereau* (Case 30/77) as any action affecting the rights of persons coming within the field of application of Article 48 to enter and reside freely in a member state on the same conditions as the nationals of the host state.

34. Public policy, public security and public health: general

Interpretation of the meaning and scope of public policy has proved to be the most contentious of these three grounds for exclusion. 'Public policy' is a translation of 'l'ordre public', a concept in French administrative law embracing wide spectrum of activities ranging from measures taken to forbid a public meeting (to prevent a disturbance) to a decree concerning the preservation of public decency on a beach. It is difficult to appreciate, from a logical perspective, how an individual's behaviour may constitute a threat to public *policy*: *Rutili* (*see* **36** below).

'Public security' has not been defined by the ECJ but is often invoked as an alternative to a threat to public policy by member states seeking to exclude an individual. Clearly, terrorist activities may pose a threat to both public policy and public security.

'Public health' may only be invoked to refuse entry or residence (for the first time) where the individual suffers from one of the diseases listed in the annex to the directive, i.e. highly infectious or contagious diseases which may be a threat to public health such as syphilis or tuberculosis and diseases or disabilities which may threaten public policy or public security, such as drug addiction and profound mental disturbance. AIDS is not listed, with the result that an AIDS sufferer may not be excluded unless coming within one of the other specified categories. The development of a disease or disability after obtaining a first residence permit does not justify the refusal to renew the permit or expulsion: Article 4(2), Directive 64/221.

35. 'Public policy'

As with other derogations from the right to free movement such as Article 36 (goods) the public policy proviso has been interpreted strictly by the ECJ: *Van Duyn* (Case 41/74), in which the Court held that, while the concept of public policy varies from state to state, its scope may not be unilaterally determined by member states without control by the EC institutions.

36. Development of the public policy proviso

The approach of the ECJ to the meaning of public policy was modified further in *Rutili* v. *Ministre de l'Intérieur* (Case 36/75) where the ECJ held that restrictions on the movement of an EC national under Article 48(3) may not be imposed unless the behaviour of the individual constitutes a genuine and sufficiently serious threat to public policy.

> *Rutili* v. *Ministre de l'Intérieur*. An Italian political activist challenged the decision of the French Minister of the Interior to restrict his activities to certain French departments. HELD (ECJ, Article 177): Restrictions may not be placed on a worker's rights to enter the territory of another member state, live there and move freely unless his presence constituted a genuine and sufficiently serious threat to public policy. This principle gives effect to Articles 8 to 11 of the European Convention on Human Rights which does not permit restrictions in the interests of national security or public safety unless they are necessary to protect those interests in a democratic society. The ECJ also held that only a total ban may be justified under the public policy proviso. Applying Article 7 of the Treaty the Court decided that a partial restriction on residence may only be imposed where such a restriction may also be placed on a national of the host state.

In *R.* v. *Bouchereau* (Case 30/77): *see* **38** below, the ECJ held that the public policy proviso may only be invoked where there is a genuine and sufficiently serious threat to one of the fundamental interests of the society.

> *Note*: Measures taken on grounds of public policy will not be justified: **(a)** on the basis of criminal convictions alone, unless the convictions show there is a present threat to public policy: *R.* v. *Bouchereau*: *see* **38** below, **(b)** where a passport or identity card used to obtain a residence permit does not justify expulsion from the territory: Article 3(3), Directive 64/221.

The right to residence derives from the Treaty not from the possession of a residence permit: *Procureur du Roi* v. *Royer* (Case 48/75). Thus, failure to comply with administrative requirements, e.g. to renew a passport or identity card, does not justify deportation although it may lead to the imposition of a penalty provided the penalty is not disproportionate. In *R.* v. *Pieck* (Case 157/79) the ECJ held that the public policy proviso did not justify *general* formalities at the frontier beyond the production of a valid identity card or passport. Article 48(3) is a means of taking measures against *individuals* who may pose a threat.

37. Personal conduct

Article 3(1) of Directive 64/221 states that measures taken on grounds of public policy or public security must be based exclusively on the personal conduct of the individual concerned. The right of residence may not be denied to a worker or his family because the worker becomes involuntarily unemployed: *Lübberson* (1984, IAT). The area of discretion left to national authorities under Article 48(3) may be examined by reference to various decisions of the ECJ: *Rutili: see above, Van Duyn, Adoui, Bonsignore* and *Bouchereau: see* below.

> *Van Duyn* v. *Home Office* (Case 41/74). Miss Van Duyn, a Dutch national, was refused entry to the UK to take up employment with the Church of Scientology. While not illegal, the practice of Scientology was regarded by the UK government as objectionable and socially harmful. Miss Van Duyn challenged the refusal before the UK courts which sought guidance from the ECJ on the meaning of personal conduct and of the basis for exclusion. HELD (ECJ, Article 177): **(a)** Past association with an organisation does not count as personal conduct although present association does; **(b)** the activities in question must constitute a genuine and sufficiently serious threat to public policy affecting one of the fundamental interests of society.

In *Van Duyn* the ECJ allowed a member state to apply a stricter standard to an EC worker than to its own nationals where the state deems that it is necessary. While the *Van Duyn* decision has been cited with approval the ECJ has moved towards a more restrictive approach in *Adoui* in which a decision to exclude must be shown to be justified.

> *Adoui and Cornaille* v. *Belgian State* (Cases 115 & 116/81). Two prostitutes sought residence permits in Belgium where prostitution is not illegal. HELD (ECJ): Member states are not entitled to refuse residence to non-nationals on account of conduct which is not illegal or controlled in nationals of the host state.

38. Previous criminal convictions

Previous (and even current) criminal convictions do not necessarily provide grounds for exclusion on public policy grounds unless they provide evidence of a present threat to public policy:

> *R.* v. *Bouchereau* (Case 30/77). B, a French national, came to work in the UK in 1975. He was convicted of unlawful possession of drugs in June 1976, having pleaded guilty to a similar offence in January 1976 (for which he

received a 12 month conditional discharge). The magistrates' court referred to the ECJ questions to determine to what extent previous convictions may be considered as a ground for exclusion. HELD: A previous criminal conviction may only be taken into account as evidence of personal conduct where it constitutes a present threat to the requirements of public policy, by indicating a likelihood of recurrence. Past conduct alone, however, may be sufficient to constitute a present threat where the conduct is sufficiently serious.

Bonsignore v. *Oberstadtdirecktor of the City of Cologne* (Case 67/74). B, an Italian working in Germany, accidentally shot his brother with a pistol. He was convicted and fined for unlawful possession of a firearm and was ordered to be deported. He challenged the deportation order in the German courts which referred to the ECJ the question of whether deportation may be justified on public policy grounds as a general preventive measure to deter others. HELD: The public policy requirement may only be invoked to justify a deportation for breaches of the peace and public security which may be committed by the individual concerned and not for reasons of a general preventive nature.

39. Procedural rights

In addition to providing the basis for derogation from Articles 48, Directive 64/221 also provides important safeguards for parties claiming rights of entry or residence in member states. These rights, being directly effective, may be invoked by individuals before the national courts.

The main safeguards under the directive include:

(a) *Right of re-entry.* Where a person holds a passport or identity card which has expired or where the holder's nationality is in doubt, the issuing state must allow the passport-holder to re-enter its territory without formalities: Article 3(4). While a decision on the granting of a first residence permit in a member state is awaited, a member state must allow the applicant temporary residence in the state. The decision must be taken as soon as possible, and not later than six months from the date of application: Article 5(1). Where the decision is to refuse a residence permit, the person must be allowed a minimum of 15 days to leave (except in cases of urgency). Where the decision is to expel, one month is the minimum period (except for emergencies): Article 7.

(b) *Grounds for decision.* The person concerned is entitled to know on which of the grounds (public policy, public health or public security) the decision is based, unless this information contravenes state security: Article 6. The grounds must be indicated in a clear and comprehensive statement, to enable the person to prepare his defence: *Rutili* (Case 36/75). Failure to comply with Article 6 led to the quashing of a deportation recommendation by magistrates in *R. v. Secretary of State for the Home Department (ex parte Dannenberg)* (1984, Court of Appeal). (*See* Steiner p. 259.)

(c) *Remedies.* Under Article 8 the person concerned is entitled to the same legal remedies in relation to a decision on entry, refusal to issue or renew a residence permit or on expulsion from the territory as a national in relation to acts of the administration. Where there is no (or only a limited) right of appeal against a refusal of a residence permit or expulsion, the host state must first obtain the opinion of a competent authority before which the person concerned enjoys such rights of defence and of assistance or representation as domestic law provides: Article 9. Thus, Article 9 supplements Article 8 and ensures that the person concerned is protected by the rules of natural justice, so that he may exercise his rights before a competent authority other than the one which adopted the decision.

In *R. v. Secretary of State for the Home Department (ex parte Santillo)* (Case 131/79) an Italian was convicted in the UK of several serious crimes of violence including rape. He was sentenced to a five year term of imprisonment, followed with a recommendation for deportation. The deportation order was, however, made by the Home Secretary after five years. The ECJ held on a reference from the High Court that the trial judge's recommendation was an opinion but that the safeguard provided by Article 9 could only be real if the opinion were close enough in time to the recommendation (otherwise the factors justifying the public policy proviso may no longer apply).

In *Pecastaing* (Case 98/79) the ECJ held that the person concerned must be able to stay long enough to initiate proceedings under Article 9, unless deportation is required as an emergency measure. No comparable suspensory procedure applies to Article 8.

Progress test 14

1. Which characteristics typify a 'worker' according to the decisions of the ECJ?

2. What are the main features of equality of treatment for a worker and his family under Article 48 and Regulation 1612/68? How has the ECJ used the concept of 'social and tax advantages' to extend equality of treatment?

3. Explain the scope of the right of the worker and his family to remain in the territory of another member state after employment in that state.

4. To what extent does Article 48(4) permit member states to exclude employment in the public sector from the free movement of workers?

5. Heidi, a German national, was offered a job in the UK working for a religious cult known as the Sun Children. She was, however, refused entry to the UK on the ground that her presence would constitute a threat to public policy as she had been convicted of theft five years previously. The UK government has recently announced that it will not permit the entry of any foreign national to work for the Sun Children while the organisation is under investigation for fraud. Advise Heidi of her legal and procedural rights.

15

THE RIGHT OF ESTABLISHMENT AND THE FREEDOM TO PROVIDE SERVICES

1. Introduction

The right of establishment and the freedom to provide services are both essential requirements of the single market. Both rights envisage the pursuit of business or professional activity. The right of establishment refers to the right of EC nationals (both natural and legal persons) to set up a business in a member state other than their own. Establishment is seen as a permanent (or near permanent) right. Freedom to provide services is the right of persons established in one member state to provide services in another state. The provision of services is, however, seen as a temporary right, not necessarily involving residence.

The Treaty provisions on the right of establishment are contained in Articles 52 to 59 and on the freedom to provide services in Articles 59 to 66.

The law on both establishment and services is largely similar. Both rights are subject to the limitation in Directive 64/221 on grounds of public policy, public security and public health (extended by Directive 75/34 to cover nationals and their families with the right to remain). However, there are significant differences between the rights of workers and the self-employed in certain areas: *see* below. There is no equivalent to Regulation 1612/68 for the self-employed. Directive 73/148 (the equivalent of Directive 73/184) provides for rights of entry and residence and Directive 75/34 (equivalent of Regulation 1251/70) provides for the right to remain after employment for the self-employed and their families.

THE RIGHT OF ESTABLISHMENT

2. The right of establishment

Article 52 provides for the abolition by the end of the transitional period of restrictions on the freedom of establishment of the nationals of a member state in the territory of another member state. This progressive abolition also applies to restrictions on the setting up of agencies, branches or subsidiaries by the nationals of any member state established in the territory of any other member state.

3. 'Nationals of a member state': natural and legal persons

As a result of the provision in Article 58, Article 52 must be read as applicable to both natural and legal persons. Article 58 provides that companies or firms formed and having their registered office, central administration or principal place of business within the EC shall, for the purpose of establishment, be treated in the same way as natural persons.

Article 52(2) requires the elimination of restrictions on the setting up of agencies, branches or subsidiaries across national frontiers; the same conditions as are applied to nationals of the host state must be applied to companies and firms covered by Article 58, subject to the provisions in the Treaty relating to capital.

Taken together, Articles 52 and 58 cause difficulties because the law regulating companies varies according to their place of incorporation. To deal with these differences, the Council and Commission were required by Article 54 to draw up a general programme for the abolition of restrictions on freedom of establishment to co-ordinate safeguards to protect the interests of members and others with a view to making these safeguards 'equivalent' across the EC.

4. The general programme for the abolition of restrictions on freedom of establishment 1961

Under the general programme companies incorporated under the law of one of the member states but having their principal place of business outside the EC must maintain an effective and continuing link with the economy of a member state. A link provided by nationality, particularly the nationality of partners or the members of the managing or supervisory body, is specifically excluded. The requirement to maintain such a link demonstrates that an organisation may not gain access to the single market merely by registering a company in one of the member states while the real business is effected outside the EC.

As a further major consequence of the programme ten directives harmonising company law have been adopted. Four further directives are in the process of adoption. It is, however, beyond the scope of this book to examine these directives in detail.

5. Recognition of companies

The Treaty provides for separate conventions between member states. In 1968 the original six member states signed the Convention on the Mutual Recognition of Companies and Bodies Corporate (to which the other six states forming the enlarged Community acceded). The Convention provides that companies formed under the law of one contracting state shall be recognised in another as having the capacity accorded to them by the law under which they were formed, subject to various derogations. However, as the Convention has not been ratified by all the signatory states, it has not yet entered into force.

6. New forms of business organisation in the EC

The European Economic Interest Grouping (EEIG) is a new form of business organisation whose purpose is to enable existing companies from more than one member state to co-ordinate certain non-profit-making activities while retaining their independence. The Commission has proposed (in the draft Fifth Directive on company law) the creation of a European Company, based on EC law. Under the proposal only companies already incorporated in the EC may form a European Company but the right is extended to the EC subsidiaries of companies incorporated outside the Community. A further framework under the Social Chapter (*see* Chapter 24) has been proposed. It would require worker consultation in EC-wide companies with at least 1000 employees and two or more sites with at least 100 staff in different member states.

7. Meaning of the right of establishment

One implication of paragraphs one and two of Article 52 is that a distinction exists between persons not yet established in a member state and those who are already established. Persons in the first category are merely entitled to establish themselves in any member state, whereas persons already established have the right to set up agencies and branches in any member state, subject to the observance of professional rules of conduct: *Klopp* (Case 107/83).

8. Direct applicability and the transitional period

In *Reyners* v. *Belgian State* (Case 2/74) the ECJ decided that Article 52 was directly applicable from the end of the transitional period and was not dependent for implementation of further directives.

> *Reyners* v. *Belgian State* (Case 2/74). R was a Dutch national, born, educated and resident in Belgium where he held a doctorate in Belgian law. He was refused admission to the Belgian bar because he was not a Belgian national. HELD (ECJ, Article 177): Article 52 was directly effective from the end of the transitional period (December 1961), being an application of the principle of non-discrimination in Article 7 EEC. The general programme and implementing directives were only of significance during the transitional period and were intended merely to facilitate legislation under Article 52.

9. Consequences of the decision in *Reyners*

The Commission decided in 1974 that no further directives should be adopted to remove restrictions on the right of establishment, considering that further directives were unnecessary and confusing. However, it could be argued that further directives might have provided useful clarification of the scope of Article 52.

10. The exercise of state authority

Activities connected with the exercise of state authority are excluded from the right of establishment: Article 55. Note, however, that the profession of advocate was considered by the ECJ in *Reyners* (Case 2/74) not to be connected with the exercise of state authority.

11. Restrictions on movement and residence

Directive 73/148 applies to both the right of establishment and the provision of services. The directive abolished restrictions on the movement and residence of:

(a) Nationals of member states who are established in one member state and wish to establish in another member state or to provide services

(b) Nationals who wish to go to another member state as the recipients of services (e.g. as tourists)

(c) Spouses and children under 21 years of nationals

(d) Relatives (both ascendant and descendant) of nationals and of spouses where dependant.

Under the directive (similar in scope to Directive 68/360 for workers) those who benefit may leave and re-enter the territory on production of the necessary identity card. Those entering for the purpose of establishment have a permanent right of residence and are entitled to a five-year, automatically renewable residence permit. Those entering to provide services may only stay for the duration of those services. A 'right of abode' document may be issued if the stay exceeds three months.

12. The right to remain

Directive 75/34 also applies to both establishment and the provision of services. It provides (like Regulation 1251/70 for workers) for the self-employed and their families to remain after retirement.

13. The freedom to provide services

Article 59 provides for the progressive abolition during the transitional period of restrictions on the freedom to provide services in respect of EC nationals who are established in a member state other than that of the person for whom the services are intended.

The Council is empowered under Article 59 to propose the extension of this freedom to the nationals of a third country (i.e. non-member state) who provide services and who are established in the EC.

Under Article 60(3) a person providing a service may temporarily pursue his activity in the state where the service is provided under the same conditions as the state imposes on its own nationals.

14. Services

'Services' are defined under Article 60(1) as those 'normally provided for remuneration, in so far as they are not governed by the provisions relating to the freedom of movement of goods, capital and persons'. They include industrial and commercial services and the activities of craftsmen and professionals, but not transport, insurance or banking, for which there is a separate provision in the Treaty.

15. Beneficiaries of the right of establishment and the freedom to provide services

Beneficiaries of the right of establishment and the freedom to provide services include EC nationals and companies formed under the law of one of the member states: *see* above.

In *Commission* v. *Germany (Re Insurance Services)* (Case 205/84) the ECJ in an Article 169 action held that an enterprise would be regarded as an establishment rather than as the provider of services where there was no branch or agency within the EC but only an office managed by the enterprise staff or other authorised independent person. Thus, it would appear to be a question of degree rather than principle which determines whether the activities of an undertaking are governed by the provisions on establishment or on services.

16. Limitation on establishment and the provision of services

Both the right of establishment and the freedom to provide services are subject (in addition to the express exceptions under Articles 55, 56 and 66) to the same conditions as govern nationals of the host state: Article 52(2) (establishment) and Article 60(3) (services). It is, however, difficult for non-nationals to satisfy the conditions laid down by law or by trade or professional bodies in relation to education or training. Rules of professional conduct may provide a further barrier: *see* below.

17. The general programme on the abolition of restrictions on the freedom to provide services 1961

In parallel with the programme relating to the right of establishment a further programme was adopted by the Council on services. While the programmes are not legally binding, they have been invoked before the courts for the purpose of interpretation: *Gravier* (Case 293/83). The Commission is also under a duty under Article 57 to draw up directives to harmonise professional qualifications: *see* below.

18. Elimination of barriers to the free movement of professional persons

There are two distinct approaches to this problem:

(a) Harmonisation of professional qualifications under Article 57

(b) Application of the principle of non-discrimination under Article 7.

19. Harmonisation of professional qualifications

A number of directives have been issued under Article 57 covering specific professions. Health professionals are at the forefront of the professions to benefit from harmonisation: there are directives covering the qualifications of doctors, nurses, dentists, pharmacists and veterinary surgeons. Architects are also the subject of a directive. Where basic training and qualifications have been harmonised, professionals have the right to establish and practise throughout the EC. Progress towards harmonisation has also been made in the fields of agriculture, the film industry, mining, gas services and catering.

20. Lawyers

In contrast to health professionals, the scope for EC-wide practice by lawyers has been more limited. Directive 77/249 enables lawyers to provide services but not to establish themselves in other member states. However, further progress on lawyers' rights of establishment is now being made as a result of Directive 89/48: see **28–30** below.

21. Beneficiaries of the right of establishment and the freedom to provide services

A person who possesses recognised or equivalent qualifications is entitled to exercise the right of establishment and the freedom to provide services even where he is a national of the state in question: *Knoors* (Case 115/78); *Broekmeulen* (Case 246/80): see **22** below.

In the absence of a specific directive recognising the mutual recognition of professional qualifications, the refusal of permission to practise a profession to a person whose qualifications have been recognised as equivalent contravenes Articles 52 (or 59, for services) and Article 7: *Thieffry* and *Patrick*.

> *Thieffry* v. *Conseil de l'Ordre des Avocates à la Cour de Paris* (Case 71/76). T, a Belgian national holding a Belgian law degree, sought to challenge the decision of the French Bar Council refusing to allow him to undertake practical training for the French bar. His law degree had been recognised by the University of Paris and he held a further qualification certificate in France for practising as an 'avocat'. HELD (ECJ, Article 177): When a national of one member state wishes to practise a profession such as advocate in another member state, having obtained a qualification in his own country recognised as equivalent by the other member state, it contravenes Article 52 to demand the national diploma as a further prerequisite to the special qualifying examination.

> *Patrick* v. *Ministre des Affaires Culturelles* (Case 11/77). P, a UK national who had trained as an architect in the UK, was prevented from practising as an architect in France. At the time there was neither a directive on architectural qualifications, nor was there a diplomatic convention. P's qualifications had, however, been recognised as equivalent to the corresponding French qualification under a Ministerial Decree of 1964. HELD (ECJ, Article 177): A person whose qualifications have been recognised as equivalent may rely on Article 52 and Article 7 to practise a profession, in the absence of a directive providing for professional recognition.

A person whose qualifications from other member states are neither harmonised nor recognised may, however, be subject to discrimination without contravention of the Treaty.

22. Additional requirements

Where a directive has been issued in relation to a particular profession, that profession may no longer insist on compliance with its own requirements from persons qualified in another member state, even where the individual in question is a national of the member state in which he seeks to practise: *Broekmeulen* (Case 246/80). In this case a doctor qualified in Belgium had been refused permission to practise as a GP in the Netherlands because he had not undertaken a further three-year training as a GP (not required under Directive 75/362 on the training of GPs). Such a requirement is clearly unenforceable.

> *Note*: Where a party seeks to exercise the right of establishment or the freedom to provide services under a directive adopted under Article 157, he may not rely on the directive until the date for implementation has passed: *Auer* (Case 136/78).

23. Application of the principle of non-discrimination

There is no secondary legislation on the right of establishment and the freedom to provide services comparable to Regulation 1612/68 (providing for co-operation between national authorities on the free movement of labour and for equal treatment). Thus, the principle of non-discrimination or equality under Article 7 of the Treaty is particularly important. (This is sometimes called the *'Cassis de Dijon'* principle from the decision on the free movement of goods: Case 120/78: *see* 9:**8**.)

By applying this principle where recognition and harmonisation have not been achieved in a particular profession it has been possible to invoke Articles 7, 52, 59 and 60 (after the expiry of the transitional period) to challenge a traditional rule which is discriminatory. 'Discrimination' has been liberally construed to cover both the taking up and pursuit of a particular activity.

Examples
(1) A German artist living in France applied to the local authority to rent a 'crampotte' (a fisherman's hut used to exhibit paintings). The application was refused because city regulations stated that the huts could only be rented by French nationals. HELD (ECJ, Article 177): Freedom of establishment under Article 52 covered not only taking up activity as a self-employed person but also the pursuit of that activity in the broadest sense: *Steinhauser* v. *City of Biarritz* (Case 197/84).
(2) A cheap mortgage facility available only to Italian nationals was HELD by the ECJ to contravene Article 7. It should have been available to all EC nationals providing services who required a permanent dwelling in the host state: *Commission* v. *Italy: Re Housing Aid* (Case 63/86).
(3) Discrimination under Greek law against land-owning by non-Greek nationals was held by the ECJ to contravene Articles 52 to 59: *Commission* v. *Greece* (Case 305/87).

(4) The manager of a company incorporated and established in the UK held a licence in the UK for the provision of manpower but not in the Netherlands where the company recruited and supplied temporary staff. He was charged with supplying manpower without the necessary licence. HELD (ECJ, Article 177): Such restrictions were only permissible where justified by the common good and to the same extent as applied to the nationals of the host state. The provision of manpower was identified as 'specially sensitive' from the occupational and social point of view, enabling a member state to impose a licensing system provided the scheme is not excessive in relation to the aim pursued: *Webb* (Case 279/80).

24. Professional rules of conduct

Professional rules of conduct may also provide barriers to the free movement of persons, particularly where a residential qualification is required.

The Court also ruled in *Van Binsbergen* that a residential qualification in a properly qualified person is not a legitimate condition of exercising a specific profession, unless it is necessary to ensure the observance of professional rules of conduct.

Van Binsbergen (Case 33/74). Van Binsbergen was represented in a Dutch court by an unqualified legal adviser, Kortman. When Kortman moved from the Netherlands to Belgium he was told he could no longer represent Van B as he was not resident in the Netherlands. HELD (ECJ, Article 177): Specific requirements on a person providing services would not infringe Articles 59 and 60 where the purpose is to apply professional rules justified by the general good which are binding on a person established in the state where the services are provided.

Analogies may be drawn between the reliance of the ECJ in *Van Binsbergen* on necessity and the rule of reason in *Cassis de Dijon*. Subsequent cases follow a similar approach, with emphasis on the principle of proportionality.

In *Gulling* v. *Conseils des Ordres des Barreaux et de Saverne* (Case 292/86) a registration requirement by the German bar for barristers wishing to establish themselves in Germany (applied equally to nationals of the host state) was held by the ECJ to be permissible. However, in *Conseil de l'Ordre de Nice* v. *Jean-Jacques Raynel* (1990, Conseil d'Etat) the Conseil d'Etat held that refusal of permission to an advocate of the Nice bar by his circuit leader to open chambers and to join the Brussels bar contravened Article 52. The Court also ruled that the freedom of establishment of an advocate in another member state does not permit a distinction between the practice of an advocate in a principal or second set of chambers.

Note: The French government passed a law in 1990 (not yet the subject of a challenge before the ECJ) forbidding foreign lawyers from providing legal services in France without first becoming a member of the local bar. This requirement would appear to contravene Directive 77/249 unless the three requirements in *Van Binsbergen* are satisfied: *see* above.

In *Vlassopoulos* v. *Ministerium für Justiz* (Case C-340/89) a Greek lawyer challenged the German rules on qualification which excluded him from practising. HELD (ECJ): Article 52 entitled the national authorities to examine the qualifications of non-nationals to see whether they are equivalent.

25. Respect for the legitimate rules and standards of member states

EC law may not be invoked to undermine the legitimate rules and standards of member states in education and training and professional rules.

Example
Under UK government rules Treasury consent was required before a company could transfer its head office to another member state. HELD (ECJ, contrary to the submissions of Advocate-General Darmon): Freedom of establishment was a fundamental right. However, in the absence of directives, Articles 52 and 58 do *not* confer on a company incorporated under the legal system of a member state in which its registered office is situated the right to transfer its management and control to another member state: *R. v. HM Treasury, ex parte Daily Mail and General Trust plc* (Case 81/87).

cf. *Segers* (Case 79/85) in which a company registered in one member state but operating entirely through an agency in another member state was held entitled to establish itself in the state in which it operated.

26. The 'Insurance' cases

Actions were brought by the Commission under Article 169 against four member states as a result of national rules requiring insurance undertakings to conduct their business in those states through persons already established and authorised to practise there: *see Commission v. Germany* (Case 205/84). Three further cases were decided against Ireland, France and Denmark.

In, for example, *Commission v. Germany* the ECJ followed the *Van Binsbergen* approach and distinguished between establishment and services. 'Establishment' was held to cover an office managed by the staff of the enterprise or by an independent person authorised to act on behalf of an enterprise. An enterprise established outside the EC but whose activities are largely directed towards the member state where services are provided (in an attempt to escape the rules of conduct of that state) is also covered. The ECJ held that Articles 59 and 60 require, in addition to the removal of discrimination based on nationality, the abolition of restrictions on the freedom to provide services imposed as a result of establishment in a member state other than that in which the services are provided.

The establishment requirement was held to be unjustified but the authorisation requirement was justified in so far as it was necessary to protect policy-holders and insured persons.

Note: The Commission has developed a new approach to the right of establishment and the provision of service in its harmonisation of financial services. A number of directives have now been adopted including banking (Directive 89/646), insurance (Directive 88/357), non-life insurance (Directive 88/357) and life insurance (Directive 90/619). The internal market in financial services is now complete. The new approach reflects the Commission's commitment to harmonisation of essential safeguards and relevant standards and the acceptance of the standards of other member states within that framework, on the principle of control and supervision by the home state. A single licence would be issued, enabling an institution licensed in one member state to offer its services to another member state (by establishing a branch or agency, or supplying its services in the other state).

27. A fresh initiative on qualifications

It became clear to the Commission that the sectoral approach to the harmonisation of professional qualifications was too slow. This approach often involved two directives for each profession or occupation, one to co-ordinate and harmonise training and another to provide for the mutual recognition of qualifications. (The architects' directive, for example, took 17 years to adopt.) The Commission, therefore, decided to speed up the recognition process as part of the 1992 Programme by creating a single system of mutual recognition of higher education qualifications based on the principle of non-discrimination entitling an individual to practise a vocation or profession.

28. Directive 89/48 on the mutual recognition of qualifications

Directive 89/48 on the mutual recognition of qualifications was adopted in December 1988 and came into effect on 1 January 1991. The directive should be directly effective against a public body from that date, being sufficiently clear, precise and unconditional. Professional bodies subject to statutory regulation are likely to be regarded as public bodies for enforcement purposes.

The directive which covers workers as well as the self-employed does not apply to those professions which are already subject to a harmonising directive, nor does it alter the rules of particular professions in individual member states.

The central element of the directive is the mutual recognition throughout the EC of higher education diplomas requiring professional education or training of three or more years' duration (or the equivalent period part-time). Directive 92/51 extended the scope of mutual recognition to qualifications involving less than three years duration.

29. The main features of Directive 89/48

(a) All professionals whose qualifications are within its scope will be entitled to recognition of their qualifications within the other member states.

(b) A professional's qualifications will be recognised where education or training is substantially the same between member states. Recognition is also accorded where the national has pursued the profession in question for at least two years in a state which does not regulate that profession: Article 3.

(c) Evidence of professional experience may be required from an applicant whose education and training is at least one year less than that required by the host state or where the applicant's period of supervised practice falls short of the host state's requirements: Article 4(a).

30. Adaptation periods and aptitude tests

An adaptation period not exceeding three years may be required by the host state where:

(a) There is a substantial difference between the matters covered by the applicant's education and training and those of the host state

(b) The activities regulated in the host state are not regulated in the home state of the applicant

(c) The profession regulated in the host state covers activities not pursued in the home state of the applicant.

In the case of **(b)** and **(c)**, an adaptation period is only required where the difference applies to specific education and training in the host state and which differs substantially from those covered by the evidence of formal requirements: Article 4(1)(b).

The applicant may opt to take an aptitude test instead of compliance with an adaptation period. A state may, however, stipulate either an adaptation period or an aptitude test where a precise knowledge of national law is required, in relation to specific professions where the practice of the profession is dependent on the constant and essential giving of advice on national law. As the requirements for professional experience and adaptation period may not be applied cumulatively, the total period may not exceed four years. The host state has discretion, on the basis of equivalence, to permit the period of supervised professional practice to be undertaken in the host state: Article 5.

Note: Directive 92/51 applicable to qualifications of less than three years was adopted in 1992 for implementation by 1994.

31. Industrial property rights and the freedom to provide services

The legitimate exercise of industrial property rights cannot be prevented by invoking Article 59 on the freedom to provide services: *Coditel* v. *Ciné Vog* (Case 62/79). In this case a Belgian film distributor, SA Ciné Vog Films, owned the performing rights in various films including one called 'Le Boucher'. Ciné Vog tried to prevent Coditel, a cable television service, from picking up 'Le Boucher' from German television and transmitting it in Belgium. Coditel argued before the national court that preventing transmission amounted to a breach of the freedom to provide services in Article 59. The ECJ held (in an Article 177 reference) that Article 59 cannot be invoked to prevent a legitimate exercise of industrial property rights unless a disguised restriction on trade is involved.

FREEDOM TO RECEIVE SERVICES

32. Freedom to receive services

Articles 59 and 60 are worded in terms of the freedom to *provide* services. There is no explicit mention of the receipt of services. However, the ECJ has extended the freedom to include the freedom to *receive* services. The issue first came before the ECJ in *Watson and Belmann* (Case 118/75) in which the Commission submitted that the freedom to receive services was the essential corollary to the freedom to provide services.

The ECJ adopted the principle proposed in *Watson and Belmann* in *Luisi and Carbone* v. *Ministero del Tesoro* (Joined Cases 286/82 and 26/83): *see* 11:**10**. These cases arose out of the criminal prosecutions of Luisi and Carbone for taking currency out of Italy in amounts greater than currency regulations permitted, the money being payments for tourism and medical services. The Court held that the freedom to provide services included the freedom to receive services. This freedom was found to entitle the recipient to visit another member state to receive services without obstruction by restrictions. Tourists, persons receiving medical treatment and persons travelling for the purpose of education or business were regarded as the recipients of services.

33. The principle of non-discrimination

The principle of non-discrimination under Article 6 EC may also be invoked in the context of the receipt of services. However, the full scope of Article 6 (previously Article 7 EEC) is not yet clear. The question has been raised in relation to the payment of fees for education: *see*, for example, *Gravier* (Case 293/83) in which the ECJ held that a discriminatory registration fee to gain access to vocational training courses contravened Article 7. (For a more detailed discussion of *Gravier* and other decisions on education: *see* below.)

More recently, the non-discrimination (or equality) principle has been applied in the case of *Cowan* v. *French Treasury* (Case 186/87). In this case the plaintiff had been attacked and robbed in the Paris Metro while on holiday. The French Criminal Injuries Compensation Board refused to pay him compensation for injuries since French law only provided for the payment of compensation out of public funds to French nationals. Cowan argued that, as his claim was based on the receipt of tourist services, the French rule contravened Article 7. The ECJ held that the recipient of services was entitled to equal protection from, and compensation for, the risks of assault as a corollary of the right to receive services.

cf. *SPUC* v. *Grogan* (Case C-159/90) where the lack of an economic element prevented the ECJ from treating the case as involving the receipt of services.

> *SPUC* v. *Grogan* (Case C-159/90) arose in the context of the protection of the right of the unborn child to life, a right which was recognised by the Irish constitution. The ECJ considered an Irish ban which prevented a student union from distributing information on abortion. The ECJ held that as no economic activity was involved there was no breach of EC law.
>
> Subsequently the Irish government applied for an injunction to prevent an Irish citizen from leaving the country to obtain an abortion abroad. While the Irish court upheld the woman's right to travel the Irish government sought to amend the protocol of the TEU (a declaration recognising that EC law does not affect the right to life) to permit the right to travel.
>
> In 1992 the Irish people voted in a referendum in favour of the TEU amendments and in December 1992 they supported the right to travel.

34. Education and vocational training: *Gravier*

The issue of the access of EC nationals to education and vocational training arose in *Gravier* v. *City of Liège* (Case 293/83).

> *Gravier* v. *City of Liège*. Gravier, a French national, had applied and had been accepted for a four-year course at the Liège Académie des Beaux-Arts in the art of the strip cartoon. She was treated by the Académie as a foreign student and was required to pay the 'minerval', a special fee not payable by Belgian nationals. Ms Gravier argued, firstly, that the 'minerval' was an obstacle to her freedom to receive services and, secondly, that to charge a higher fee for a vocational course to an EC national was discriminatory under Article 7: *see Forcheri* (Case 152/82) – *see* 12:**22**. HELD (ECJ, Article 177): Vocational training was covered by Article 7. (There was no ruling on the first argument raised.) The ECJ also held that 'vocational training' covered all forms of teaching leading to a particular profession, trade or employment, or which provides the necessary skills for such a profession, even if the programme involves an element of general education.

The reasoning which enabled the ECJ in *Gravier* to rule that vocational training was covered by Article 7 derives from an imaginative interpretation of Article 128 (empowering the Council to lay down general principles to implement a common vocational training programme) and from the provisions on workers and their children in Regulation 1612/68, Articles 7(3) and 12. The Court held that this general provision in Article 128 brought vocational training within the scope of coverage of EC law, as a result of which such training was subject to the equality principle of Article 7. Article 128 was thus treated as directly effective, although it is hard to see how the criteria for direct effect were satisfied. (*See* Steiner p. 249.)

35. Education and training after *Gravier*

The scope of 'vocational training' was not clear after *Gravier*. However, several cases followed, making definition more straightforward.

In *Blaizot* v. *University of Liège* (Case 24/86), relying on *Gravier*, a number of university students of veterinary studies claimed reimbursement of the 'minerval'. The ECJ held that a university course may be considered vocational training not only where the final examinations constitute the required qualification but also where the course provides specific training in the form of the knowledge necessary to practise a trade or profession (even in the absence of a formal requirement for such knowledge).

The implication of this decision is that most university undergraduates courses will qualify as 'vocational'. Only those courses designed to improve general knowledge (e.g. a general arts degree) rather than preparation for an occupation would be excluded. Thus, those degrees such as medicine and veterinary studies involving an academic and vocational stage would effectively be considered as a single 'vocational' stage.

Two further cases referred by the Belgian courts were decided on the same day: *Belgian State* v. *Humbel* (Case 263/86) and *Commission* v. *Belgium* (Case 42/87).

Belgian State v. *Humbel* (Case 263/86). The Belgian authorities claimed the payment of the 'minerval' for a one-year vocational course in Belgium which formed part of general secondary education received by the son of a French national living in Luxembourg. HELD (ECJ, Article 1177): Such a course must be regarded as 'vocational' if it forms an integral part of an overall programme of education.

Commission v. *Belgium* (Case 42/87). Belgian rules limited access to higher education in Belgium to only two per cent of non-nationals. HELD (ECJ, Article 169): The rules contravened Article 7 in so far as they applied to vocational training.

As a result of the decision in *Gravier* and the subsequent rulings of the ECJ, EC nationals must be granted access to courses which (overall) are vocational on terms equivalent to those granted to the nationals of the host state, even when the courses are subsidised by that state.

36. Grants and scholarships

Doubts expressed in *Gravier* over the question of whether the access of EC nationals to vocational training also carried entitlement to grants and scholarships were resolved in the cases of *Brown* (Case 197/86) and *Lair* (Case 39/36): *see* 14:**19**. In both cases, the ECJ held that maintenance grants fell outside the scope of the EEC Treaty, being a matter of educational and social policy, and were thus not subject to Article 7.

37. ERASMUS and other EC schemes

Educational schemes (identified by acronyms such as ERASMUS, COMETT, LINGUA and SOCRATES) are proliferating. The best known scheme, ERASMUS, was drawn up to facilitate student and staff mobility in university exchange programmes within the EC by providing financial assistance. The Council decision (based on Articles 128 and 235) setting up the ERASMUS scheme was challenged by the Commission in *Commission* v. *Council* (Case 242/87). The ECJ held that in principle the Council could rely on Article 128 to adopt the decision. In relation to vocational training, the ECJ upheld the decision in *Gravier* and the subsequent decisions, ruling that as most university activities under ERASMUS were concerned with vocational training, the programme was covered by Article 128. The ECJ also held that as the research elements of the programme could not be covered by Article 128 it was legitimate to invoke Article 235 as a further legal basis for the decision.

Other programmes adopted by the EC include COMETT which aims to promote technological development and LINGUA to improve the quality and range of language teaching. The scope of the LINGUA programme, originally proposed to apply to both university and school levels of education, was reduced to exclude specific reference to schools after objections by the UK government. The legal basis for EC action in education has been strengthened in the TEU: *see* 26:**28**

RESIDENCE RIGHTS OF NON-WORKERS

38. Residence rights for non-workers

Under Directive 90/364 residence rights are to be granted to the nationals of member states who do not enjoy this right under other provisions of EC law, and also to members of their families (as defined by Article 10(1) of Regulation 1612/68). The date for implementation of the Directive was 30 June 1992. The right of residence is, however, only granted to those persons who are covered by sickness insurance in respect of all risks and who have sufficient resources to avoid becoming a financial burden on the social assistance system of the host state. Evidence of the right of residence will be required in the form of a residence permit, granted for five years and automatically renewable. Validation of the permit may be demanded by the host state after two years.

Beneficiaries of rights under this Directive must be treated on the same basis as nationals of the host state for some of the purposes of Directive 68/360 (on the abolition of restrictions on movement and residence of EC workers and their families). The spouses and families of beneficiaries will also be entitled to take up employment or self-employment within the host state. Similar principles govern the right of residence of former employees and the self-employed after employment, and their families: Directive 90/365.

39. Students' rights of residence

Directive 90/366 was adopted to provide for the residence rights of students, their spouses and dependent children, provided the students were enrolled in recognised educational establishments to pursue vocational training. However, the directive was annulled by the ECJ in *Parliament* v. *Council* (Case C-295/90) because the measure had been wrongly based on Article 235 rather than Article 7 EEC. The ECJ ruled that Directive 90/366 would continue to be applied pending its replacement by a correctly based directive. This was achieved by Directive 93/96.

To benefit from the right of residence, such students must make a declaration that they have sufficient resources to avoid becoming a burden on the social assistance scheme of the host state. Unlike other non-workers, the right of residence of students is limited to the duration of their studies. It does not carry the right to receive a maintenance grant: *see* above.

40. Derogation

Derogation from the right of residence for non-workers is only permissible on grounds of public policy, public health and public security under Directive 64/221.

41. Union citizenship

One of the significant innovations introduced by the TEU was the status of 'citizenship of the Union', according rights as a result of membership of the

Union rather than the EC. Article 8 of the EC Treaty states that 'Citizenship of the Union is hereby established. Every person holding the nationality of a member state shall be a citizen of the Union.'

Under Article 8a Union citizens will have the right to move and reside freely within the territories of the member states subject to the limitations and conditions laid down in the Treaty and by measures adopted to give it effect. This right is clearly not directly effective since it required implementation by unanimous vote by the end of 1994. The deadline has not been met.

At first sight it would appear that the link between economic status and the freedom to move and reside has been broken. However the wording of Article 8a (referring to the adoption of provisions with a view to *facilitating* free movement) will allow the retention of existing conditions which prevent the economically inactive from becoming a burden on the social services of the host state (*see* Wyatt and Dashwood p. 659).

On implementation of Article 8a Union citizenship will bestow the following rights in addition to the right to move and reside freely within the EU:

(a) The right to vote and stand as a candidate in municipal elections and elections to the European Parliament in a member state in which the Union citizen is resident but not a national: Article 8b. The right has been implemented in relation to municipal elections by Directive 94/80 (in force from January 1996) and to EP elections by Directive 93/109 (in force from 1993).

(b) The right to receive diplomatic and consular protection in the state in which the Union citizen is resident on the same terms as a national of that state: Article 8c. This right is not yet implemented.

(c) The right to petition the European Parliament and the new Community Ombudsman: Article 8d: *see* Chapter 2.

Progress test 15

1. Which rights are enjoyed by natural and legal persons under Articles 52 and 58? Which conditions must be satisfied for a legal person to enjoy these rights?

2. Following the end of the transitional period, are further directives necessary to implement Articles 52 and 58?

3. How has the legal position of lawyers differed from that of other professionals in relation to the right of establishment and the freedom to provide services?

4. How has the principle of non-discrimination been invoked to hasten the right of establishment and the freedom of professionals to provide services? In what way has the principle inspired Directive 89/48 on the mutual recognition of qualifications?

5. To what extent is the freedom to receive services a corollary of the freedom to provide services?

6. In what circumstances is it legitimate for a university to charge a fee to an EC national from another member state to attend an undergraduate course?

7. How will the rights of non-workers be improved as a result of Directives 90/364 and 365 and Directive 93/96?

8. What new rights will be enjoyed by citizens of the Union?

16

SOCIAL SECURITY

1. Introduction

The free movement of workers, the self-employed and their families would be of limited value if such movement entailed the loss of social security benefits such as unemployment benefits and state pensions.

2. The EC approach

There is no EC system of social security. The approach adopted in the EC Treaty to answer this problem is set out in Article 51. Under this Article the Council was required to adopt measures to ensure the implementation of two basic principles:

(a) Aggregation, for the purpose of acquiring and retaining the right to benefit and of calculating the amount of benefit, of all periods taken into account under the laws of several countries.

(b) Payment of benefit to persons resident in the territories of member states.

REGULATION 1408/71

3. The purpose of Regulation 1408/71

Regulation 1408/71 (as amended and updated by Regulation 2001/83 and implemented by Regulation 547/72) was adopted to give effect to these objectives, superseding Regulation 3/58. Regulation 1408/71 is concerned with social security schemes and pensions. When first introduced, the Regulation applied only to workers and their families; it was amended by Regulation 1390/81 to include the self-employed. Its purpose is not to establish a common scheme of social security but to co-ordinate the different national schemes in accordance with Article 51. The Regulation thus ensures that claimants' contributions in different member states are aggregated (i.e. cumulated to ensure continuity of contribution record), and that benefits may be collected by those entitled in whichever member state they are resident: *Borowitz* v. *Bundesversicherrungsanstalt für Angestellte* (Case 21/87). The ECJ reaffirmed in the same case that the Regulation does not prohibit national legislation from granting broader social security benefits than those provided by the Regulation.

4. Abolition of territorial restrictions

The EC scheme is intended to abolish as far as possible territorial restrictions on the application of different social security schemes within the EC: *Knappschaft v. Maison Singer et Fils* (Case 44/65). National social security schemes are likely to require amendment to comply with these principles. Any conflict between national and EC law must be resolved in favour of EC law: *Simmenthal SpA* (Case 106/77).

5. Scope of coverage

Article 2(1) of the Regulation provides that it should apply to the employed, the self-employed, their families and survivors, stateless persons and refugees. The first two categories, however, do not correspond exactly to the decisions of the ECJ on 'workers' under Article 48 or on the beneficiaries of the right of establishment and the freedom to provide services under Articles 52 and 59.

Instead, a pragmatic approach was taken to the definition of 'employed' and 'self-employed' in Article 1(a)(i) of the Regulation (as amended by Article 1(2)(a) of Regulation 1390/81).

6. Employed and self-employed persons

The employed and self-employed persons covered by the Regulation are defined in Article 1(a)(i) (as amended by Regulation 1390/81, Article 1(2)(a)) as any person who is insured (either on a compulsory or optional continued basis) for one or more of the contingencies covered by the branches of a social security scheme for employed or self-employed persons. The original coverage under Regulation 3 was limited to 'wage earners and comparable workers', interpreted by the ECJ in *Hoekstra (née Unger)* to include persons compulsorily insured at the outset who continued to make voluntary contributions after ceasing employment. Regulations 1408/71 and 574/72 were amended by Regulations 1390 and 3795/81 to include the self-employed.

It is clear from *Hoekstra* that 'worker' in the context of social security has a Community meaning and may be applied to all those who are covered by national social security systems, irrespective of whether the scheme in question is compulsory or voluntary.

The following insured persons have been held to be covered by the Regulation:

Examples
(1) Persons working outside the EC: *Laborero* and *Sabato* (Cases 82 and 1031/86).
(2) Persons who have always worked in their country of origin: *Laumann* (Case 115/77). In this case the orphaned children of a worker who had never left his home state were covered as a result of the change of residence to another member state by the *children*.
(3) Persons not currently insured under a scheme who have been insured in the past: *Hoekstra*.

(4) Persons who are insured but are moving within the EC for a purpose other than work: *Hessiche Knappschaft* v. *Maison Singer et Fils* (Case 44/65). In this case, a German holiday-maker was killed while driving in France. The German social security authorities who had paid his dependents claimed against the driver who had caused the accident in France, relying on their rights of subrogation. The ECJ held that the concept of worker under Article 51 was not limited to migrant workers or to workers who are obliged to move in the course of their work.

Note: Students, although eligible for employment, are *not* considered to be workers for social security purposes: *Kuyken* v. *Rijksdjenst voor Arbeidsvooziening* (Case 66/77).

7. Members of the family and survivors

A 'member of the family' is defined under Article 1(f) of the Regulation as any person defined or recognised as a member of the family or designated as a member of the household by the legislation under which benefits are provided. As members of the family may claim only those rights which are recognised by national law as deriving from the relationship with the insured person, the meaning of the term 'member of the family' is bound to vary from state to state. Where national law regards as a member of the family only those persons living under the same roof as the insured person, it is enough if the person in question is dependent on the insured person: Article 1(f).

The ECJ has on some, but not all, occasions applied a liberal interpretation to the expression 'member of the family' to avoid restricting the free movement of workers. In *Mr and Mrs F* (Case 7/75) the ECJ allowed the dependent child of a worker to claim a handicap benefit in his own right. This approach was not, however, followed in *Kermaschek* (Case 40/76), nor in *Franscogna* (Case 157/84).

A 'survivor' means any persons defined or recognised as such by the legislation under which the benefits are granted: Article 1(g). In most cases, families and survivors may only claim benefits under the insurance of the worker or self-employed persons, unless they themselves are appropriately insured. However, where an employed or self-employed person visits another member state, Article 22(3) of Regulation 1408/71 vests rights to sickness and maternity benefits directly in his family members. There has for some time been a trend towards claiming such benefits which do not derive from the worker's insurance as a 'social advantage' under Article 7(2) of Regulation 1612/68. *See* below.

8. General principles of social security

A number of general principles are stated in the preamble to Regulation 1408/71 to underline the approach to social security. (*See* Steiner, chapter 21, and Wyatt and Dashwood, chapter 11.) Their purpose is to ensure that the migrant worker is not disadvantaged by movement within the EC:

(a) Non-discrimination on grounds of nationality

(b) Payment regardless of residence

(c) No entitlement to double benefits

(d) The single state principle

(e) Aggregation.

9. Non-discrimination

The principle of non-discrimination is set out in Article 3(1) of Regulation 1408/71, reflecting the general principle of non-discrimination in Article 6 of the EC Treaty (previously Article 7 of the EEC Treaty). Article 3(1) provides for the equal treatment of persons resident in the territory of one of the member states. Such persons shall (subject to the special provisions of the Regulation) be subject to the same obligations and enjoy the same benefits under the legislation of any member state as the nationals of that state.

Discrimination may be direct (overt) or indirect (covert). Both forms are prohibited.

Example

An Italian woman claimed an allowance payable under the French Social Security Code to married women of French nationality over sixty-five years of age who were of insufficient means and who had brought up five children for at least nine years before the age of sixty. Although the French authorities waived the nationality requirement for the claimant herself, they were not prepared to do so in the case of her children, five of the seven being of Italian nationality. HELD (ECJ): Article 3(1) applied not only to overt discrimination (such as would have applied if the mother herself has been discriminated against) but also to covert discrimination in the form of disguised discrimination which had the same result, such as a condition relating to the nationality of the children: *Palermo* (Case 237/78).

> *Note:* 'Indirect' discrimination was also condemned in *Sotgiu* (Case 152/73), unless the discrimination was based on objective factors. In *Palermo* the ECJ rejected the argument of the French authorities that the implementation of demographic policy (the growth of the French population) amounted to an objective factor justifying discrimination. Regulation 1408/71 did not distinguish between schemes on the basis of demographic policy.

The position of reverse discrimination in social security under Regulation 1408/71 is not completely clear. In *Kenny* (Case 1/78) an Irish national claimed sickness benefit while in prison in Ireland. No payment of benefit under the rules would have been payable to a claimant while in prison in the UK. The social security authorities refused payment, arguing that the rules meant that imprisonment outside the UK was also covered, on the basis that any other decision would discriminate against UK nationals contrary to Articles 7 and 48 of the Treaty because migrants would be more likely than UK nationals to serve their prison sentence abroad. The decision, while not conclusive on reverse discrimination, states that it is for the national authorities to decide the conditions governing benefits which must be applied without discrimination to the nationals of the state concerned and to those of the other member state.

> *Note:* There are some exceptions to the principle of non-discrimination. EC law may not be applied: (1) to rectify any disadvantage arising from national rules of affiliation to a social security scheme: *Schmitt* (Case 29/88); (2) to determine the temporal effect

of its social security rules: *Jordan* (Case 141/88). In *Jordan* the ECJ ruled that EC law may not be invoked to allow new non-retrospective social security rules to be applied in circumstances arising before their introduction.

10. Payment in any of the member states

Articles 10(1) of Regulation 1408/71 protects the worker who moves to another member state (e.g. to retire to his country of origin) other than the state responsible for the payment of his benefit. Article 10(1) provides that invalidity, old age or survivors' cash benefits, pensions for accidents at work or occupational diseases and death grants acquired under the legal system of another member state shall not be reduced, modified or otherwise affected because the recipient resides in a state other than the state responsible for payment.

Note: Certain forms of benefit are excluded from Article 10(1): sickness benefits and family benefits are covered by the special provisions in Regulation 1408/71 and Regulation 574/72.

11. No entitlement to double benefits

While Regulation 1408/71 is intended to ensure that employed and self-employed people are not prejudiced in that they gain advantage by such improvement, i.e. persons who have contributed to the social security schemes in more than one member state may not claim double benefit.

Article 12(1) of the Regulation provides that the Regulation can neither confer nor maintain the right to several benefits of the same kind for one and the same period of compulsory insurance, thus avoiding the purposeless overlapping of contributions in several states: *Caisse de Pension des Employés Privés de Massonet* (Case 50/75). This provision does not apply to benefits in respect of invalidity, old age, death (pensions) or occupational disease awarded by the institutions of two or more member states. For these benefits, special provision for apportionment between the member states applies. In effect, the migrant worker is credited with notional insurance periods spent in one member state when these periods were, in fact, spent in another member state.

The application of Article 12 could result in the claimant receiving less from one member state than he would be entitled in another. To rectify this injustice, the ECJ has ruled in a number of cases that the worker is entitled to the difference between the two sums, to be paid by the competent institution of the state paying the larger amount. *See*, for example, *De Felice* (Case 128/88): retirement pensions; *Georges* (Case 24/88): family allowances. (*see* Steiner p. 266.)

Article 12(2) upholds the right of member states to make legislative provision for reduction, suspension or withdrawal of overlapping benefits, even where the right to such benefits arises in another member state or when the income arises in another member state.

Benefits in respect of invalidity, old age, death (pensions) or occupational disease are again excluded. This exclusion has been interpreted by the ECJ as meaning that national rules for the reduction of a pension to take account of a pension arising in another member state must not be applied: *Celestre* (Case 116/80).

12. The single state principle

Article 13 provides that a worker to whom the Regulation applies shall be subject to the legislation of a single member state only: *see* **18** below.

13. Aggregation and apportionment

The principle of aggregation requires the social security system of one member state to take into account periods of employment completed under the legislation of another. Without aggregation the immigrant's contribution record might not be sufficient to sustain a pension (or other benefits).

The corollary of aggregation is apportionment. Under the principle of apportionment, the financial cost of rights acquired under the social security systems of various member states may be shared between the various institutions of the member states in proportion to the length of time worked in each. Article 50 protects the worker from being prejudiced by this principle by providing that the worker cannot receive as a total sum less than would have been his entitlement if he had received his entire pension under the law of his state of residence.

The principle of aggregation is applied specifically to each individual benefit:

Examples
(1) Sickness and maternity benefit: Article 1(3).
(2) Old age and death pensions: Article 45. This article provides for the aggregation of insurance periods only in relation to the acquisition, retention or recovery of benefit rights. Affiliation to social security schemes is governed by national law: *Brunori* (Case 266/78).
(3) Death grants: Article 64.
(4) Unemployment benefits: Article 67.
(5) Family benefits: Article 72.

Under the various specific provisions for aggregation account must be taken where necessary of periods of contribution, employment and residence in all the member states in which the migrant has worked for the purpose of deciding eligibility to benefit and the amount of benefit to which he may be entitled.

14. Subrogation

The principle of subrogation has also been applied in EC law. 'Subrogation', in a general insurance context, means the right of the insurer to step into the shoes of the insured and make any claim to which the insured would have been entitled. If a person receives benefit under the legislation of one member state and is entitled to claim compensation for that injury from a third party in that other state's territory, any subrogation rights vested in the institution responsible for payment of benefit under the law applicable to it shall be recognised in the other member states.

Example
A worker was killed in France by the negligence of a third party. As a result of the accident his widow received a pension from the German social security institution. HELD (ECJ): The German social security institution may be

subrogated according to German law to the widow's rights against the third party in France: *Töpfer* (Case 72/76).

15. Benefits to which Regulation 1408/71 applies

Article 4(1) provides that the Regulation should apply to all legislation relating to the following branches of social security:

(a) Sickness and maternity benefits

(b) Invalidity benefits (including benefits intended to maintain or improve working capacity)

(c) Old age benefits

(d) Survivors' benefits

(e) Benefits in respect of accidents at work and occupational diseases

(f) Death grants

(g) Unemployment benefits

(h) Family benefits.

Under Article 4(2)(a) the Regulation is stated to apply to all general and special social security schemes, whether contributory or non-contributory. Article 4(2)(a) extends the application of Regulation 1408/71 to special non-contributory benefits provided under legislation other than that covered by Article 4(1) where such benefits (*i*) supplement or act as a substitute for the social benefits under the Regulation, or (*ii*) are intended solely to protect the disabled, or (*iii*) are intended to guarantee a minimum income.

EXCEPTION: The Regulation does *not* apply to social and medical assistance, to benefit schemes for victims of war or its consequences, or to special schemes for civil servants and people treated as such: Article 4(4).

16. Social assistance

The term 'social assistance' is not defined in Regulation 1408/71. It constitutes the major exception to entitlement to benefit under Article 4 and has been narrowly defined by the ECJ. (*See* Steiner p. 268.)

In *Frilli* v. *Belgian State* (Case 1/72) the ECJ applied a 'double function' test to determine which benefits qualify as social security. The test reflects the dual nature of certain benefits which resemble social assistance as they are based on need, while also conferring rights on beneficiaries in the same way as in the social security benefits. Such benefits must therefore be considered to be social security benefits. In *Frilli* a benefit in the form of a non-contributory guaranteed minimum income unrelated to insurance which was payable in Belgium either to Belgian nationals or to persons living in Belgium for a minimum period of five years was treated as social security, being assimilated to the old age pension. In *Callemeyn* v. *Belgian State* (Case 187/73) a special handicap benefit which was not dependent on employment or contributions had been refused to the wife of a migrant worker by the Belgian authorities. The ECJ held that the payment was assimilated to invalidity benefit and constituted social security.

In a third case where the ECJ followed a similar line of reasoning, the claimant, the 14-year-old handicapped son of an Italian migrant worker in Belgium, was refused a grant for handicapped persons because he failed to fulfil the fifteen year residence requirement. Despite the fact that the benefit appeared to be social assistance, being neither a family benefit nor a benefit related to contributions, the ECJ ruled that the benefit was social security. The ECJ also stated that such a claimant was entitled, as a dependent, to equal treatment while his parents were resident in a member state, even after achieving the age of majority: *Mr and Mrs F* v. *Belgian State* (Case 7/75).

The ECJ continued to rule on the question of which benefits constitute social security and which social advantage in a number of further decisions. The following were held to be social security benefits:

Examples
(1) A payment in Germany for the purpose of combatting tuberculosis (because payment was linked to the membership of a public social security pension scheme): *Heinze* (Cases 14–16/72).
(2) A handicap payment sought under the same legislation as applied in *Callemeyn* by a claimant with no pre-existing social security entitlement: *Mazzier* (Case 39/74).
(3) Benefits sought by claimants as 'victims of war': *Fossi* (Case 79/76) and *Tinelli* (Case 144/78). In both of these cases the ECJ held that a benefit may only be excluded as 'social assistance' where it involves a discretionary assessment of need or personal circumstances.

17. Social advantages

Since the 1980s the ECJ has adopted a new approach to benefits which might appear to be 'social assistance'. Departing from its previous, sometimes dubious, reasoning in regarding nearly all benefits as social security under Regulation 1408/71, the ECJ turned instead to the concept of 'social advantage' under Article 7(2) of Regulation 1612/68. The scope of 'social advantage' had been extended in cases such as *Fiorini* (Case 32/75), *Even* (Case 207/78), *Reina* (Case 65/81) and *Frascogna* (Case 157/84). *See* 12:**17(b)**.

Applying the newly established concept of 'lawful residence' the ECJ held that various forms of benefit amounted to a 'social advantage'.

Example
An Italian mother living with her pensioner son in Belgium after he had worked there was held to be entitled to a guaranteed income paid to old people in Belgium: *Castelli* (Case 261/83). (*See* also *Hoecks* (Case 249/83); *Scrivner* (Case 122/84); *Frascogna* (Case 157/84); *Lebon* (Case 316/85): *see* 12:**19(b)**.)

Claims which might, in the past, have failed to be classified as social security are more likely to succeed on the basis of social advantage. This will be particularly beneficial for workers who are not insured within a social security scheme.

However, if a worker wished to 'export' a benefit, this is only possible in relation to a social security benefit under Regulation 1408/71. No machinery exists within the member states for processing claims in relation to 'social advantage' claims. Similarly, any claimant relying on aggregation must be able to bring the claim within Regulation 1408/71: *see Campana* (Case 11/85) in which special aid for vocational training for unemployed workers was assimilated to unemployment benefit and was brought within Regulation 1408/71, entitling the claimant to qualify for the benefit through aggregation.

18. Which law should be applied?

This question is of vital importance, for example, to the worker living in one state and working in another. Each state retains control over the type of benefits provided and the conditions of eligibility. The basic rule governing the applicable law is that it is the law of the state of employment: Article 13(2)(a) of Regulation 1408/71. This rule is known as the *'lex laboris'*. The rule is modified only where its application would cause either administrative inconvenience or the cumulative application of the legislation of several member states.

Under Article 13(2)(b) a person who is self-employed in the territory of one member state is subject to the legislation of that state even if he resides in another member state.

The law of the state of employment takes effect as soon as a person takes up employment. Applying the rule, it follows that the state of employment must be the state with which he is insured. In that state, known as 'the competent state', the institution responsible for insurance is also responsible for payment of benefits and is known as the 'competent institution': Article 1(o).

The law applicable to an unemployed person is the law of the state of last employment and insurance contribution (subject to various exceptions): Article 70. Special rules are provided for civil servants: Article 13(2)(d), the armed forces: Article 13(2)(e), and seamen on board a vessel which is flying a member state's flag: Article 13(1)(c).

19. Exception to the *lex laboris* rule

There are three exceptions to the *lex laboris* rule under Article 14. They are:

(a) the temporary worker

(b) the worker employed in two or more member states

(c) the frontier worker.

20. The temporary worker

Article 14(1)(a) (as amended) provides that a person employed in the territory of one member state who is posted to another member state to work there for the undertaking continues to be subject to the legislation of the first member state, provided the posting is not anticipated to last more than 12 months and that he has not been sent as a replacement for another person who has completed his term of posting. (The 12 month period may be extended under Article 14(1)(b).)

Examples

(1) A French skilled worker posted for three days to Germany by an employment agency was injured in an accident at work. He claimed reimbursement of the cost of medical treatment. HELD (ECJ, Article 177): A worker posted to another member state on a temporary basis was covered by Regulation 1408/71, provided he was attached to an undertaking which paid him and to whom he remained answerable: *Manpower Sàrl* (Case 35/70).

(2) A commercial traveller, paid by commission, representing undertakings established in one member state, who spent nine months of each year in another member state was held to be outside the scope of the Article 14(1)(a) (originally Article 13(1)(a)): *Hakenberg* (Case 13/73).

It is clear from decisions of the ECJ such as *Niemann* (Case 191/73) and *Petroni* (Case 24/75) that the EC social security rules should only be invoked to improve the position of the claimant, not to take away his rights under national law. In *Ten Holder* (Case 302/84) the ECJ held that the rules in Regulation 1408/71 dealing with social security amount to a complete system of conflict rules which remove from the legislature of member states the power to determine the scope of coverage of national provisions for persons who are the subject of the Regulation.

21. The worker employed in two or more member states

This exception covers the worker in international transport: Article 14(2)(a), and 'others': Article 14(2)(a). The law to be applied under Article 14(2), in order of priority, will be:

(*i*) the law of his state of residence if, as a worker in international transport, he is employed there principally or, as an 'other', he is employed there partly

(*ii*) the law of the state of employment where he is employed by a permanent branch or agency

(*iii*) the law of the state where the registered office or place of business of the undertaking with which he is employed is situated.

22. The frontier worker

The frontier worker is defined under Article 14(2)(b) as a person employed in the territory of one member state by an undertaking which has its registered office or place of business in the territory of another member state and which straddles the common frontier of these states. In this case the applicable law is the law of the state in which the undertaking has its registered office or place of business.

There are similar rules applicable to the self-employed under Article 14(a). Once the applicable law has been decided, the competent institution within that state must apply the principle of aggregation: *see* above. Under this principle contributions paid under the legislation of another member state must be counted as far as this is necessary in order to decide on eligibility to benefit: Article 10.

These benefits may be either in cash (according to the law of the competent state) or in kind (according to the law of the state of residence). 'Cash benefits' are benefits to compensate for the loss of earnings arising from incapacity; 'benefits in kind' include health and welfare services administered under the relevant legislation and certain cash payments, for example to reimburse the cost of health and welfare services. Article 19 sets out the general basis of the scheme and various articles (e.g. Article 25: unemployment benefits) provide specifically for individual benefits. Unlike claims for social advantage under Article 7(2) of Regulation 1612/68 for which no mechanism appropriate for reciprocity exists, claims under Regulations 1408/71 and 574/72 are processed on a reciprocal basis by the competent institution responsible for payment of benefits in both cash and kind: Article 19: institutions responsible for payment.

23. Persons resident outside the competent state: special rules for payment of benefit

(a) *Unemployment provisions*. Regulations 1408/71 makes special provision for the migrant worker to claim unemployment benefit when visiting another member state to seek employment. Under Article 69(1) of the Regulation a person wishing to retain his entitlement to benefit must register as a person seeking employment with the employment services of the competent state, and remain available for work for at least four weeks after becoming unemployed. The competent institution may then authorise his departure before that time has expired. The next step under Article 69(1) is for the unemployed person to register as a person seeking work with the employment services of each member state to which he goes within seven days of the day when he ceased to be available to the employment services of the state he left.

Compliance with these requirements will ensure that entitlement to benefits from the competent state will continue for up to three months (provided the claimant is eligible for benefits for this period). Benefits may be paid in the claimant's state of origin: Article 70. Failure to find work, leading to a return to the competent state within the three month period, also ensures the continuation of entitlement to benefits. If, however, the claimant does not return within the three month period, he will lose all entitlement to benefit under the legislation of the competent state: Article 69(2), unless, exceptionally, the time-limit has been extended by the competent institution.

(b) *Family benefits*. The general rule on the payment of benefits regardless of residence is contained in Article 73(1) of the Regulation which provides that family benefits are to be provided under the law of the member state of employment. In *Bronzino* v. *Kindergeldkasse, Nüremburg* (Case C-228/88) and *Gatto* v. *Bundesanstalt für Arbeit* (Case 12/89) the German authorities had refused payment of family allowances to Mr Bronzino and Mr Gatto because their unemployed children (aged between 16 and 18 years) were not available for work in Germany, being resident in another member state. The ECJ held under Article 177 that a refusal to grant family allowances in such circumstances constituted an obstacle to the free movement of workers. Articles 73 and 74 of Regulation 1408/71 would be satisfied where the unemployed family member was available for work in the member state in which he lived. Under Article 73(2), however, an exception is provided where the state of employment is France, in which case the level of family benefits is determined by the law of the state in which the family is residing. (The exception was included at the demand of France where family benefits were more generous than in other member states.)

The exclusion of France was successfully challenged in the *Pinna* case (Case 41/84). Mr Pinna, an Italian living in France, was refused family allowances under French law for periods when his two children were visiting him from Italy. The ECJ held that in creating two systems of social security for migrant workers (a general system and another for migrant workers subject to French law) EC social security rules created more difficulties for the free movement of migrant workers. It followed that EC law should not add to these existing disparities. Although the provision applied equally to French families, the effects of the provision were more likely to be experienced by the families of migrant workers. Thus the residence criterion for the members of a family in a member state other than France failed to provide for equality of treatment under Article 48 and could not be used to co-ordinate national social security schemes. Special rules for the avoidance of overlapping benefits are provided in Article 10(1)(a) of Regulation 574/72: *see Beeck* (Case 104/80) and *Georges* (Case 24/88) above.

Progress test 16

1. Explain the operation of the aggregation of benefits under Regulation 1408/71. Which categories of persons are covered by the Regulation?

2. To what extent does Regulation 1408/71 permit reverse discrimination?

3. What is the principle of no overlapping of benefits? How has the principle been modified by the ECJ to avoid unfairness?

4. What is meant by the terms 'social assistance' and 'social advantage'?

5. Explain the operation of the *lex laboris* rule and its exceptions.

6. To what extent does Regulation 1408/71 provide for the payment of benefit to persons resident outside the competent state?

17

CAPITAL MOVEMENTS AND ECONOMIC AND MONETARY UNION

1. Introduction

The EC Treaty maintains the distinction in the EEC Treaty in its separate provision for capital movements and economic policy. The EEC Treaty covered these areas in a somewhat sketchy fashion. The provisions were not directly effective. Member states were reluctant to implement the free movement of capital, perceiving implementation as a loss of control over economic policy. The TEU represents a sharp dividing line in the treatment of these areas of law and policy. It repealed the original provisions of the EEC Treaty, replacing them with new, more ambitious provisions and provided for a programme to achieve full economic and monetary union before the end of the century.

CAPITAL MOVEMENTS UNDER THE EEC TREATY

2. The basic provisions

The main Treaty provisions were contained in Articles 67 to 73, implemented by Directives 88/361 (*see* **5** below) and 89/646 (providing for a minimum capital requirement for first authorisation of credit institutions and the principle of home-country control of credit institutions). These two directives gave broad effect to the free movement of capital: *Ministerio Fiscal* v. *Bordessa* (Cases C-358 & 416/93).

3. Abolition of restrictions

Article 67(1) provided for the abolition of:

(a) all restrictions on the movement of capital belonging to persons resident in the member state

(b) discrimination based on the nationality or place of residence of the parties or on the place where the capital is invested.

4. Implementation

Article 67 required implementation by the Council under Article 69. Lack of enthusiasm among the member states for the abandonment of exchange control regulations limited progress until 1988.

5. The Directive on capital movements

Directive 88/361 on capital movements was an important step towards the completion of the internal market and made it easier, for example, to open a bank account or obtain a loan from a bank in another member state. The directive has been implemented by all member states except Greece and Portugal which have an extension until the end of 1995.

6. The main features of the directive

(a) It provides for the abolition of:

    (*i*) all restrictions on the actual transfer of capital
    (*ii*) any measure limiting the carrying out of the underlying transaction
    (*iii*) discriminatory measures (e.g. discriminatory taxation of investors).

(b) It requires capital transfers to be effected on the same terms as current payments.

(c) It allows member states, in exceptional circumstances (where the operation of monetary and exchange rate policies are seriously disrupted by short-term capital movements), to restrict capital movements, but only for limited periods of time and subject to the control of the Commission.

(d) It requires member states to try to reach the same level of liberalisation in transactions with third countries as they achieve with the residents of other member states.

> *Note*: While Directive 88/361 contributed significantly to the completion of the internal movements, other measures outside the scope of this book (on tax harmonisation and financial services) have also played a part.

ECONOMIC POLICY UNDER THE EEC TREATY

7. Balance of payments

Under Article 104 each member state was responsible through its economic policy for maintaining equilibrium in its balance of payments and currency stability. However, under Article 107 all member states were required to treat their exchange rate policy as a matter of common concern. Changes by a member state which were inconsistent with Article 104 and which distorted competition could, if authorised by the Commission, lead to counter-measures by other member states. Where a member state was in difficulties or under serious threat of difficulties, the Commission could recommend the state concerned to take certain measures: Articles 108. Otherwise, in a balance-of-payments crisis, the member states concerned could take the necessary protective measures: Article 109.

8. The regulation on medium-term financial support for member states' balance of payments

Regulation 1969/88 set up a system of financial support to provide assistance to member states facing actual or imminent balance-of-payments problems or which had liberalised capital movements despite balance-of-payments problems.

9. Obligations of the member states

Article 106 imposed three obligations on member states:

(a) to liberalise cross-frontier payments in line with the movement of goods, persons and services within the EC

(b) to undertake further liberalisation of payments so far as the economic situation in general and the balance of payments state in particular permit

(c) not to introduce any new restrictions on transfers connected with invisible transactions (as listed in Annex 3 of the Treaty).

10. Banking transactions

Provisions have been adopted to speed up and simplify banking transactions within the EC and internationally, as part of a European Code of Conduct. Prior to the final stage of economic and monetary union, national banknotes will carry a clear indication of their ECU value printed on them (*see* below). Other proposals take account of the development of methods of electronic and cross-border dealings.

11. Decisions of the Court of Justice

There have been two major decisions relating to capital movements and payments:

> *Casati* (Case 203/80). Casati, an Italian businessman living in Germany, was charged with the attempted illegal exportation of deutschmarks from Italy. He had brought the money into the country to buy equipment for commercial purposes. Having failed to buy the goods Casati attempted to re-export the money. The Italian court referred several questions to the Court of Justice on the meaning of Articles 67, 69, 71 and 106.
>
> HELD (Article 177): Article 67(1) means that restrictions on the exportation of banknotes may not be regarded as abolished by the end of the transitional period, irrespective of the provisions of Articles 69. The Court interpreted Article 106 as meaning that the Article in practice ensures the free movement of goods by authorising the necessary currency transfers. Thus, the right of non-residents to re-export banknotes previously imported to finance a commercial transaction but not used is not guaranteed under EC law.

(That is, the Court decided that the movement of banknotes may still be restricted, but such restrictions will not be justified if their effect is to impede the free movement of goods and services.)

Luisi and Carbone v. *Ministero del Tesoro* (Joined Cases 286/82 and 26/83). Mrs Luisi and Mr Carbone were fined under Italian law for exporting foreign currency in amounts greater than permitted under Italian law. They challenged the validity of the fines on the basis that the Italian law restricted the freedom to travel throughout the EC, Mrs Luisi maintaining that she had exported the money to pay for medical treatment in France and Germany, Mr Carbone to finance his three month stay in Germany as a tourist. HELD (Article 177): The freedom to provide services includes the freedom, for the recipient of those services, to go to another member state to receive a service there, without being obstructed even in relation to payments, and that tourists, persons receiving medical treatment and persons travelling for the purposes of education or business are to be regarded as recipients of services.

However, the Court also ruled in *Luisi* that the physical transfer of banknotes may not be classified as a movement of capital where the transfer arises out of an obligation to pay for the transaction involving the movement of goods and services. Thus, payments for tourism or travel for business, education or medical purposes cannot be classified as movements of capital even where they are effected by the physical transfer of banknotes.

12. The European Monetary System

The provision on economic and monetary policy in Articles 104 to 109 could be seen to be weak in that they did not provide for the mechanism for exchange rate management between the currencies of the member states. An attempt to regulate European currencies was made in 1972 by means of the 'snake', a scheme which permitted limited currency fluctuation. This first scheme was not entirely successful and was later abandoned.

In 1979 the nine member states, prior to the second accession, formed the European monetary system (EMS), a scheme to create closer monetary co-operation leading to a zone of monetary stability in Europe. There are two main elements in the EMS, the exchange rate mechanism (ERM), and the creation of the European currency unit (the ECU). The UK joined the ERM in 1990 but, with Italy, suspended membership after a currency crisis. Greece, Spain and Portugal remain outside the ERM.

13. The Exchange Rate Mechanism

Each member state participating in the ERM has a central currency rate set against the ECU. This central rate can be realigned if the participants agree. Under the ERM the participating states must control their exchange rates, for example by adjusting interest rates, so that the value of the currency moves within fixed limits (currently a wide band, but EMU requires adherence to a narrow band before moving to the third stage: *see* **20** below).

14. The European currency unit (the ECU)

The precursor of the ECU was known as the European unit of account, a gold-based currency used to express the operations of the European Monetary Co- operation Fund. From 1979 the Fund's activities were expressed in a unit of account known as the ECU (Regulation 3180/70), defined as the sum of specified amounts of the currencies of member states. In other words, the ECU is based on a 'basket of currencies', including the deutschmark and the pound sterling.

Originally, the ECU was used mainly for the purpose of bookkeeping within the EC institutions and in the allocation of grants and subsidies. However, the ECU is being used increasingly for international accounting. The ECU will become the single currency of the EC under the third stage of economic and monetary union: *see* below. At present the ECU is legal tender only in Belgium.

15. The Single European Act

The SEA added a new Article 102A to the Treaty providing that:

> In order to ensure convergence of economic and monetary policies, which is necessary for the future development of the Community, member states shall co-operate in accordance with the objectives of Article 104. In so doing they shall take account of the experience required in co-operation within the framework of the European Monetary System and in developing the ECU and shall respect existing powers in this field.

This vague and bland provision did not appear to take the EMS much further forward. Further development could only happen in the context of progress towards economic and monetary union.

ECONOMIC AND MONETARY UNION

16. Introduction

The introduction of the Economic and Monetary System was the first step towards economic and monetary union (EMU). Adoption of the Single European Act represented a further step in that direction by the member states. The European Council at its meeting in Hanover in June 1988 appointed a Committee chaired by Jacques Delors, the President of the Commission to make proposals on stages for achievement of EMU for consideration by the meeting of the European Council in Madrid in June 1989.

17. The report of the Delors Committee

The Report of the Delors Committee was issued in May 1989. It proposed that the EEC Treaty should be amended to make the institutional changes necessary to achieve full economic and monetary union. Progress towards union should be seen as a single process, involving three stages.

The first stage would involve greater convergence of economic and monetary policy. In the second stage the economic and institutional basis for EMU including a European Central Bank would be set up. In the third stage of full EMU the ECU would become the single currency of the EC, fixed at an irrevocable exchange rate.

18. The meetings of the European Council at Madrid and Rome

In June 1989 the Madrid Council decided that Stage One would begin on 1 July 1990. At the first Rome Summit in 1990 eleven member states, excluding the United Kingdom, agreed to complete the Second Stage by the end of 1994. At the second Rome Summit in 1991, following a change of Prime Minister, the United Kingdom stressed willingness to participate fully in the current inter-governmental conferences. These conferences were concluded in 1991, leading to the signing of the Treaty on European Union (TEU) at Maastricht.

19. The Treaty on European Union

Intergovernmental conferences were convened to consider economic and monetary union (and, in parallel, political union). By December 1990 the member states had reached agreement on the terms of EMU, but only after two member states, the UK and Denmark, had secured 'opt outs' from the commitment to EMU through Protocols annexed to the Treaty. The Treaty on European Union (TEU) was signed at Maastricht in February 1991. Full ratification was not completed until November 1993 (see Chapter 1). As a result the UK and Denmark may choose at a later date whether they wish to apply for full participation in EMU. In the case of the UK no decision to apply will be taken without the matter being put before the Westminster Parliament.

20. The commitment to EMU

The legal foundation for EMU was incorporated into the Treaty by the TEU. It requires 'the close co-ordination of economic policies' (Article 3(1) EC) to be established as a matter of common concern within the framework of policy guidelines set by the Council following the decision of the European Council (Articles 102(a) and 103(2) EC). It is based on the three-stage approach of the Delors plan as follows:

Stage 1 Member states must comply with the provisions of the Treaty on the free movement of capital. In addition they must liberalise their financial institutions (Article 104) and work towards lasting convergence in economic policy (Article 109(e)(1)). The first stage began on 1 July 1990 and finished on 31 December 1993. During that time the Exchange Rate Mechanism, seen as a cornerstone of economic policy, suffered from speculative pressures on the international currency market. As a result the UK and Italy had to leave the ERM in 1992. By permitting a wider band for currency fluctuation the ERM has been effectively suspended since 1993. The completion of the internal market in capital and payments required by the TEU has largely been achieved (but note that Portugal and Greece have a derogation until 31 December 1995): see 5 above.

Stage 2 Stage 2 began on 1 January 1994 as a preparation for full EMU in Stage 3. The European Monetary Institute (based in Frankfurt) was established in 1994 to foster co-operation between national central banks, co-ordination and consultation on monetary policy, the EMS and the use of the ECU including preparation of ECU banknotes. Other responsibilities include cross-border payments and the regulatory framework for the European Central Bank in the third stage, to be set out by 31 December 1996.

Stage 3 According to Article 109(j)(4) of the EC Treaty the third stage of full economic and monetary union must commence no later than 1 January 1999 when the single currency will be introduced. Despite the economic problems created by the recession the European Council meeting at Cannes in June 1995 reaffirmed its commitment to the Treaty deadline as the final date for the introduction of the single currency. It remains to be seen whether this timetable is retained at the 1996 IGC.

The European Council will decide by qualified majority by the end of 1996 if a majority of member states achieve the stated economic convergence criteria to proceed to stage 3 and, if so, to set a date. The convergence criteria are demanding, including limits on inflation, avoidance of excessive government budgetary deficits, observance of the narrow band of the ERM for two years and restrictions on average long-term interest rates. Few member states currently meet these requirements.

Once the date for the third stage has been set the European Central Bank (ECB) and European System of Central Banks (ESCB) must be established (Article 109(1)). The value of the ECU is to be fixed irrevocably by the unanimous decision of the participating states (Article 109(g)). The ECU will operate as a currency in its own right (Article 109(1)(4)) under the control of the ECB.

The ECB will operate as an independent bank along similar lines to the German Bundesbank on which it is modelled. The primary objective of the ECB is price stability. Only the EC will be entitled to issue ECU banknotes, but coins may be minted by member states (Article 105(1a)(i)).

21. A two-speed Europe?

It will not be possible for all 15 member states to participate in full EMU at the outset, either because of 'opt-outs' or through failure to meet the convergence criteria. In the future new member states from the Eastern bloc would be without immediate prospect of joining EMU. This raises the question of a 'two-speed Europe' or 'Europe of variable geometry' as this prospect is sometimes called. To some extent a two-tier approach to European integration may be seen as implied by the political compromises agreed at Maastricht on the single currency and other issues. A flexible approach in the future will be needed to accommodate an increasing number of member states with different levels of development and commitment to integration.

Progress test 17

1. How has Directive 88/361 contributed to the free movement of capital?

2. What degree of independence was permitted to member states by the EEC Treaty in maintaining stability in relation to balance of payments and currency?

3. To what extent were restrictions on the free movement of banknotes permissible under the EEC Treaty?

4. What provision was made in the EEC Treaty for the EMS?

5. Explain the operation of the ERM and the ECU.

6. How did the SEA amend the EEC Treaty in relation to EMU?

7. Outline the 3 stages to EMU proposed by the Report of the Delors Committee.

8. Which member states have agreed to participate in full EMU? What is the UK position and how is it secured?

9. At which stage of EMU are the member states at present? Identify the criteria which must be satisfied before full EMU may be achieved.

10. Why is it likely that European integration in future may proceed at more than one speed?

Part Three

COMPETITION LAW AND POLICY

18

INTRODUCTION TO COMPETITION

1. Terminology

It is useful to become familiar with some of the economic terms in competition policy:

Barriers to entry: legal restrictions (e.g. patents, licensing requirements) on entering the market.

Cartel: a combination of undertakings which agree to restrict competition (e.g. by fixing prices).

Concerted practice: a practice falling short of an actual agreement which is illegal under Article 85.

Dominance: the enjoyment by an undertaking of market power; abuse of a dominant position is illegal under Article 86.

Duopoly: where market power is held by two sellers who react to each other's conduct.

Exclusive dealing: an arrangement for the distribution of goods within an identified area, usually involving supply by a producer to a single franchised dealer who agrees not to sell competing goods.

Horizontal agreement: agreement or merger between undertakings operating at the same level in the chain of distribution (e.g. a cartel between distributors).

Information agreement: agreement to provide competitors with advance information on prices.

Market power: the extent to which an undertaking may influence prices and output in a particular market.

Monopoly: where market power is held by a single undertaking.

Oligopoly: where a few sellers hold market power and react to each other's conduct.

Parallel imports: situation which arises where the price of goods is much higher in one member state than another, making it cost-effective to buy goods in the state where they are cheapest and sell in the state(s) where the price is highest. Eventually, this practice should lead to price equalisation.

Quantitative restriction (quota): a restriction on the quantity of goods to be produced or imported, including an absolute prohibition (nil quota) on production or importation.

Vertical agreement: agreement between firms operating at different levels in the chain of distribution (e.g. agreement between a producer and a supplier or between a supplier and customer).

2. The theory of competition: perfect competition

The modern approach to competition from the latter part of the nineteenth century onwards derives from the theory of perfect competition. As a model rather than an account of what happens in real life, perfect competition assumes various factors: that all markets contain a large number of buyers and sellers, that the sellers produce identical (or interchangeable) products, that resources can flow freely from one area of economic activity to another, and that there are no 'barriers to entry or exit' (i.e. restrictions on new businesses entering or existing businesses leaving the market).

Applying the theoretical model, any producer will be able to sell his product at a price no higher than the market will bear. Because there are many producers no single producer will be able to dictate prices. Under conditions of perfect competition an efficient distribution of resources is achieved. A producer acting rationally has an incentive to make more profits by expanding production up to the point where it costs more to produce a further unit than the price of the product (the 'marginal cost'). Output would be maintained at this point (the 'optimal level'). Consumers would be free to buy as many goods as they need at the price they are willing to pay (an efficient allocation of resources).

Without regulation, according to the traditional view, market power would be concentrated in the form of monopoly or oligopoly. As a result, the monopolist would prosper at the expense of the consumer, whose choice of products would be restricted. There would be little pressure to keep down prices and resources would be misallocated because it is in the interest of the monopolist to limit output, using 'too few' of society's resources, while more resources are channelled into the production of less valuable goods. Similar objections may be levelled against oligopolies where undertakings tend to behave as if acting in a cartel by responding rapidly to the behaviour of rival undertakings with similar behaviour ('conscious parallelism').

The traditional view of economists was based on an acceptance that perfect competition does not exist in the real world. State intervention was, therefore, necessary if economic activity was to be brought closer to perfect competition, thus protecting both consumer choice and opportunities for small businesses (now known within the EC as 'small and medium sized enterprises'). This approach underlay much early anti-trust (competition) law in the USA such as the Sherman Act 1890. It was also adopted in Europe after the Second World War, particularly in Germany where it was seen as a means of avoiding dominance by larger producers, and, to a lesser degree, in France.

3. An opposing view of competition: the Chicago school

An opposing view has emerged through the writings of the Chicago school of economists who believe that perfect competition *is* reflected in the real world, rendering state intervention largely unnecessary. It follows that only the most serious anti-competitive activities need to be controlled. Even monopolies are not necessarily to be prohibited unless they prevent competition from new entrants to the field.

4. A compromise approach: 'workable competition'

Some economists have adopted a compromise approach based on the idea of 'workable competition'. These economists accept that perfect competition is impossible, but consider that firms should strive to attain the most competitive structure which can be achieved, i.e. a workable competitive structure, which would benefit production and performance. The theory of workable competition has been invoked on a number of occasions by the EC Commission and by the ECJ (e.g. in the *Pronuptia* decision: see 19:14). If the theory of workable competition is followed, competition rules will have to deal with certain problems, including the need to prevent firms from entering into agreements which restrict competition without any beneficial features and the need to control the abuses of their position by monopolists or those in a dominant position; workable competition will have to be maintained in industries in which there are only a few sellers and mergers controlled to avoid a concentration of market power.

5. The theory of 'contestable competition'

According to the theory of 'contestable competition', the best allocation of resources is achieved by ensuring that firms operate only in a 'contestable' market. This theory emphasises the need for freedom to enter and leave the market without incurring costs. Such a market need not be perfectly competitive. While the importance of this theory in EC competition law is hard to assess at present, its likeliest application would appear to be in relation to deregulation, e.g. of the airline industry.

6. The purpose of competition law in the EC

Competition law in the EC and elsewhere does not aim solely to maximise consumer welfare by drawing up legal rules to provide for the most efficient allocation of resources and the maximum reduction of costs. There is no single competition policy. Instead, competition law and policy within the EC reflect changing values and social aims and cannot be restricted to the narrow application of any one economic theory. Article 2 refers to the task of the EC as the promotion of the harmonious development of economic activities by the creation of a common market and the progressive approximation of the economic policies of the member states. The main objectives of competition policy within the EC may be summarised as follows:

(a) to create and maintain a single market for the benefits of producers and consumer ('market integration')

(b) to prevent large undertakings from abusing their power ('equity')

(c) to persuade firms to rationalise production and distribution and to keep up to date with technical progress ('efficiency').

7. The legal framework of competition law in the EC

Competition law and policy in the EC are based on Article 3(f) of the EEC Treaty which requires the institution of a system ensuring that competition in the common market is not distorted. The competition rules are seen as an essential adjunct to the provisions on the free movement of goods in Articles 30 to 36. Articles 85 and 86 of the Treaty provide a framework for competition rules on concerted practices in Article 85, and abuse of a dominant position in Article 86. Articles 90 and 91 provide for similar rules to be applied to public undertakings. State aids are covered in Article 92(1). The main secondary legislation is found in Regulation 17/62. Competition law is a highly developed branch of EC law; thus it is only possible in the ensuing chapters to consider the main principles applicable to the subject.

8. Criticism of EC competition policy

The competition policy of the EC has been criticised on the ground that all agreements which restrict competition are illegal (unless they are subject to individual or block exemptions). Although some form of restrictive practices such as vertical agreements may prove to be beneficial to consumers they are treated in the same way as horizontal agreements which are more likely to produce detrimental consequences. Another criticism of EC competition policy has been that the completion of the internal market by the end of 1992 has been accorded a higher priority than equity or efficiency in the administration of competition law and policy. The role of competition law and policy will remain a key issue in the development of the European Economic Area and in the possible future enlargement of the EU to include the Eastern European States.

Progress test 18

1. Why, according to the theory of perfect competition, is it necessary to regulate the operation of market power?

2. Which theory (or theories) of competition have influenced the development of competition law and policy within the EC?

3. What are the main objectives of competition law within the EC and how are these objectives reflected in the EC Treaty?

4. Are all forms of anti-competitive agreements detrimental to consumers?

19

ARTICLE 85

1. Introduction

Articles 85 and 86 are directly effective: *BRT* v. *SABAM* (Case 123/73). They should be read together as a seamless web to prevent avoidance, but *see Tetra Pak Rausing SA* v. *Commission* (Case T-51/89) below, in which the Court of First Instance (CFI) stated that Articles 85 and 86 are complementary in that they pursue a common general objective under Article 3(f). However, they constitute two independent legal instruments addressing different situations: Article 85 concerns agreements, decisions of associations of undertakings and concerted practices; Article 86 concerns unilateral activity of one or more undertakings.

> *Note*: Competition decisions are identified as follows (P = pourvoi or appeal; T = tribunal):
>
> **(a)** Commission decisions: D year
> **(b)** CFI decisions: Case T-number/year.
> **(c)** ECJ decisions: Case C-number/year P or Case number/year

2. Article 85: the prohibition

Article 85(1) prohibits all agreements between undertakings, decisions by associations of undertakings and concerted practices which may affect trade between member states and which have as their object or effect the prevention, restriction or distortion of competition within the common market. This general prohibition is followed by examples of anti-competitive practices in Article 85(1)(a) to (e) such as price fixing and market sharing. Article 85(2) provides that any agreement in breach of Article 85(1) shall be automatically void. However, it should be noted that a procedure under Article 85(3) enables the Commission to 'exempt' agreements fulfilling certain conditions. Alternatively the Commission may grant negative clearance, a declaration that the agreement does not infringe Article 85(1): *see* Chapter 21.

3. Infringement of Article 85(1)

The basic elements which must be present for there to be an infringement of Article 85(1) are considered under the following headings:

(a) Agreement

(b) Undertakings

(c) Decisions by associations of undertakings

(d) Concerted practices

(e) Effect on trade between member states

(f) Prevention, restriction or distortion of competition

(g) Object or effect

(h) Within the EC.

4. Agreements

The word 'agreement' is not defined in the Treaty. However, it has been widely interpreted by the Commission to include an agreement not normally regarded as a contract such as a 'gentlemen's agreement': *Cartel in Quinine* (D1969) because it was enforceable through arbitration, and a voluntary undertaking to limit freedom of action without a contract: *Franco-Japanese Ball Bearings Agreement* (D1974). An agreement may be oral or in writing.

5. Undertakings

(a) *Undertakings generally*
'Undertaking' is not defined but, like 'agreement' has been liberally interpreted by the Commission and the ECJ to include any legal or natural person engaged in economic or commercial activity involving the provision of goods or services: *Polypropylene* (D1986). This activity need not be pursued for a profit: *P and I Clubs* (D1985). The following have been considered to be 'undertakings':

Examples
(1) Individuals engaged in sporting or cultural activities, e.g. opera singing: *Re UNITEL* (D1978).
(2) Trade associations: *FRUBO* v. *Commission* (Case 71/74).
(3) State-owned corporations: *Italian State* v. *Sacchi* (Case 155/73). (NB: The competition rules are extended to the public sector by Article 90(1): *see* Chapter 23.)
(4) Undertakings related to agriculture: *Milchforderungs Fonds* (D1985).
(5) Coal, steel and atomic energy, where the matter is not already covered.
(6) Transport organisations: *Commission* v. *Belgium* (Case 156/77).

(b) *Transport undertakings*
It is clear from the decision of the ECJ in *Ministère Public* v. *Adjes* (Cases 209–213/84) that Articles 85 and 86 apply in principle to air and sea transport. Action may not be taken by individuals in their national courts, however, until implementation measures have been taken by the EC institutions or the member states. A package of two regulations, a directive and a decision was adopted in 1987 as a first step towards completion of the internal market in air travel, with effect from 1 January 1988. Regulation 3975/85 enabled the Commission to enforce competition rules in the air transport sector. From 25 August 1992 Regulation 2410/92 extended the application of EC competition rules to air transport within a single state. Regula-

tion 3975/87 does not, however, apply to air transport between an EC and non-EC airport. Regulation 2672/88 enabled the Commission to issue block exemptions in this field. In *Ahmed Saeed Flugreisen* v. *Zentrale zur Bekämpfung unlauteren Wettbewerbs* (Case 66/86) the ECJ held that tariff agreements for flights to destinations outside the EC remained covered by Articles 88 and 89, being outside the implementing regulations. Flights within the EC are covered by the Regulation, with the result that anti-competitive agreements relating to such flights will automatically be void unless they have been notified. Further regulations were proposed in 1989 to extend the scope of Articles 85 and 86 to flights within the EC. Article 86 was held to apply to air transport without distinction.

In *London European Airways* v. *Sabena* (D1989) the Commission fined Sabena 100,000 ecus, the first time the competition rules had been invoked against an airline. In 1992 Aer Lingus was found by the Commission to have breached Articles 85 and 86 by making it difficult for British Midland to compete on the Heathrow to Dublin route (*British Midland* v. *Aer Lingus*, D 1992). Completion of the internal market in air transport has largely been achieved following several packages of measures between 1987 and 1995.

Regulation 4056/86 which applied the competition rules to sea transport took effect in July 1987.

(c) *Public authorities*
Agreements and concerted practices entered into by public authorities engaged in commercial activities would appear to be covered by Article 85(1). In *Bodson* v. *Pompes Funèbres des Régions Libérées SA* (Case 30/87) the ECJ held that Article 85 did not cover a licensing arrangement over certain funeral services to the Société des Pompes Funèbres. In this case the local authority was acting in its capacity as a public authority. If the authority had been active in the course of commercial activities rather than as a public authority, the authority would be likely to be covered. In the *ARD* decision in 1989 the Commission held (in *Film Purchases by German Television Stations*) that an association representing a number of German television companies, a public institution under national law, constituted an undertaking under Article 85(1).

(d) *The 'economic entity' principle*
Agreements between undertakings which form a single economic unit do not infringe Article 85(1). Thus an agreement between a parent company and its subsidiary over a matter controlled by a parent is covered by the 'economic entity' principle and is not regarded as a decision between undertakings: *Viho Europe BV* v. *Commission* (Case T-102/92). A parent company may, however, be liable for the acts of its subsidiary in relation to third parties when the subsidiary is acting on the instructions of the parent: *Béguelin Import Co.* v. *G.L. Export-Import SA* (Case 22/71). The Commission may examine the relationship between the parties to determine its true nature: *Pittsburg Corning Europe* (D1973).

6. 'Decisions by associations of undertakings'

The most usual type of 'association' covered by Article 85(1) is the trade association: *Vereniging van Cementhandelaren* v. *Commission* (Case 8/72). Where such trade associations co-ordinate their activities, there may be an anti-competitive effect without a formal agreement. The expression 'decisions by associations of undertakings' has been widely interpreted by the ECJ.

Examples
(1) A non-binding recommendation of trade association: *NV IAZ International Belgium* v. *Commission* (Case 96/82).
(2) A non-binding code of conduct: *Re The Application of the Publishers' Association* (D1989) (upheld by the CFI but overruled by the ECJ on a different point in 1995).

7. 'Concerted practices'

Concerted practices arise where positive steps short of an agreement have been taken to align the activities of undertakings, for example following a recommendation to exchange advance information on intended prices. In *Imperial Chemical Industries Ltd* v. *Commission (Dyestuffs)* (Case 48/69) the ECJ defined a concerted practice as a form of co-operation between undertakings which have not entered into a formal agreement but which have "knowingly substituted practical co-operation . . . for the risks of competition."

Imperial Chemical Industries Ltd v. *Commission.* On three occasions in 1964 ten major producers of dyestuffs, including ICI and CIBA, who produced 80 per cent of the dyes sold in the EC, announced price rises of about 10 per cent. Similar price rises occurred on two further occasions. There was evidence of collusion: on the first occasion four of the parent companies had sent telex messages to their subsidiaries within an hour of each other. Two further messages had been sent within the next two hours, all messages being similarly worded. The ECJ upheld the decision of the Commission, holding that their behaviour contravened Article 85(1), and imposed heavy fines on the undertakings concerned. HELD: Parallel behaviour does not necessarily amount to a concerted practice under Article 85(1) unless it leads to competition which does not accord to normal conditions of the market.

The decision has been criticised on the ground that in a market dominated by a few sellers normal price increases involving parallel pricing without co-operation may result in a breach of Article 85(1).

In the *Sugar Cartel 'Suiker Unie'* cases (Cases 40 etc./73) the ECJ held that the Commission must consider the characteristics of the market in deciding whether the parallel behaviour is an independent response to the market or the result of intentional co-operation ('a concerted practice').

On a number of occasions the Commission has issued decisions which clearly recognise the distinction between genuine, independent price rises and concerted practices. It is more likely that a concerted practice will be identified in the context of a distribution agreement with emphasis placed by the Commission and the ECJ on the spirit rather than the letter of a practice.

Example
An EC national challenged the service charge made for transferring funds to Italy, arguing that the charge, apparently uniformly applied by a number of banks,

amounted to a concerted practice. HELD (ECJ): such a charge could be a concerted practice where co-operation could be shown provided there was a sufficient effect on competition: *Züchner* v. *Bayerische Vereinsbank* (Case 172/80). c.f. The *Eurocheque* case (D1992) where uniform bank charges under the Eurocheque system were approved due to the clear advantages to tourists and other travellers.

8. Effect on trade between member states

The agreement, decision or concerted practice must affect inter-member trade to infringe Article 85(1). Thus an agreement which is concerned with trade within one member state or with exports outside the EC is, on the face of it, not covered by Article 85(1). The test defining the circumstances in which an agreement is brought within Article 85(1) was stated by the ECJ in *Société Technique Minière* v. *Maschinenbau* (Case 56/65) as follows: 'It must be possible to foresee with a sufficient degree of probability on the basis of a set of objective factors of law or of fact that the agreement in question may have an influence, direct or indirect, actual or potential, on the pattern of trade between member states.'

This test has been applied on a number of occasions, e.g. in *Windsurfing International Inc.* v. *Commission* (Case 193/83) where the ECJ emphasised the need to look at restrictions in the context of the agreements as a whole.

Examples
(1) An attempt to partition the market on national lines: *Pronuptia* (Case 161/84). In this case a franchising agreement between Pronuptia in France, the franchisor, and the franchisee in Germany, limiting the franchisee's power to operate outside a defined territory, was found by the ECJ to contravene Article 85(1). There was no evidence that the franchisee intended to operate outside the area of restriction. However, a potential effect on trade was enough.
(2) A scheme fixing the price of cement in the Netherlands contravened Article 85(1) by strengthening existing division of the market: *Vereniging van Cementhandelaren* (Case 8/72).
(3) The operators of a cartel in the Belgian roofing-felt sector were fined for contravention of Article 85(1). Although the agreement was limited to sales in one member state, it was capable of affecting inter-member trade: *Belasco* v. *Commission* (Case 246/86).

   c.f. *Publishers Association* v. *Commission* (Case C-360-92P) in which the ECJ set aside part of the decisions of the commission and CFI. The ECJ held that the refusal of exemption to the net book agreements (a system of price maintenance for books) had failed to take sufficient account of the single language area formed by the British and Irish book markets.

9. Prevention, restriction or distortion of competition

Competition law in the EC is concerned with distortion of competition rather than the question of whether inter-member trade has been increased or decreased. This, and a number of other important principles, were decided in the case of *Consten and Grundig* v. *Commission* (Cases 56 and 58/64).

Consten and Grundig v. *Commission.* Grundig, a German manufacturer of electronic goods, entered into an exclusive dealing agreement with Consten SA. Under the agreement Consten had the sole right to distribute Grundig products in France and also exclusive use of the Grundig trade mark (GINT) in that country. In return Consten agreed not to re-export Grundig products into any of the other member states, effectively banning parallel imports and exports. However, another French undertaking, UNEF, purchased Grundig products in Germany and resold them in France, undercutting Consten's prices. As a result, Consten brought an action against UNEF in the French courts for trade mark infringement. UNEF applied for and obtained a decision that the decision between Grundig and Consten contravened Article 85(1). HELD (ECJ): The object of the agreement was to eliminate competition at the level of supply by the wholesaler to the distributor (i.e. inter-brand competition).

(a) *Principles established by the Consten and Grundig decision*

> **(a)** The list of examples in Article 85(1)(a) to (e) is illustrative not exhaustive. The general words in Article 85(1) govern the particular words in the examples.

> **(b)** The prohibition applies to vertical as well as horizontal agreements.

> **(c)** An agreement should be examined in the light of the whole network of agreements (where such a network exists).

> **(d)** Only those parts of the agreement which restrict competition and affect trade between member states should be prohibited.

> **(e)** A particular agreement may be condemned without a full market analysis of actual effects where the object of the agreement is to restrict competition: *see* **10** below.

> **(f)** Trade mark rights may not be enforced where their use partitions the market.

(b) *Criticism of the Consten and Grundig decision*

The main criticism of the decision has been that it brought vertical agreements (such as those between producers and distributors, or distributors and retailers) clearly within the scope of Article 85(1). It has been argued that vertical agreements are often beneficial to consumers since they lead to improvements in the promotion and distribution of products. However, such agreements are equally capable of partitioning the market. In *Consten and Grundig* the ECJ found that the agreement aimed to insulate the French market for Grundig products.

10. 'Object or effect'

The decision of the Court in *Consten and Grundig* that a market analysis is not necessary where the object of an agreement is clearly to restrict competition was upheld in *Société Technique Minière* v. *Maschinenbau Ulm GmbH* (Case 56/65). An analysis would only be required in the case of an overtly anti-competitive agreement to confirm that the agreement was incapable of restricting competition. This approach was confirmed in *Sandoz* v. *Commission* (Case C-277/87) in which imports were stamped 'Export prohibited'. The invoices were held to constitute agreements. *See* also: *Tipp-Ex* v. *Commission* (Case C-279/87).

Where an agreement does not have the restriction of competition as its object (e.g. a research and development agreement) a market analysis is required to establish whether effects of the agreement infringe Article 85(1). The issues to be covered in such an analysis were set out in *Société Technique Minière* v. *Maschinenbau Ulm GmbH* (Case 56/65), an Article 177 reference from the Court d'Appel in Paris arising out of a claim by STM that the distribution agreement into which they had entered contravened Article 85(1). The issues under consideration in an exclusive dealing agreement include:

(a) The nature or quantity of the products to which the agreement relates

(b) The position and size of the parties in the market of the producer and the exclusive dealer

(c) Whether the agreement is isolated or part of a network

(d) The severity of the restrictions

(e) Whether the agreement allows re-exportation and parallel importation of the products concerned.

As a result of such an analysis, the agreement between STM and MU was found not to contravene Article 85(1). (*see* Steiner p. 148 and Whish pp. 216–221.)

11. Within the EC

While Article 85(1) specifically bans agreements between undertakings located within the EC, undertakings situated outside the EC are within the scope of Article 85(1) if the *effects* of their agreements or practices are felt within the EC: *Béguelin Import Co.* v. *G.L. Export-Import SA*. In *Imperial Chemical Industries Ltd.* v. *Commission (Dyestuffs)* (Case 48/69), *see* **7** above, four of the parties were established outside the EC. Because the effects of their concerted practices were felt within the EC they were held liable by the Commission for infringements of Article 85(1). This decision was upheld by the ECJ. It should, however, be noted that ICI (UK) Ltd was found liable for the acts of its subsidiary in the Netherlands at a time prior to UK membership of the EC. The *Dyestuffs* decision does not represent total commitment to the 'effects' doctrine: action against subsidiaries established in the EC circumvented the issue.

However, in *Wood Pulp* (Cases 89, 104, 114, 116–117, 125–129/85) the ECJ upheld a Commission decision in relation to a number of undertakings established outside the EC, not acting through subsidiaries, but who supplied two-thirds of the EC consumption of wood pulp. The ECJ held that the key factor was the place where the agreement or concerted practice was *implemented*. As the agreement in question had been implemented within the EC, the undertakings were fined for a breach of Article 85(1).

12. Minor agreements: the *de minimis* principle

Only agreements which affect competition to a noticeable extent are covered by Article 85(1). An insignificant effect will escape the prohibition under Article 85(1): *Völk* v. *Etablissements Vervaecke Sprl* (Case 5/69). In this case, Völk, a manufacturer of washing machines in Germany, and Vervaecke, a Dutch distributor of electrical goods, entered into an agreement giving Vervaecke exclusive rights to distribute Völk's products in Belgium and Luxembourg, reinforced by a ban into these countries of parallel imports by third parties of Völk's products. Völk produced only 0.2 to 0.5 per cent of washing machines in the German market and his share of the Belgian and Luxembourg market was even smaller (about 200 machines sold annually). The Court held that, taking into account the position of the parties in the Belgian and Luxembourg market, there was no noticeable effect on competition.

Once an agreement is found to fall within the *de minimis* rule there will be no breach of Article 85(1) even if the parties clearly intend to restrict competition.

In 1986 the Commission issued the Notice on Minor Agreements which provides that, in most cases, agreements between undertakings whose share of production and distribution of goods and services does not exceed 5 per cent of the total market in the area covered by the agreement will not contravene Article 85(1) provided the undertakings' aggregate turnover is no more than 200 million ecus. However, it should be remembered that notices are not legally binding, although they do indicate the likely approach of the Commission. Where an agreement covered by the Notice contravenes Article 85(1) because of its effect on competition, the Commission will not normally fine the undertaking.

13. Agreements likely to infringe Article 85(1)

Article 85(1) (a) to (e) provides a list of examples (not exhaustive) of agreements likely to infringe Article 85(1) including the following: price-fixing, control of production, markets or technical development, application of dissimilar trading terms, and the application of extraneous obligations. Where the agreement is not covered by the *de minimis* principle and has an effect on inter-member trade, it infringes Article 85(1). Agreements relating to those matters listed in Article 85(1) (a) to (e) are usually automatically void. Certain agreements may, however, be found not to infringe Article 85(1), in which case they will benefit from negative clearance. Other agreements will be found to infringe Article 85(1) but to be eligible for exemption under Article 85(3) either on an individual or a block basis.

14. The rule of reason

The rule of reason is a concept borrowed from US anti-trust law. Under s. 1 of the Sherman Act 1890 contracts in restraint of trade were prohibited without definition or exemption. The US courts compromised on the harshness of the statute by applying the 'rule of reason', i.e. by weighing the pro- and anti-competitive effects of the agreement to decide whether the agreement was permissible. (*see* Whish pp. 206–211; Steiner pp. 156–157.)

Under Article 85(3) of the EC Treaty exemptions may be granted to agreements which restrict competition by the Commission. Increasingly overwhelmed by its workload the Commission decided to issue block exemptions categorising practices deemed to be acceptable, thus avoiding the need for individual applications where the conditions were satisfied: *see* **21–25** below.

An alternative approach may be seen in the practice of identifying elements of an agreement deemed essential although restrictive. This approach may be followed by the national courts as well as the EC institutions since Article 85(1) is directly effective, unlike Article 85(3). The following restrictions have been found by the ECJ to be essential and therefore justifiable under Article 85(1):

Examples

(1) Provisions in franchising agreements to protect the intellectual property rights of the franchisor and to maintain the identity of the franchise system: *Pronuptia* v. *Schillgalis* (Case 161/84).

(2) Restrictive covenants on a vendor of a business and its goodwill which were considered necessary to the transfer in question: *Remia Nutricia* v. *Commission* (Case 42/86).

(3) An exclusive purchasing obligation in an agreement between a brewery and tenant was not illegal if, in its economic and legal context, it did not prevent access to the market by competitors: *Delimitis* v. *Henninger Bräu* (Case C-234/89).

15. Distribution agreements

The rule of reason is particularly relevant to distribution agreements (*see* Weatherill and Beaumont pp. 622–644). Many benefits flow from the opening-up of new markets through distribution agreements provided strong competition remains between brands. While block regulations cover exclusive distribution and franchising agreements, selective distribution agreements may only be exempted on an individual basis.

The ECJ made an important ruling in the *Metro-Grossmärkte GmbH* v. *Commission* (Case 26/76), holding that selective distribution systems will not infringe Article 85(1) provided dealers are chosen on the basis of objective criteria of a qualitative nature relating to the technical qualification of the dealer and his staff and the suitability of his trading premises, and that such conditions are laid down uniformly and not applied in a discriminatory fashion. The Court also emphasised that price competition is not the only form of competition, basing its analysis on the concept of 'workable competition' (*see* **18:4**) defined as 'the degree of competition necessary to ensure the observance of the basic requirements and the attainments of the objectives of the Treaty, in particular the creation of a single market . . .'

The ruling in *Metro* was upheld in a number of subsequent decisions, e.g. *Lancôme* v. *ETOS BV* (Case 99/79); *L'Oréal NV* v. *de Nieuwe AMCK* (Case 331/80). However, it is clear that the *Metro* principle applies only to the type of goods in relation to which the Commission or the Court considers that it is appropriate to restrict outlets for distribution.

Examples

(1) Technically complex products, e.g. cameras: *Kodak* (D1970); computers: *IBM Personal Computers* (D1984).

(2) Products where the brand image is significant, e.g. ceramic tableware: *Villeroy Boch* (D1984); gold and silver jewellery: *Murat* (D1983).

(3) Newspapers (since the short shelf-life necessitates effective distribution): *Binon* v. *Agence et Messageries de la Presse* (D1985); *but not* plumbing fittings: *Re Ideal/Standard Agreement* (D1988).

Any restrictions imposed in a selective distribution agreement must go no further than is necessary to protect the quality of the product: *L'Oréal* (Case 31/80). In *Hasselblad* (Case 86/82) the Commission objected to provisions enabling the producers to supervise advertising by distributors as this control would have included control over advertisements including price cuts.

The ECJ in *Metro* distinguished between qualitative and quantitative restrictions. In a selective distribution system, qualitative restrictions of an objective nature (e.g. relating to the suitability of premises) are permissible where they are justifiable. Quantitative restrictions are only permissible where they do not exceed the requirements of a selective distribution system. Where they are excessive, an individual exemption is still a possibility and was granted in the following decisions in which there were territorial restrictions:

Examples

(1) A franchise system in which the franchisor selected or produced the goods sold by the franchisee but was not permitted to start a business on the territory of another franchisee: *Pronuptia* v. *Schillgalis* (Case 161/84).

(2) A franchise where the franchisee had complete freedom to purchase microcomputers: *Computerland* (D1989).

(3) A franchise system for the sale of medium and top quality shoes: *Charles Jourdan* (D1989).

Restrictions on imports and exports involving an absolute territorial ban designed to partition the market infringe Article 85(1) and hardly ever qualify for exemption: *see*, for example, *Consten and Grundig*.

16. Invalidity under Article 85(2)

Under Article 85(2) any agreements or decisions prohibited pursuant to this Article shall be automatically void. However these words belie the Commission's competence to grant exemptions under Article 85(3). This power is vested solely in the Commission, causing complications for national courts which must avoid giving decisions which could conflict with those of the Commission: *Delimitis* (Case C-234/89).

17. Informal consultations, 'comfort letters' and notices

The Commission encourages undertakings to consult informally about agreements, but this has the disadvantage of placing the Commission on notice of matters which it may investigate. The Commission sometimes issues a 'comfort letter' stating either that, in its opinion, the agreement does not infringe Article 85(1) or that it does not contravene Article 85(1) but is suitable for exemption. Unfortunately for the recipients these letters do not have the status of a decision (issued after an investigation and consultation in accordance with Regulation 17/62). In the *Perfume* cases, e.g. *Lancôme* v. *ETOS*, the ECJ held that comfort letters are administrative letters outside the framework of the Treaty and do not bind national courts, nor can they be invoked before the ECJ in annulment procedures.

Another form of non-binding guidance is the Commission Notice, e.g. the Notice on Co-operation Agreements in 1968 and the Notice of Cooperation in 1993.

EXEMPTIONS

18. General

The power exists under Article 85(3) to declare that Article 85(1) does not apply to any agreement or category of agreement between undertakings, or any decision or category of decision by associations of undertakings which contributes to improving the production or distribution of goods or to promoting technical or economic progress, while allowing consumers a fair share of the resulting benefit, provided the agreement etc. does not:

(a) impose on the undertakings concerned restrictions which are not indispensible to the attainment of objectives

(b) afford such undertakings the possibility of eliminating competition in respect of a substantial part of the products in question.

19. Notification

The procedure for obtaining an individual exemption is set out in Regulation 17/62. Under Article 4(1) of the Regulation it is essential that agreements are notified to the Commission if exemption is sought. Exemption will not otherwise be granted. Before a decision is taken the parties have the right to be heard: Article 19(1), as have third parties who can show 'sufficient interest': Article 19(2). When the Commission has decided on eligibility for exemption it issues a decision to the parties. This decision must be published in the *Official Journal*: Article 21, and may be challenged under Article 173 before the Court of First Instance. An action for annulment under Article 173 also arises for breach of an essential procedural requirement, such as denial of the right to be heard: *see* Chapter 21.

20. Conditions for exemption

There are four conditions which must be satisfied before an exemption may be granted under Article 85(3), two positive and two negative. They are as follows.

(a) *It must contribute to improving the production or distribution of goods or to promoting technical or economic progress.* This requirement is probably the most important of the four, with a broad interpretation given to the arguments which may be raised.

(*i*) *Production*. Benefits in production have frequently been found to arise from agreements to specialise in particular areas of production: *see*, for example, *Re Jaz/Peter (No. 1)* (D1969), or to collaborate in research and development, avoiding unnecessary duplication of effort. Such benefits include a reduction in costs or increase in productivity as a result of economies of scale. Similarly, there may be an improvement in output or in the quality or range of goods produced as a result of plant modernisation or rationalisation.

Examples

(1) The French producers of several different types of lightweight paper used in cigarettes entered into a specialisation agreement. An exemption was granted despite a combined market share in the EC of over 50 per cent due to the strength of competition from outside the EC: *Fine Papers* (D1972).

(2) One company agreed to cease manufacturing needles and sold its plant to the other in return for shares, undertaking to buy all its needles in future from the other company. The agreement, although within the financial limits, did not qualify under the block exemption because of the lack of reciprocity. However, an individual exemption was granted, taking into account factors such as reduction in price of the needles: *Prym/Beka* (D1973).

(*ii*) Improvements in distribution usually arise as a result of exclusive supply, dealership or distribution agreements. Such agreements (particularly exclusive distribution agreements) facilitate market penetration and improve the promotion of products, continuity of supply, technical expertise and after-sales services. Thus, despite the wording of Article 85(3), improvement in services as well as the goods is covered: *Re ABI* (D1987) in which agreements restricting competition between Italian banks were exempted because they simplified and standardised banking procedures. *See* also *Transocean Marine Paint Association* (D1967) in which various small and medium sized manufacturers of marine paint in the EC collaborated to rationalise the production and marketing of marine paints on the world market. The Commission granted an exemption, accepting that a global distribution network was established and that the gain in international competition outweighed the reduction in competition between members.

(*iii*) *Technical progress*. Technical progress may result from various agreements, particularly specialisation agreements which involve research and development. Applications for exemption were successful in the following:

Examples

(1) Discovery and application of new technology, the development of newer and safer products, improvements in energy savings: *see*, for example, *Re X/Open Group* (D1987) in which a number of computer manufacturers collaborated to produce a standard which would enable users to switch the hardware and software from different sources. HELD: The agreement would promote technical progress by enabling the development of programmes for which there might not otherwise be a market.

(2) Improved exploitation of inventions through patent and know-how licensing agreements: *Re United Reprocessors* (D1976).

(3) A joint venture between three UK companies manufacturing switch-gear for the research and development of vacuum interrupters: *Re Vacuum Interrupters (No. 1)* (D1977).

(*iv*) *Economic progress*. Economic progress has not been specifically invoked as a ground for exemption as often as the factors outlined above. However, it was invoked in the *Davidson Rubber Co.* (D1972) where a patent licensing agreement resulting in economies of scale was exempted.

(b) *The agreement must allow consumers a fair share of the resulting benefit*. The term 'consumer' has been broadly interpreted to include all purchasers, not merely end users: see e.g: *ACEC* v. *Berliet* (D1968) where the resulting benefit of an agreement between two French manufacturers on the production system for a prototype bus was passed on to the 'middleman' in a commercial transaction.

In most cases where there is vigorous competition in the same product market, benefits in the form of lower prices, an increased range of products or a better service, will be passed on to consumers: *Re KEWA* (D1976); *Re United Reprocessors* (above). Failure to pass on such benefits would result in a loss of business to the parties to the agreement.

(c) *There must be no unnecessary restrictions*. The restrictions must not exceed what is absolutely necessary for the agreement (an application of the principle of proportionality). Clauses which provide absolute territorial protection are unlikely to succeed: *Consten and Grundig* above. However, limited territorial protection for a franchisee may be acceptable: *Pronuptia* above.

The Commission may insist on the dropping of certain terms of an agreement before granting exemption: *see* e.g. *Re Optical Fibres* (D1986) where the Commission required one party in a joint venture to reduce its voting right in the other.

(d) *There must be no elimination of competition*. The agreement must not allow the possibility of elimination of competition in respect of a substantial part of the common market. The range of competing products must be identified, taking into account the parties' market share and structure of the market in which they are competing.

Examples
(1) Where there is lively competition, the market may be the EC as a whole: *Re Fine Papers* above, or the world market: *Re Vacuum Interrupters (No. 1)* above.
(2) Where competition is more limited, it may be the territory of a single member state where the agreement is performed: *Van Landewyck* v. *Commission* (Cases 209–215 and 218/78).

BLOCK EXEMPTIONS

21. The Commission's response

The practice of issuing block exemptions developed as the response of a Commission to the need to focus on unusual or complex agreements and the uncertainty of firms about to enter into agreements over the validity of those agreements. A series of regulations has been issued in areas where agreements are generally beneficial rather than anti-competitive. As a result, many undertakings draft their agreements in order to take advantage of the provisions of these block exemptions. Where a block exemption applies, there is no need for undertakings to notify an agreement falling within its scope.

22. The block exemptions

Regulations have been issued granting exemptions in relation to agreements within the following categories including:

(a) Exclusive distribution: Regulation 1983/83

(b) Exclusive purchasing: Regulation 1984/83

(c) Specialisation: Regulation 417/85

(d) Research and development: Regulation 418/85

(e) Patent licensing: Regulation 2349/84

(f) Motor vehicle distribution: Regulation 123/85

(g) Franchising: Regulation 4087/88

(h) Know-how licensing: Regulation 556/89.

23. The pattern of the regulations

The regulations typically lay down the permitted restrictions deemed essential to the agreement (the 'white' list), followed by a list of forbidden restrictions (the 'black' list). In some cases there is a further category of restrictions subject to the 'opposition' procedure (the 'grey' list) under which restrictions must be notified to the Commission. If they are not opposed within six months they are considered to be exempt.

24. Features of certain block exemptions

(a) *Specialisation.* Exemption is currently available only for undertakings with a combined annual turnover of no more than ECU 1000 million and a market share not exceeding 20 per cent in the goods covered by the agreement. When these limits are exceeded, the opposition procedure may be invoked.

(b) *Research and development.* The current upper limit on the parties' combined market share is 20 per cent. (There is no turnover limit.)

(c) *Franchising.* This Regulation applies to franchising in distribution and servicing but not manufacturing. The franchisee pays for the right to use the franchisor's know-how in return for the right to sell goods or services according to a standard business format (or marketing style and premises).

25. The white and black lists

Examples of permissible practices (the white list) include:

(1) Restrictions on active searching for business outside the member's own territory in a distribution agreement.
(2) Exclusivity in exclusive purchasing and distribution agreements.

Examples of forbidden restrictions (the black list) include:

(1) Absolute territorial restriction in exclusive purchasing or distribution agreements.
(2) Closed exclusive patent licences.

Where a restriction is not covered by the white list or the grey list, or where upper limits are exceeded, exemption is only available as a result of an individual application.

Progress test 19

1. How have the words 'agreement' and 'undertaking' been interpreted by the ECJ in the context of Article 85?

2. To what extent do the competition rules apply to air and sea transport?

3. Three undertakings with registered offices outside the EC have entered into an agreement to fix prices within the EC. The undertakings all manufacture cars outside the EC for distribution within the EC by subsidiary companies. Advise the three undertakings whether their agreement is subject to EC competition rules.

4. A, B and C are retail undertakings in the UK. Noticing that A and B had both raised the price of their goods to the same figure, C followed with an identical price rise. Advise C whether the undertaking may be in breach of Article 85. Would your advice differ if A, B and C had agreed to exchange advance information before raising prices?

5. Can an agreement between undertakings limited to one member state contravene Article 85?

6. Consider the relevance of obtaining a market analysis where the object of an agreement is to prevent or distort competition.

7. D, a UK undertaking, entered into an agreement with E by which E agreed to operate an exclusive distribution network within the Netherlands for child car seats. D holds 1 per cent of the market for child car seats in the UK and 3 per cent of the market in the Netherlands. Advise D and E whether it is necessary to notify the agreement to the Commission.

8. In which ways is a typical franchise agreement likely to infringe Article 85?

9. How has the US concept of the 'rule of reason' influenced the development of competition law in the EC?

10. What is the effect on the agreement of a breach of Article 85(1)? Do 'comfort' letters serve a useful purpose?

11. Which factors does the Commission bear in mind when deciding an application for exemption?

12. H SA is the largest producer of apple juice in France. H intends to enter into an agreement with J plc, a UK company manufacturing tins and cartons for drinks. Under the agreement H SA will stop making its own containers and will instead purchase all its containers from J plc. The agreement will enable H SA to penetrate the UK fruit juice market and J plc the French food packaging market. There will be a reduction in price which will be passed on to the consumer who, in the words of H SA and J plc, will be offered a 'superior product'. Advise H SA and J plc on the need to notify the Commission of the agreement.

13. Why did the Commission decide to make certain types of agreement subject to block exemptions? Explain the operation of a typical block exemption.

20

ARTICLE 86

1. Introduction

Article 86 regulates the activities of undertakings in a dominant position whereas Article 85 controls the activities of independent undertakings which collude (*see* Chapter 19).

2. Article 86: the prohibition

Under Article 86 any abuse by one or more undertakings of a dominant position within the common market or in a substantial part of it is prohibited as incompatible with the common market in so far as it may affect trade between member states. This prohibition is followed by an illustrative list of abusive practices.

It is important to note that it is not *dominance* but *abuse of a dominant position* which is illegal under Article 86: *Michelin (NV Nederlandsche Bander-Industrie Michelin* v. *Commission* (Case 322/81)). Such abuse must be controlled because it is anti-competitive and leads to the inefficient distribution of resources: the customer of a monopolist charging high prices cannot obtain alternative goods or services from another supplier. The monopolist, on the other hand, may be able to profit excessively from his market position.

3. 'Undertakings' and the control of oligopoly

Prior to the *Flat Glass* decision (D1989) it was generally thought that Article 86 did not apply to the activities of independent undertakings but only to those covered by the 'enterprise entity' concept, i.e. where parent and subsidiary are treated as indivisible: *Continental Can* (Case 6/72). Thus oligopolies could be controlled under Article 85 (which required proof of an agreement or concerted practice) but not Article 86. In *Flat Glass* the Commission decided that a group of undertakings held a dominant position in the flat glass market in Italy. Although the CFI partly annulled the Commission's decision (in Cases T-68/89, T-77/89 and T-78/89) it did not rule against the relevance of Article 86 for oligopolies. (*See* Weatherill and Beaumont p. 606.)

4. Essential elements

There are three essential elements in establishing a breach of Article 86:

(a) a dominant position

(b) abuse of that position

(c) an effect on inter-member trade caused by the abuse.

> *Note*: Unlike Article 85 there is no procedure for negative clearance or exemption under Article 86. A negative clearance procedure does, however, exist for mergers under the Merger Regulation (Regulation 4064/89: *see* **18** below).

5. Dominance

Dominance was defined in *United Brands* v. *Commission* (Case 27/76) as 'the position of economic strength enjoyed by an undertaking which enables it to prevent effective competition being maintained on the relevant market by giving it the power to behave to an appreciable effect independently of its competitors, and ultimately of its consumers.'

This definition of dominance was repeated in *Hoffman-la Roche* (the Vitamins case, Case 85/76) and extended as follows: 'Such a position does not preclude some competition . . . but enables the undertaking which profits by it, if not to determine, at least to have an appreciable effect on the conditions under which that competition will develop, and in any case to act largely in disregard of it so long as such conduct does not operate to its detriment.'

Where there is effective competition from alternative products or from a challenge to the undertaking's market share by another firm (*see* Weatherill and Beaumont pp. 654–58) there will be no breach of Article 86.

To prove dominance it is necessary to establish the relevant market. This is identified by examining the product market, the geographical market and, sometimes, the temporal market.

6. The product market

It is in the interests of an undertaking whose activities are being investigated under Article 86 to argue that the market should be defined as widely as possible, since this reduces the opportunity for dominance. A producer of, say, wheels for sports cars will hold a smaller share of the market if the product market is wheels for cars generally rather than for sports cars. Where services are in issue the 'relevant service market' should be identified: *Decca Navigator System* (D1980).

The importance of identifying the relevant product market in establishing dominance was shown in the first case to come before the ECJ under Article 86, *Continental Can (Europemballage Corp.* v. *Continental Can* (Case 6/72): *see* below). The Commission's failure to identify the product market market in this case led to the annulment of its decision by the ECJ.

Continental Can (Case 6/72). Continental Can (CC), a powerful US multinational company, through its wholly owned subsidiary, Europemballage (E), held 86% of the shares in Schmalbach (S). S had a dominant position in Germany for tins of meat and fish and for metal lids for glass containers. E proposed to take over a Dutch packaging firm, Thomassen (T). At the time of the proposed takeover S and T were operating in adjacent areas but were not competitors. E offered for the shares held in T by third parties, as a result of which the CC holding in T rose to 91%.

The dominance of S was imputed under the enterprise entity concept to CC. The Commission held that CC (and S) had a dominant position in three separate markets: cans for meat, cans for fish, and metal tops. The elimination of *potential* competition between S and T and the reduction in consumer choice in the supply of products amounted to an abuse. The Commission decided that the takeover of T by CC (through E) amounted to a breach of Article 86.

While agreeing in principle with the Commission that the takeover could be an abuse, the ECJ held that the Commission had failed to identify the relevant product market and to give reasons for its decision. The Commission decision was annulled.

7. Product substitution

The product market should be defined by reference to the question of product substitution, that is whether there is 'a sufficient degree of interchangeability between all the products forming part of the same market in so far as a specific use of such products is concerned': *Hoffman-la Roche* (Case 27/76). Thus, the product market covers goods which are identical or are regarded by customers as interchangeable, similar in relation to the characteristics of the product, its price, quality or use. (*See* Steiner, chapter 14; Green, Hartley, Usher, chapter 18.)

Two key factors in identifying the product market emerge from the reasoning of the ECJ in *Continental Can* and later decisions:

(a) Cross-elasticity of demand (i.e. the extent to which the customer can obtain similar goods or acceptable substitutes)

(b) Cross-elasticity of supply (the extent to which other undertakings can supply goods or acceptable substitutes).

DECISIONS ON THE PRODUCT MARKET

8. Bananas or fresh fruit?

In *United Brands* v. *Commission* (Case 22/76) the Commission alleged that United Brands, one of the world's largest producers of bananas (marketed under the brand name 'Chiquita'), handling 40 per cent of the EC trade in bananas, had infringed Article 86 in various ways. The Commission claimed that the product market was bananas (branded and unbranded). United Brands, on the other hand, claimed that the market was fresh fruit. The ECJ upheld the Commission definition, accepting that there was a separate market for bananas. Bananas were consumed particularly by the very young, the old and the sick, consumption being little affected by pricing or consumption of other fruits.

9. Raw materials or end product?

In *Commercial Solvents* (*Instituto Chemicoterapico* (Cases 6, 7/73) the ECJ decided that there may be a separate market for raw materials and the end product.

> *Commercial Solvents.* Commercial Solvents Corporation (CSC) and its Italian subsidiary refused to supply Zoja, an Italian company, with aminbutanol, the best and cheapest raw material used to make ethambutol, a drug for treating tuberculosis. CSC had a near-monopoly in ethambutol. Other substitutable drugs existed but were less satisfactory. Zoja could not readily adapt its production process to these alternatives. The ECJ upheld the Commission decision that the product market was aminobutamol, not the raw materials for making ethambutol.

10. Other examples of the product market

The following product markets have been identified by the ECJ or CFI:

(1) Tyres for heavy vehicles, as distinct from tyres for cars and light vans (production processes were different; customers came from separate groups): *Michelin* (*NV Nederlandsche Baden-Industrie Michelin* v. *Commission* (Case 322/81).
(2) Vitamins, each of which occupied a separate market depending on its properties and functions: *Hoffman-la-Roche* (Case 85/76, *see* above).
(3) Spare parts for independent repair of cash registers. The parts were supplied by a Swedish firm to a firm in the UK through its subsidiary, illustrating how small the relevant market may be in contrast with, for example, *United Brands* (Case 22/76): *Hugin Kassaregister AB* v. *Commission* (Case 22/78).
(4) Different types of cartons for fresh pasteurised milk and UHT (ultra high temperature) treated milk. Fresh and UHT milk taste different and were not regarded by consumers as interchangeable: *Tetra Pak (No. 1)* (Case T-51/89).
(5) Plasterboard and wet plaster (the latter requiring to be laid by skilled, trained plasterers): *British Plasterboard Industries plc* v. *Commission* (Case T-85/89).

11. The geographical market

Article 86 is only infringed where dominance occurs within the common market or a substantial part of it. Thus it is essential to determine the geographical market, i.e. the market in which there are available and acceptable substitutes 'where the conditions of competition are sufficiently homogenous for the effect of economic power on the undertaking to be evaluated': *United Brands* (Case 22/76). A useful point to start the identification of the geographical market is by reference to the sales area. The geographical market is not necessarily synonymous with the sales area and is influenced by factors such as:

(a) *Costs and feasibility of transportation.* Where the product is easy and cheap to transport such as nail cartridges in *Hilti* v. *Commission* (Case T-30/89) the market may be the whole of the EC (cf. highly perishable products such as fresh seafood which will have a more restricted local market).

(b) *Consumer preferences.* The pattern and volume of consumption may be examined to determine whether the territory of a member state could be a substantial part of the common market. In *Suiker Unie* (Cases 40/73, etc.) Belgium and Luxembourg were considered sufficiently large to amount to a substantial part of the common market.

> *Notes*: (1) The geographical market is not necessarily identical with the physical size of the market. However, it is now generally accepted that the territory of each member state (or even part of such a territory), e.g. the port of Genoa: *Corsica Ferries* (Case C-18/93), may be a substantial part of the common market.
>
> (2) It is possible for the market to be the whole of the EC or even of the whole world where competition is on a global scale.

12. The temporal market

Seasonal considerations affecting opportunities for product substitution may be a factor. Although the Commission did not define the banana market according to the time of year in *United Brands*, it did consider the time factor in *RE ABG Oil* (D1977). In this case the Commission limited the oil market to the crisis period after the OPEC action in the early 1970s, during which companies had a particular responsibility to supply customers on fair terms.

13. Assessing dominance

To assess dominance a detailed economic analysis is required, the main elements of which are:

(a) *Market share of the undertaking.* This is a key feature in establishing dominance. In *Continental Can* the share of the German market held by CC was 70 to 80 per cent. The share of 3 of the 7 vitamin markets held by Roche in *Hoffman-La Roche* was more than 80 per cent. Such a high market share will be regarded by the ECJ as proof of dominance.

(b) *Market share of competitors.* A relatively low market share by the undertaking (such as 40 to 45 per cent in *United Brands*) may indicate dominance where the market is fragmented by competitors (in that case holding 10 and 16 per cent).

(c) *Financial and technical resources.* Ready access to the international capital market was significant in *Continental Can*. Possession of superior technology has been identified by the ECJ in several cases, e.g. *Michelin*, *United Brands*, etc.

(d) *Control of production and distribution.* Control of production and distribution (sometimes called 'vertical integration') was regarded as significant in *United Brands* where the undertaking owned the plantations and the means of transport and also marketed the bananas itself. Roche's highly developed sales network in *Hoffman-la Roche* amounted to a similar commercial advantage over competitors.

In *ICI and Tioxide* (D1990), notified under the Merger Regulation (*see* below), the Commission found that ICI's acquisition of Tioxide did not contravene Article 86. Before the acquisition Tioxide supplied most of ICI's requirement for titanium dioxide in paint manufacturing. The acquisition did not affect access to markets, titanium dioxide and paints being seen as separate markets.

(e) *Conduct and performance.* An undertaking's conduct and performance may provide evidence of dominance, e.g. discriminatory pricing: *Michelin.* Economic performance may also indicate dominance, e.g. where it shows that there is 'spare' or 'idle' capacity: *Hoffman-la Roche.* A temporary loss made by United Brands did not prevent a finding of dominance in the light of the undertaking's success in retaining its market share.

ABUSE OF A DOMINANT POSITION

14. General

Article 86 does not prohibit dominance, merely abuse of a dominant position: *see* 2 above. The list of abusive practices which follows the prohibition in Article 86 provides examples including unfair prices, limiting production, discrimination in contractual terms and the imposition of supplementary obligations.

15. Comparison with Article 85

There are many parallels between the types of behaviour prohibited under Article 85 and Article 86. Both Articles must be interpreted in the light of the objectives of Article 3(g) of the Treaty. However, there is no mechanism for negative clearance under Article 86 equivalent to Article 85(3). In *Tetra Pak Rausing* (Case T-51/89) the CFI held that the grant of exemption under Article 85(3), either as a result of individual or block exemption, could not render inapplicable the prohibition under Article 86. The Commission has developed the concept of 'objective justification' where behaviour which is apparently anti-competitive is found not to constitute an abuse. In most cases the behaviour has not been found to be objectively justified (see e.g. *Hilti*).

16. Categories of abuse

Two main categories have been identified by the Commission and the ECJ (*see* Whish, *Competition Law,* chapter 18; Steiner, chapter 14). These are:

(a) *Exploitative abuses:* where the dominant undertaking takes advantage of its position by imposing harsh or unfair trading conditions, e.g. unfair pricing.

(b) *Anti-competitive abuses:* abuses which are not harsh or unfair but which reduce or eliminate competition, e.g. refusal to supply. In these circumstances the undertaking uses its market dominance to undermine or eliminate competitors or to prevent new entrants from entering the market. Since the decision in *Continental Can,* mergers have been regarded as exploitative abuses within the scope of Article 86. However, since its adoption mergers have increasingly been considered under the Merger Regulation (Regulation 4064/89). Mergers (or 'concentrations' as they are known under the Regulation) are examined separately at the end of the chapter.

Many types of abuse, e.g. price discrimination, fall into both categories. These categories should not be regarded as sacrosanct. If the undertaking's activities are considered by the Commission to be without objective justification abusive and thus abusive, there is a breach of Article 86.

17. Examples of abuse

(a) *Unfair prices.* An unfair price was defined in *United Brands* as a price which bears no reasonable relation to the economic value of the product. Such prices may be excessively high or (occasionally) excessively low as a result of pressure from a dominant purchaser.

(b) *Discriminatory prices.* Discriminatory prices arise where different customers are charged different prices without objective justification. Differential pricing based on national markets was rejected in *United Brands* as the basis for objective justification. Price discrimination may take many different forms, e.g. predatory pricing (undercutting a rival product at below cost price): *AKZO Chemie BV* (Case C-62/86); loyalty rebates: *Hoffman-la Roche*; discounts intended to keep imports outside a dominant firm's territory: *BPP Industries plc v. Commission* (Case 50/89).

(c) *Unfair trading conditions.* Conditions imposed by a copyright society on its members could be unfair if they exceeded what was necessary for the society to manage its rights effectively: *BRT v. SABAM* (Case 127/73).

(d) *Refusal to supply.* Refusal to supply has been considered an abuse on a number of occasions by the Commission and the Court, e.g. *Commercial Solvents* (*see* 9 above), in which a competitor was driven out of business as a result, and *United Brands,* in which the undertaking refused to supply a Danish wholesaler who had taken part in a sales campaign by a rival supplier. In the *Magill TV Guide* cases the refusal by television companies to supply information about weekly programme listings to a competing producer of a guide was an abuse: *RTE, BBC and ITP v. Commission* (Case C-241/91 P). Refusal to supply a service was also considered an abuse in *Belgian Telemarketing* (Case 311/84).

(e) *Import and export bans.* Import and export bans constitute an abuse, not only restricting competition but also hindering market integration (*see* Whish, chapter 8). In *BL v. Commission* (Case 226/84) the ECJ upheld the Commission's finding that BL's pricing policy requiring type approval certificates on cars reduced imports into the UK and constituted an abuse.

MERGERS AND CONCENTRATIONS

18. Merger control under Article 86

Article 86 was invoked for the first time in the context of merger control in *Continental Can* (Case 6/72): *see* 6 above. The ECJ ruled, in principle, that mergers which eliminate competition infringe Article 86, without the need to show a causal link between dominance and abuse. (Note, however, that the Commission decision that there was a breach of Article 86 was annulled for failure to examine the relevant product market.)

Examples

(Both of the following decisions were taken prior to the application of the Merger Regulation.)

(1) In *Tetra Pak 1 (BTG Licence)* (D1988) the Commission held that it was an abuse to take over a firm to acquire an exclusive licence for patents and know-how which had the effect of excluding other operators from the market. The subsequent appeal to the CFI was withdrawn on this point although it went ahead on a number of other issues. While holding that the acquisition of an exclusive licence is not itself an abuse, the CFI recognised that the acquisition had strengthened Tetra Pak's market dominance and was likely to delay competition from fresh entrants (*see* Goyder, *EC Competition Law*, chapter 18).

(2) In *Metaleurop SA* (D1990) two undertakings, one holding 11 per cent of the zinc market and the other holding 18 per cent of the lead market, decided to merge their non-ferrous metal production in a new company, Metaleurop SA. As a result of the merger the new company's share of the zinc market rose to 20 per cent. The Commission held that despite the size of the merger neither of the undertakings held a dominant position in lead or zinc. The presence of other producers and a steady flow of imports from outside the EC made it unlikely that the merger would prevent effective competition. There was no breach of Article 86.

19. Merger control under Regulation 4064/89

The possibility of a merger infringing Article 85 arose for the first time in *BAT & Reynolds* v. *Commission* (Cases 142 and 156/84). This case provided the stimulus to revive the proposal for a regulation to control mergers. Regulation 4064/89 was adopted in 1989, with effect from October 1990.

Under the regulation the Commission is obliged to investigate mergers, known as 'concentrations', where certain threshold levels are involved. Mergers above these thresholds must be notified to the Commission. In a Notice in 1990 the Commission stated that a joint venture will be considered to be a 'concentration' where it involves the performance of functions of an autonomous economic entity and the lack of co-ordinated activity. Joint ventures not covered by this definition will be considered to be 'co-operative' and will be outside the control of the Commission.

The regulation applies to concentrations which satisfy the following criteria:

(a) The undertakings concerned have a combined worldwide turnover exceeding ECU 5000 million (or 10 per cent of assets for banks and insurance companies); and

(b) At least two of the undertakings have an EC-wide turnover of at least ECU 250 million; provided

(c) Each of the parties does *not* derive two thirds of its business in the EC in a single member state.

These turnover limits were due to be reviewed after 4 years. While the Commission is anxious to lower the limits (and extend its competence) this view is not shared by the national competition authorities (*see* below). It could be argued that further loss of control by the member states contravenes the principle of subsidiarity.

20. Procedures and decisions under the regulation

Once a proposed concentration has been notified to the Commission the undertakings concerned must suspend activities for three weeks. Where the concentration does not impede effective competition it will be declared compatible with the common market; otherwise the Commission has one month in which to initiate proceedings, followed by a further four months in which to issue a decision.

Factors taken into account by the Commission in reaching its decision include the structure of the markets concerned, the market position of the parties, actual and potential competition (from within and outside the EC), freedom of choice for third parties, barriers to entry, the interests of consumers, and technical and economic progress.

The procedures under the regulation appear so far to be operating reasonably smoothly. Of the concentrations notified to date only one has been found to be incompatible with the common market: *Aerospatiale/Alexia/De Havilland* (1991) in which the Commission based its analysis in the world market for commuter aeroplanes, thus according a high market share to the parties and thus substantial economic strength. The decision has been subject to criticism, indicating the general sensitivity of control of concentrations at EC level. In a number of other decisions the Commission has, however, imposed conditions with a view to reducing market power resulting from the concentration. An appeal lies from the Commission decision to the CFI (see e.g. the appeal against Nestle/Perrier decision in *Comité Central de l'Enterprise de la Societe General des Grandes Sources* v. *EC Commission* (Case T-96/92R)).

21. 'One-stop shopping' or national control

Part of the purpose of the regulation was to provide a single forum for the examination of concentrations with the EC. This has not proved possible as member states have sought to retain an element of control over concentrations covered by the regulation. Provision is made for involvement by the national authorities where there are distinct national markets or legitimate notifiable interests.

(a) *Distinct national markets.* A member state is entitled under Article 9(2) of the regulation within 3 weeks of receiving a copy of a notification of a concentration to inform the Commission that a concentration threatens to strengthen a dominant position, significantly impeding competition in a distinct national market.

If the Commission decides that there is both a threat and a distinct market, it may either consider the case itself or refer it to the member state's competition authorities. A member state, in the event of a referral, must within 4 months reach a decision, limiting itself to measures necessary to safeguard competition. The Commission and Council declared in 1990 that the procedure should only be invoked in exceptional circumstances.

The procedure was used for the first time in *Streetley/Tarmac* (D1990) when a notification relating to brick and clay tiles was referred back to the UK authorities. If the concentration were allowed to go ahead it would give the new company a dominant position where previously three undertakings had been active. The concentration was likely to cause significant barriers to entry in the relevant market in the UK, while having little impact on other parts of the EC. In the circumstances it was appropriate for the issues to be decided by the UK authorities.

Conversely a member state may invoke a procedure under Article 22(3) requesting the Commission to apply the regulation to a concentration in its own territory without an EC dimension.

(b) *The protection of legitimate interests.* Although Article 21(2) of the regulation states that member states shall not apply their national legislation on competition to a concentration with an EC dimension it must be read subject to paragraph (3) which entitles member states to take appropriate measures to protect legitimate interests outside the regulation provided they are compatible with EC law.

Under paragraph (3) member states may intervene at their own instigation in three areas:

(*i*) 'public security' (i.e. defence interests)
(*ii*) 'plurality of the media' (i.e. the need to maintain diversified information and news)
(*iii*) 'providential rules' (i.e. surveillance of financial bodies, e.g. solvency rules).

Member states wishing to intervene to protect legitimate interests in other matters of public interest must notify the Commission.

22. Effect on inter-member trade

For an infringement of Article 86 an effect on inter-member trade must be proved. The phrase has the same meaning as applied to Article 85. It is important to note that alterations in the competitive structure of the common market amount to an effect on inter-member trade: *Commercial Solvents*.

Progress test 20

1. What does Article 86 prohibit and how does it differ in scope from Article 85?

2. Define 'a dominant position'.

3. Explain the importance of identifying the relevant product market in

establishing a breach of Article 86. What was the relevant product in *United Brands* v. *Commission* (Case 22/76)?

4. What are the two main categories of abuse of a dominant position? Give examples of the most common types of abuse. Can a merger amount to an abuse under Article 86?

5. A plc, a UK company, has an EC-wide turnover of ecu 200 million. It wishes to merge with BSA, a French company with an EC turnover of ecu 300 million. Both companies manufacture car tyres. Advise A and B whether the merger must be notified to the Commission and of the consequences of notification. Would your advice differ if either company carried out all its business in a single member state?

21

ARTICLES 85 AND 86: ENFORCEMENT AND PROCEDURE

1. Introduction

The powers and procedures of the Commission in enforcing EC competition law are laid down in Regulation 17/62. The regulation came into force on 13 March 1962. Although it has been amended a number of times the legal mechanism remains substantially the same. EC competition law is administered by Directorate General IV (D/G IV) within the Commission, with the national courts also involved in the application of Articles 85 and 86.

THE ROLE OF THE COMMISSION: REGULATION 17/62

2. Power to grant exemption and negative clearance

Only the Commission has the power to grant exemptions or negative clearance, following notification on Form A/B: Article 9 of the Regulation. However, the national courts retain their competence to apply Articles 85 and 86 until the Commission initiates any procedure under Articles 2, 3, or 6: *see* below.

Note: Mergers are not covered by Regulation 17 but by Regulation 4064/89: *see* Chapter 20.

3. Effects of notification

Notification may lead to immunity from fines: Article 15(5)(a) unless the agreement is found to infringe Article 85(1), without being eligible for exemption: Article 15(6). Notification cannot, however, attach provisional validity (except in the case of 'old' agreements, i.e. agreements made before Regulation 17/62 came into effect) or pre-accession agreements: *Brasserie de Haecht* v. *Wilkin (No. 2)* (Case 48/72).

4. The right to be heard

Under Article 19(1) of the Regulation, before taking a decision adverse to the applicant, the Commission must allow the applicant the right to be heard on matters to which the Commission has objected. Persons showing a sufficient interest also have the right to be heard: Article 19(2). Before taking a decision favourable to the applicant, the Commission must publish a summary of the application, inviting interested parties to submit comments: Article 19(3).

5. Alternative procedures

Owing to the heavy nature of its workload, the Commission adopted various procedures to speed up the decision-making process. In some cases the matter is dealt with informally without the need for notification. In others, the agreement may be covered by a block exemption. Agreements covered by block exemptions need not be notified provided no unnecessary terms are included. Comfort letters following notification save time and paperwork but are not legally binding: see 19.**17**. In some cases, the opposition procedure is used, often requiring no action by the Commission: see 19.**23**. The main drawback of informal procedures is that they deny interested parties the opportunity to challenge them before the CFI.

Note: Actions for annulment of Commission decisions were heard by the ECJ until the creation of the CFI in September 1989.

6. Termination of infringement

The Commission, acting either on its own initiative or on application, may issue a decision requiring the undertaking or association of undertakings to terminate its infringement of Article 85 or Article 86: Article 3. The application may be brought either by a member state or by legal persons claiming a legitimate interest. The Commission may, before issuing a decision, issue recommendations for termination. An action for annulment of a Commission decision may be brought in the CFI under Article 173, or for inaction under Article 175. There is a right of appeal from the CFI to the ECJ on a point of law.

7. Date of effect, duration and revocation of decision under Article 85(3)

The Commission must state the date of effect of the decision not earlier than the date of notification, except in relation to those agreements not covered by Articles 4(2) and 5(2) and those not notified in time under Article 5(1). The decision must last for a specified period only but may be renewed if Article 85(3) continues to be satisfied. A list of circumstances in which the Commission may revoke or amend a decision or prohibit specified acts by the parties is given in Article 8(3)(a) to (e). All final decisions in which negative clearance or exemption is either granted or refused must be published in the *Official Journal*.

8. Interim measures

The power to take interim measures is not expressly provided by Regulation 17. However, the ECJ held in *Camera Care* v. *Commission* (Case 792/79 R) that the power is implied in Article 3, annulling a Commission decision refusing to make an interim order requiring Hasselblad to supply its cameras to Camera Care. The ECJ ruled that the Commission may take interim measures provided that:

(*i*) they are urgent and necessary to avoid serious or irreparable damage to the party seeking the remedy or in a situation intolerable to the public interest.
(*ii*) there is a reasonably strong case of prima facie infringement of the competition rules
(*iii*) the principle of proportionality is observed
(*iv*) the decision is temporary and capable of review by the CFI.

Note: (a) The essential procedural safeguards under Article 19 of the Regulation must be observed. The interim measure may be challenged before the CFI. (b) The ECJ ruled in *Ford of Europe* v. *Commission* (Cases 228 and 229/82) that an interim order may only be granted if it falls within the framework of the final decision.

Example
A Commission decision declaring the net book agreements void was temporarily suspended as there were clear prima facie arguments against the decision: *Publishers' Association* v. *Commission* (Case T-66/89). An appeal to the CFI was unsuccessful but this decision too was suspended pending hearing by the ECJ (Case 56/89). The ECJ set aside parts of the earlier decisions: *see* 19:**8**.

INVESTIGATIVE POWERS

9. Extensive powers

To enable it to carry out the market analyses necessary to grant negative clearance or exemption the Commission has been given extensive powers of detection and investigation under Regulation 17/62. The Commission may begin proceedings on its own initiative or on application by a member state or individual (e.g. in *ICI* v. *Commission* ('*Dyestuffs*') (Cases 617/73) in which complaints had been made by the printing industry). Under Regulation 17/62 these powers include:

(a) Requests for information: Article 11. The Commission may make a written request for information, stating the purpose for which it is needed and the possible fines for incorrect information. If the information is not forthcoming the Commission may order the production of information by formal decision.

(b) Sector enquiry. If economic trends indicate that competition is being restricted or distorted, the Commission may order a sector enquiry: Article 12. In this case, the Commission may request every undertaking in a particular sector to provide details of their agreements or concerted practices or information about structure and practices if the undertaking is in a dominant position.

(c) Investigations.

(1) *Powers*. Under Article 14 the Commission may authorise its officials to:
(*i*) examine the books and records of an undertaking
(*ii*) take copies of books and records

(*iii*) ask for an 'on the spot' explanation

(*iv*) enter the land, premises and vehicles of undertakings.

(2) *Failure to allow investigation.* Failure to allow such an investigation may lead to a decision ordering an investigation. Further failure to comply may lead to a fine and a penalty. While the Commission may compel an undertaking to provide all necessary information about facts of which it has knowledge, an undertaking may not be compelled to incriminate itself: self-incrimination contravenes the right to a fair hearing: *Orkem (formerly CDM)* v. *Commission* (Case 374/87). The onus rests with the Commission to establish a breach of either Article 85 or 86. *See* also *Solvay & Co.* v. *Commission* (Case 27/88 decided on the same day and on virtually identical facts as in *Orkem*). In *Otto BV* v. *Postbank NV* (Case C-60/92) the ECJ held that information learned by the Commission and national authorities from proceedings before national courts may not be used in evidence in proceedings which may lead to the imposition of a penalty.

(3) *Privilege.* Privilege may be claimed for correspondence between a client and independent lawyer in the EC or with an establishment in the EC, after proceedings have been initiated by the Commission. Correspondence with in-house lawyers, however, is not privileged: *Australian Mining & Smelting Europe Ltd* v. *Commission* (Case 155/79). It is the function of the CFI (or ECJ) to decide which documents are privileged.

(4) *Voluntary or compulsory investigations.* Investigations may be either 'voluntary' under Article 11(2) or 'compulsory' under Article 14(3) (e.g. *National Panasonic (UK) Ltd* v. *Commission* (Case 136/79)). Prior warning of an investigation must be given to member states. But in *National Panasonic* no prior notice of a 'dawn raid' was given to Panasonic. The ECJ rejected Panasonic's claim that prior notice should have been given and found that the Commission was entitled to carry out such undertakings as are necessary to reveal any breaches of Articles 85 or 86. National Panasonic was found to have engaged in concerted practices contrary to Article 85.

(5) *Powers of entry and search.* Powers of entry and search relate only to undertakings and not to the premises of individuals. A 'dawn raid' was also carried out in *Hoechst* v. *Commission* (Cases 46 and 227/88). The Commission's investigation was challenged by Hoechst on the grounds that it breached the inviolability of the home and that the Commission's decision was insufficiently precise. The ECJ held that where the Commission intended to carry out an investigation without the co-operation of the undertakings concerned, it must observe procedural guarantees laid down by national law. The fundamental right to the inviolability of domicile applied to private residences and could not be extended to commercial premises. The Commission's statement of reasons was found to be drafted in general terms but containing sufficient detail about the products in which a cartel was suspected contrary to Article 85(1).

This decision was upheld in *Dow Benelux NV* v. *Commission* (Case 85/87) and *Dow Chemical Iberica SA* v. *Commission* (Cases 97–99/87).

(6) *Investigation by the authorities of member state.* Under Article 13 the Commission may request the authorities of a member state to carry out the investigations

which it considers necessary under Article 14(1) or which it has ordered under Article 14(3). The officials of the national competition authority usually accompany the Commission officials in an investigation.

CONFIDENTIAL INFORMATION

10. Professional secrecy and business secrets

The Court is obliged under Article 19(2) of Regulation 17/62 to have regard to the 'legitimate interest of undertakings in the protection of their business secrets'. Under Article 20(2) the Commission must not disclose 'information acquired as a result of this Regulation and of the kind covered by the obligation of professional secrecy' to the national authorities, e.g. courts: *DGDC* v. *AEB* (Case C-67/91).

In *AKZO Chemie BV* v. *Commission* (Case 53/85) the ECJ held that it was for the Commission (subject to review by the Court) to decide whether a document contains business secrets. Once it is clear that a document contains business secrets (e.g. details of joint ventures agreements, market shares or expansion plans) its contents must not be divulged. The degree of protection attaching to 'professional secrecy' is less clear: the Commission may be prepared to divulge information covered by professional secrecy where it considers that this is necessary.

In *Adams* v. *Commission* (Case 145/83) Stanley Adams, formerly a senior executive at Hoffman-La Roche in Switzerland, succeeded in obtaining damages against the company in an action under Article 215. While employed by Hoffman-La Roche the applicant had secretly passed documents to the Commission which showed that the company was breaching Article 86. Although Adams requested confidentiality from the Commission, Hoffman-la-Roche was able to identify Adams from the documents. As Adams had committed an offence by revealing the documents to the Commission he was charged with industrial espionage on re-entering Switzerland from Italy. While he was in custody his wife committed suicide. Adams was convicted and given a one-year suspended jail sentence. He sued the Commission for damages, claiming that his credit-worthiness had been damaged by the conviction and that his business had been destroyed. Although damages were awarded they were reduced by half on account of his contributory negligence, namely his failure to warn the Commission that he could be identified from the documents and his return to Switzerland despite the risk of prosecution.

11. Procedural rights of the parties, third parties and member states

Under Article 19 of Regulation 17/62, and Regulation 99/63, before ordering termination of an infringement or the imposition of fines or penalties, the Commission must give notice to the parties of the case against them, to enable them to present their case and be heard. The same rights apply to interested third parties and to member states.

FINES AND PENALTIES

12. Fines and penalties

Under Article 15 the Commission may impose fines for infringements of Articles 85 and 86 which are intentional or due to negligence, ranging from 1000 ecus to one million ecus, or 10 per cent of the undertaking's turnover, whichever is greater. In calculating turnover, fines are based on group turnover worldwide in the relevant sector: *Re Benelux Flat Glass Cartel* (D1985).

13. Factors taken into account

Factors taken into account in calculating the fine (*see* Whish p. 308; Steiner p. 188) include:

(a) The duration and gravity of the infringement

(b) The behaviour of the parties (open or concealed)

(c) The economic importance of the parties and the share of the relevant product market

(d) Whether the parties have already been found to have infringed Article 85 or 86: *Hercules* v. *Commission* (Case T-7/89)

(e) Whether the infringement is deliberate

(f) The profits from the illegal activities: *Eurocheque: Helsinki Agreement* (D1992).

14. Examples of fines

The Commission has imposed heavy fines on undertakings for clear breaches of the competition rules. See, for example, *Musique Diffusion Française* v. *Commission* (Cases 100–103/80) in which the ECJ held that it was permissible for the Commission to impose a fine which was high enough to act as a deterrent to others. In that case the ECJ reduced by 2.5 million ecus the Commission's fine of 7 million ecus for partitioning the market (because of certain inaccurate assessments by the Commission). More recently the Commission has imposed fines of ECU 57.85 million for price fixing and market sharing: *Polypropylene* (D1986) and ECU 60 million for similar infringements: *Polythene* (D1989). In 1994 the CFI upheld the fine of ECU 75 million against Tetra Pak for its pricing policies: *Tetra Pak* (Case T-83/91). This decision is subject to appeal to the ECJ.

15. Mitigating factors

Various factors may be accepted in mitigation by the Commission. These include recession in the industry in question and the parties' willingness to terminate the offending behaviour: *Wood Pulp* (D1985). (Extensive parts of this decision were annulled on appeal to the ECJ in Cases 89/85 etc.) An undertaking to establish a programme to ensure that the firm does not in future infringe the competition rules was a factor in *John Deere* (D1985).

16. Annulment proceedings

When annulment of a Commission decision is sought under Article 173 the case will be examined according to the principles under that Article. Annulment actions rarely succeed, but do quite frequently lead to a reduction in the fine. Firms no longer invoke the annulment procedure as a delaying tactic, since the ECJ rules in *AEG-Telefunken* (Case 107/82) that interest may be charged from the date of the Commission decision.

17. Failure to supply information; daily penalties

Fines from 100 to 5000 ECUs may be imposed on undertakings which, intentionally or negligently, fail to supply information: Articles 11, 12 or 14: *see* **9(c)(2)** above. Under Article 16 a daily penalty of 50 to 1000 ECUs may be imposed on undertakings failing to co-operate in investigations under Article 11(5) or Article 14(3).

18. Parallel fines: double jeopardy

If an agreement contravenes both EC law and the laws of a member state or other competition authority, it may be fined twice.

Examples
  (1) The parties were fined under both EC and US law for price fixing, quotas and market division: *Quinine Cartel* (D1969).
  (2) Fines were imposed by both German and EC authorities; *Dyestuffs* (Case 48/69).

19. Enforcement through the national courts

Under Article 88 EEC the national competition authorities may administer the competition rules in the national courts until these powers are removed by the Commission by negative clearance, exemption or investigation. The ECJ ruled in *BRT* v. *Sabam* (Case 127/73) that the competence of national courts derives from the direct effects of Articles 85 and 86, not from Regulation 17/62. A dilemma faces the national court where an exemption seems appropriate on the facts. Only the Commission may grant an exemption but the national court must make a ruling in the case under consideration. The court may thus:

(a) decide there is no breach, if the legal position is clear from previous decisions of the ECJ or the Commission; or

(b) stay the action if parallel proceedings have been started by the Commission; or

(c) make an Article 177 reference to the ECJ. (*See* Steiner p. 169).

20. Remedies in the national courts

Breach of Article 85 or 86 should lead to the application of the same remedies as are available for similar breaches of national law: *Rewe-Zentralfinanz* (Case

33/76); *see* also *Comet* v. *Produktschap* (Case 45/76). In interlocutory proceedings an injunction or declaration may be obtained, but the national courts (particularly in the UK) are divided about whether or not damages are available: *Garden Cottage Foods* (HL 1984).

In addition to reliance on Articles 85 and 86 in the national courts, an individual claiming a legitimate interest may request that the Commission investigates an alleged infringement of EC competition rules: Article 3(2) Regulation 17/62. Where such a request is made to the Commission an interim order may also be sought from the national court: *see*, for example, *Cutsforth* v. *Mansfield Inns Ltd.* (High Court, 1986) in which the plaintiffs succeeded in obtaining an interim injunction to prevent the application of agreements to which they were not a party. The agreements in question were tenancy agreements between the defendants, brewers who had taken over a group of tied houses, and the tenants of those houses. Prior to the agreement the applicant had supplied pin-tables and other gaming equipment to the public houses in the group, but under the agreement the tenants were obliged to purchase such equipment only from named suppliers. The applicants were excluded from the list. The applicants complained to the Commission and succeeded in obtaining an interim injunction from the English High Court.

Such applications, however, do not always succeed: *see Argyll Group plc* v. *Distillers Co. plc.* (Court of Session, 1986) in which the Scottish court refused to grant an interim interdict (injunction) to prevent a merger between Distillers and Guinness, stating that no prima facie case had been made out. Injunctions were also refused in *Plessey* v. *GEC* (High Court, 1990) and *Megaphone* v. *British Telecom* (High Court, 1989). In a Co-operation Notice in 1993 the Commission stated that interim measures may be more quickly and readily obtained in the national courts than before the Commission although the Notice states that the Commission will close the file if the complainant could pursue a directly effective right in the national courts. On occasion it may, however, be necessary to pursue actions before both the national courts and the Commission. (*See* Steiner pp. 196–197.)

Progress test 21

1. What are the practical advantages of notification?

2. What action may be taken by the Commission where it considers that there has been a breach of either Article 85 or Article 86?

3. In what circumstances is the Commission empowered to take interim measures?

4. What powers are held by the Commission to enable it to investigate possible breaches of the competition rules?

5. How does the case of *Adams* v. *Commission* (Case 145/83) illustrate the importance of confidentiality in the dealings of the Commission?

6. What rights are held by third parties and member states in proceedings before the Commission?

7. Which factors are considered by the Commission in deciding the amount of a fine?

8. What action may be taken by individuals affected by breaches of EC competition rules?

22

INTELLECTUAL PROPERTY

1. Introduction

The term 'intellectual property' is used in this book to cover both industrial and artistic property. 'Industrial property' covers valuable rights connected with the production and distribution of goods and services (e.g. patents and trade marks). 'Artistic property' covers artistic and literary property (e.g. copyright). The term used in the EC Treaty is 'industrial and commercial property': *see* Article 36.

2. Scope of intellectual property rights

Intellectual property rights usually provide for the exclusive enjoyment of valuable property rights by the holder against the world in general. The granting of intellectual property rights has traditionally been left to the national authorities. There is clearly a need for unification of intellectual property rights if market division on rigid national lines is to be avoided. The creation of intellectual property rights at a regional, European level, is therefore innovatory. Progress towards the recognition of European rights has been made in the two patent conventions, the Trade Mark Directive 89/104 and Regulation 40/94, and the Copyright Directive 93/83 on satellite broadcasting. Without further harmonisation of intellectual property rights the continued use and enjoyment of such rights on a national basis may disturb the free movement of goods and distort competition within the EC. Thus, it is necessary to consider intellectual property rights in the context of Articles 85 and 86 and also Articles 30 to 36.

Example
Grundig had appointed Consten to be the exclusive distributor of Grundig products in France. The exclusive dealing agreement was reinforced by the sole use in France by Consten of Grundig's international trade mark, GINT. An action for annulment of the Commission decision refusing exemption was brought by the parties under Article 173 in the ECJ. The ECJ rejected the appeal and upheld the Commission decision: *see* **16.16**. HELD: Articles 36 and 222 EEC allow for the *existence* of national industrial property rights but their *exercise* is subject to Community control: *Consten and Grundig v. Commission* (Cases 56 and 58/64). The purpose of the GINT trade mark was not to protect the holder's legitimate rights but to partition the market, providing absolute territorial protection for Grundig products in France, in breach of Article 85(1). (*See* also *Terrapin v. Terranova* (Case 119/75), below.)

INTELLECTUAL PROPERTY RIGHTS AND THE FREE MOVEMENT OF GOODS

3. Treaty provision

While the competition rules may be invoked to prevent the division of the market on national lines by intellectual property rights: see below, they do not provide a comprehensive answer to this problem. It is thus necessary to invoke the provisions in the free movement of goods in Articles 30 to 36 in the courts both at national level and in the ECJ (or CFI).

4. Relationship between EC law and national law

The key question arising in the context of intellectual property rights is: how far may the holders of national intellectual property rights rely on those rights to exclude imports from another member state? Article 222 states that the Treaty shall 'in no way prejudice the rules in member states governing the system of property ownership'. Article 222 must, however, be read subject to Article 36 which states that the prohibitions of Articles 30 to 36 'shall not preclude prohibitions or restrictions on imports, exports or goods in transit justified on grounds of . . . the protection of industrial and commercial property. Such prohibitions or restrictions shall not, however, constitute a means of arbitrary discrimination or a disguised restriction on trade between member states'.

5. A compromise approach

In order to satisfy the requirements of Article 222, the ECJ has adopted a compromise approach. In *Terrapin* v. *Terranova* (Case 119/75) a German firm known by the trade name 'Terrapin' sought to prevent a UK firm from registering the name 'Terranova'. The German company claimed that consumers would be confused as both companies made building materials. The ECJ held in Article 177 proceedings that Article 36 could be invoked to prevent the importation of goods under the name which causes confusion where these rights are held by different proprietors under different national laws, provided they do not operate as a means of arbitrary discrimination nor as a disguised restriction on trade between member states.

In *Terrapin* the Court again distinguished between the *existence* of intellectual property rights (recognised by national law) and the *exercise* of those rights (which may be restricted under the Treaty). However, the ECJ qualified this approach by stating that Article 36 only permits exceptions to the principle of the free movement of goods to the extent to which such exceptions are justified for the purpose of safeguarding the rights which constitute the specific subject-matter of that property.

See also the earlier decision in *Deutsch Grammophon Gesellschaft mbH* v. *Metro-SB-Grossmärkte GmbH & Co. KG* (Case 78/70), in which the ECJ drew a similar distinction between the existence and exercise of rights, this time in relation to copyright protection. While copyright protection under national law is legitimate, a prohibition on parallel imports resulting from the use of copyright to prevent goods moving from one member state's territory to another would be an improper exercise of those rights (and would be unjustifiable under Article 36).

6. Exhaustion of rights

Where the holder of an intellectual property right puts goods into circulation in his own member state's territory, he loses the right to prevent their importation from that state into another member state. His rights are said to be 'exhausted'. See *Centrafarm BV v. Sterling Drug Inc.* (Case 15/74) (patents) and *Centrafarm BV v. Winthrop* (Case 16/74) (trade marks). Goods may be put into circulation either directly by the owner of the right or by the grant of a licence to a third party.

Examples
(a) *Patents*: The application sought to prevent the importation into the UK of portable lavatories made by the Italian company, on the basis that the products infringed a UK patent. HELD (ECJ): as the patent was valid under national law (although it would not have been granted elsewhere in the EC) the patent was protected under Article 36: *Thetford Corp. v. Fiamma Spa* (Case 335/87).

(b) *Trade marks*. (1) Centrafarm obtained drugs in the UK which the company repacked before selling in Germany. Hoffman-La Roche, the holder of the German trade mark for the drug, sued Centrafarm for trade mark infringement. HELD (ECJ): enforcement of the trade mark would constitute a disguised restriction on trade between member states contrary to Article 36 where the marketing system adopted by the trade mark holder involves an artificial partitioning of the market, provided repackaging cannot adversely affect the condition of the product and that the repackaging firm does not confuse users. The repackaging firm must state that the goods have been repackaged and must notify the trademark holders of its intention to repackage: *Hoffman-La Roche* (Case 102/77).

(2) Centrafarm bought drugs in the UK under the trade 'Serenid D', reselling them in the Netherlands under the name 'Seresta'. American Home Products Corporation owned both trade marks, marketing an almost identical drug in the Netherlands under the name 'Seresta'. HELD (ECJ): the holder of a trade mark was entitled to prevent the unauthorised fixing of trade marks, unless the trade mark was being used to divide the market along national lines (as this would constitute a disguised restriction on trade between member states, falling outside Article 36): *Centrafarm BV v. American Home Products Corporation* (Case 3/78).

(3) Dahlhausen distributed blood filters in the Federal Republic of Germany which it imported from Italy. The filters and packaging were marked 'Miropore', followed by the letter R in a circle. Pall sought to prevent Dahlhausen from using the R symbol after the 'Miropore' trade mark on the ground that it constituted misleading publicity contrary to German law. HELD (ECJ): Article 30 prohibits the application of a national rule on unfair competition enabling a trader to seek, in the territory of a member state, the prohibition of the distribution of a product bearing the letter R in a circle next to the trade mark, where that mark had been registered in another member state, but not in the state in which the prohibition was sought: *Pall Corporation v. P.J. Dahlhausen & Co.* (Case C-238/89).

(c) *Copyright*. (1) GEMA, the German copyright association, sought to rely on its

German rights to prevent parallel imports of records from the UK which had been put on the market without GEMA's consent. HELD (ECJ): (i) Copyright in artistic works is within the term 'industrial and commercial property' in Article 36 and is therefore subject to the exhaustion principle. (GEMA was thus unable to use the German rights to keep out parallel imports.) (ii) It was irrelevant that the royalty rate in the UK was 2 per cent lower than in Germany, leading to a loss of profits by GEMA in Germany: *Musik-Vetrieb Membran* (Cases 55 and 57/80)

(2) The copyright in the records of Cliff Richard had expired in Denmark but not in Germany. Patricia and other German recording companies sought to buy recordings in Denmark and import them for resale in Germany. HELD (ECJ): although the recordings had been lawfully placed on the market, they had not been marketed by the holder of the copyright or with the holder's consent, but only because the copyright had expired. Thus, the copyright holder was able to rely on the mark, the disparity between the national laws amounting to an obstacle to the free movement of goods: *EMI v. Patricia* (Case 341/87).

(3) Local (Danish) law recognised a separate copyright in video rental rights from sale rights. HELD (ECJ): imports from one member state to another could be blocked in relation to video rental rights (rights not exhausted), but not in relation to sale (rights exhausted): *Warner Brothers v. Cristiansen* (Case 158/86).

(d) *Registered designs.* (1) The proprietor in the Netherlands of a registered design for a handbag sought to prevent the importation into the Netherlands of an identical bag, made in France to a design registered to another owner. HELD (ECJ): the proprietor of the right was entitled under Article 36 to rely on the right to prevent importation from France where the bags had been manufactured without the consent of the owner of the right: *Nancy Keane Gifts BV* (Case 144/81).

(2) Renault sought to enforce its registered patent rights in designs for ornamental car body parts to prevent the copying of the designs, or marketing such parts in other member states. HELD (ECJ): the holder of the right could rely on it to prevent the manufacture or marketing of copies of such parts in another member state without the consent of the holder of the right: *Consorzio Italiano della Componentistica de Ricambio per Autoveicoli v. Regie Nationale des Usines Renault* (Case 53/87). *See also Volvo v. Eric Veng* (Case 238/87), below.

(e) *Plant breeders' rights.* The holder of plant breeders' rights sought enforcement of licensing agreements with various companies to propagate seeds for sale. HELD (ECJ): the plant breeder, having invested in the development of the basic product, should be able to protect himself against improper handling of the seed varieties and to control resale prices: *Erauw Jacquery v. La Hesbignonne* (Case 27/87). (This decision could be relevant to other circumstances such as the licensing of computer software.)

7. The common origin principle

Until the recent decision in '*Hag II*': *see* below, it was considered unlawful, where different persons in different member states held trade marks with a common origin, to prevent the sale in one member state of goods subject to one of the national marks purely because the holder of the mark had national protection in that member state: *Van Zuylen Frères v. Hag AG ('Hag I')*

(Case 192/73). The common origin principle was restricted to trade marks. Trade marks relate to the reputation of a particular product and last indefinitely, unlike other intellectual property rights such as patents and copyright which protect creative activity and are of limited duration. Trade marks were thought to pose a more serious threat to the free movement of goods than other property rights.

The ECJ, however, reversed the decision in *Van Zuyen Frères* ('*Hag I*'). In *SA CNL-Sucal NV v. Hag GF AG* ('*Hag II*') (Case C-10/89) the ECJ recognised the role of trade marks in retaining customers' goodwill by permitting them to link the mark with a particular manufacturer's products or services.

> *SA CNL-Sucal NV v. Hag GF AG* ('*Hag II*'). Hag GF AG was a German company which produced and distributed decaffeinated coffee according to the process it had devised. It registered two trade marks under the name 'Kaffee Hag' in Belgium where it established a wholly owned subsidiary company, Café Hag SA. The subsidiary company held several trade marks, one of which bore the mark 'Café Hag'. Café Hag SA was sequestrated in 1944 as enemy property, being subsequently sold by the Belgian authorities to the Van Oevelen family. In 1971 Café Hag SA transferred the trade marks in Benelux to Van Zuylen Frères, a Belgian firm which was later transformed into a company known as SA CNL-Sucal NV. The German company, Hag GF AG, claimed that its product 'Kaffee Hag' was a famous brand in Germany, superior to the coffee produced by Sucal, and sought in the German courts to restrain Sucal from infringing its trade mark. HELD (ECJ, Article 177): Articles 30 and 36 EEC did not prevent national legislation from allowing an undertaking which was the proprietor of a trade mark in one member state from opposing the importation from another member state of similar goods bearing an identical or confusingly similar trade mark to the protected mark. Reliance on a trade mark in these circumstances remained possible even when the mark under which the disputed product had been imported had initially belonged to a subsidiary of the undertaking which was opposing the importation and had been acquired by a third undertaking following the sequestration of that subsidiary.

> *Note*: National laws on intellectual property may not be invoked (in the absence of unfair competition) merely because the public may be misled as to the origin of the goods: *Theodor Kohl KG v. Ringelham and Rennett SA* (Case 177/83).

8. Goods from third countries

Where undertakings within the EC seek to enforce their rights in intellectual property to prevent goods from third countries entering the EC, there is no contravention of Articles 30 to 36 on the free movement of goods: *EMI v. CBS* (Case 51/75). In this case trade mark disputes had arisen before the courts in the UK, Denmark and Germany over the importation of records manufactured by CBS in the USA with the trade mark 'COLUMBIA'. EMI was therefore entitled to enforce the trade mark which it held throughout the EC against CBS, the holder (through a subsidiary) of the US trade mark.

INTELLECTUAL PROPERTY RIGHTS AND COMPETITION LAW

9. Introduction

Intellectual property rights by their nature restrict competition. There is a clear distinction drawn by the ECJ between the *existence* of such rights and their *exercise*: *Consten and Grundig* v. *Commission* (Cases 56 & 58/64): *see* **2** above. The existence of intellectual property rights does not necessarily infringe competition law: *Sirena srl* v. *EDA srl* (Case 40/70). The exercise of these rights may, however, restrict competition under Article 85 or constitute an abuse of a dominant position under Article 86.

10. Improper exploitation of intellectual property rights

Any exploitation of intellectual property rights which contravenes Articles 85(1) is illegal: *Consten*. Any agreement or concerted practice or abuse by a dominant undertaking such as the maintenance of artificial price levels or imposition of discriminatory conditions may contravene either Article 85 or Article 86, depending on the circumstances.

Example
GEMA, a performing rights society in Germany, required copyright holders who wished to become members to assign all their rights, present and future, throughout the world until five years after leaving the society. Contractual rights were extended to cover non-copyright works. Only German residents could become ordinary members, foreign residents being excluded from valuable rights. HELD (Commission): The unfair conditions imposed as a result of the dominance of GEMA constituted an abuse under Article 86: *Re GEMA* (D1971).

11. Non-discrimination and intellectual property rights

Discrimination against EC nationals on grounds of nationality in intellectual property rights contravenes Article 6 EC. Such a breach (then of Article 7 EEC) was found by the ECJ in *Patricia* v. *EMI* (Case C-326/92). The case arose out of the failure of German law to allow Cliff Richard the same level of protection as German nationals in relation to unauthorised recordings of his music. A similar breach occurred in relation to Phil Collins. The ECJ held in a joint ruling with Case C-326/92 that denying the rock star the right to prevent unauthorised recordings made in Germany of concerts in the USA infringed Article 7: *Collins* v. *Imtrat Handelsegesellschaft* (Case C-92/92).

12. Licences

The ECJ confirmed in *Parke, Davis & Co. Ltd.* v. *Probel* (Case 24/67) that the distinction between the existence and exercise of rights in relation to trade marks applied equally to patent licences. The Commission followed the same line of reasoning in a series of patent licensing cases, culminating in *Windsurfing International Inc.* v. *Commission* (Case 193/83), a decision upheld by the ECJ.

Windsurfing International Inc. v. *Commission.* The owners of patent licences in a special sail rig which comprised sail, mast, mast foot and curved booms for use with sailboards sought to impose on its licensees restrictions contrary to Article 85(1). These restrictions required the licensee: (i) to sell only complete sailboards rather than the patented rig on its own, with royalties charged on the complete sailboard, (ii) to exploit the patents for the rigs, only to make sailboards using hulls approved by Windsurfing International, (iii) to manufacture only at a specified plant and (iv) not to challenge the licensed patents. HELD (ECJ, Article 173): such provisions constituted an improper exercise of intellectual property rights contrary to Article 85(1).

In *Volvo AB* v. *Eric Veng* (Case 238/87) the ECJ affirmed that the refusal by the holder of an intellectual property right of a licence to another manufacturer is not an abuse of a dominant position, even though that manufacturer has offered to pay a reasonable royalty. (The right in question was the design right owned by Volvo for the manufacture of spare parts, a similar issue to that in the *Renault* case (Case 53/87): *see* **6(d)**.) But see the decision of the ECJ in the *Magill TV Guide* case (Case C-241/91 P) upholding the decision of the CFI: below.

'No-challenge' clauses restraining the licensee from challenging the validity of an intellectual property right are usually illegal. However, in *Bayer & Hennecke* v. *Sulhoffer* (Case 65/86) the ECJ held that no-challenge clauses included as part of a settlement in a dispute over ownership or validity of intellectual property rights do not infringe Article 85(1).

In *Ottung* v. *Klee* (Case 320/87) the ECJ held that an obligation on a licensee to continue paying royalties after the expiry of a patent does not necessarily restrict competition, unless the licensee may not terminate on giving reasonable notice or the licence restricts the licensee's freedom of action under termination.

13. The specific subject-matter of the property

The Commission has ruled, in a number of decisions, that intellectual property rights may only be exercised to protect the specific subject matter of the property concerned:

(a) *Patent rights.* Patent rights require protection to reward the original effort of the inventor: *Centrafarm BV* v. *Stirling Drug Inc.* (Case 15/74). Patent licensing agreements, however, usually infringe Article 85(1) and require exemption to be enforceable. The approach of the Commission to individual exemptions follows the lines of the block exemption on patent licensing (Regulation 2349/84), prohibiting, for example, absolute territorial protection: *L.C. Nungessor KG* v. *Commission* (Case 258/78).

(b) *Trade marks.* The ECJ defined the specific subject-matter of a trade mark in *Centrafarm BV* v. *Winthrop BV* (Case 16/74): it is the protection of rights in the product, in order to protect the owner from competitors who sell goods improperly bearing the mark. Trade mark rights may not be invoked to prevent the parallel importation of goods bearing legitimate trade marks.

(c) *Copyright.* There is no clear definition of the specific subject-matter of copyright. Conditions which are unnecessarily restrictive and discriminatory infringe the competition rules. A reciprocal copyright agreement between copyright management societies does not infringe Article 85 unless the terms of the agreement exceed what is necessary to protect the interests of members: *Ministère Public* v. *Tournier* (Case 395/87).

In the *Magill TV Guide* cases (Cases T-69/89, T-70/89 and T-76/89) Magill, a publisher, complained to the Commission that the copyright in the listing of television programmes held by the *Radio Times, TV Times* and *RTE Guide* (for Ireland) contravened Articles 85 and 86. Under these copyright arrangements no publisher could publish a weekly programme schedule. The Commission decided that the refusal to allow third parties to publish a weekly schedule amounted to an abuse of a dominant position. The copyright owners were ordered to permit third parties to publish schedules by the grant of licences for which royalties would be paid.

The decision was upheld by the CFI which accepted that the three television companies were dominant in the weekly listing of tv programmes which constituted a separate market from the daily tv listings. While the existence of copyright did not necessarily amount to an abuse, the refusal to supply information to Magill was an abuse. The CFI considered that the essential function of copyright was 'to protect the moral rights in the work and to ensure a reward for the creative effort, while respecting the aims of, in particular, Article 86'. As the compilation of information on tv listings was not considered to involve creative effort the companies were obliged to supply the information. The ECJ upheld the CFI decision in 1995 (Case C-241/91 P).

14. Relationship between Articles 30 to 36 and Articles 85 and 86

The prohibitions in Article 30 and Articles 85 and 86 apply cumulatively to intellectual property. As the provisions on the free movement of goods are fundamental to the EC, any conflict between the rules on free movement and the competition rules should be resolved in favour of Article 30.

HARMONISATION OF INTELLECTUAL PROPERTY

15. Patents

The wide differences in national approaches to intellectual property rights has led to a demand for integration at European level. There are two contentions in relation to patents:

(a) *The European Patent Convention.* The European Patent Convention (in force since 1977) is not an EC convention. Its signatories include all the EC member states except Ireland and Portugal and certain EFTA countries. Under the Convention it is possible to obtain patent protection in some or all of the signatory states through a single application to the European Patent Office (EPO) in Munich. Patent rights, however, will have to be enforced separately in each country.

Example

Biotechnology: In 1990, in the 'Harvard Mouse' appeal, the EPO considered the patentability of a mammal with chromosomes modified by Harvard scientists to increase the chance of cancerous cell growth. The EPO decided that animals which are the products of microbiological processes are patentable.

> *Note*: In 1988 the Council proposed a directive on the legal protection of biotechnical inventions, aiming to adapt existing patent law principles to establish a harmonised framework of standards to protect inventions.

(b) *The Community Patent Convention.* The Community Patent Convention was signed in 1975 but has not been fully ratified. Under the Convention any litigation will take place in Community Patent Courts in each member state with effect throughout the EC, with a right of appeal to a Common Appeal Court.

16. Trade marks

As part of the 1992 programme the first trade marks directive (Directive 89/104) was adopted for implementation in December 1991. Under the directive national trade marks will continue to exist. Member states will, however, be required to harmonise their trade mark laws in a number of areas such as the rights conferred by a registered trade mark. The Council has recently adopted Regulation 40/94 harmonising trade marks within the EC. Under the regulation a Community trade mark will exist in parallel with national marks. A single application would be made to the Community Trade Marks Office. Rights would be enforced in Community Trade Mark Courts designated by the member states.

17. Copyright

A common level of copyright protection has applied within the EC as all member states are signatories of the Berne Copyright Convention. The copyright directive (Directive 93/98) has finally been adopted harmonising the duration of copyright and related rights. Copyright protection lasts for 70 years from the death of the author while the period of related rights (e.g. for performers) lasts for 50 years. The directive also provides that distribution rights will not be exhausted except by sale in the EEA (i.e. the EC and most of EFTA) by the copyright holder or with his consent.

Directive 91/250 on computer programs was adopted in 1991, providing for protection of computer programs in the way that they are expressed but not of the underlying principles.

The Commission has published a proposal for a regulation on design rights. Under the proposal an EC design office would administer the rules protecting designs throughout the EC.

18. Semiconductors

Directive 87/54 harmonises the law relating to the design (topography) of the internal layout of semiconductor integrated circuits. Under the Directive, member states must provide legal protection against the unauthorised use of original topographies.

Progress test 22

1. Define 'intellectual property'.

2. Why is it necessary to unify intellectual property rights within the EC?

3. What does the decision in *Terrapin* v. *Terranova* (Case 119/75) demonstrate on the relationship between Article 36 and Article 222?

4. When are rights in intellectual property said to be 'exhausted'? Give examples in relation to patents, trade marks, copyright and registered designs.

5. How did the decision in the '*Hag II*' (Case 10/89) alter the common origin principle expressed in '*Hag I*' (Case 192/73)?

6. In what way(s) may intellectual property rights infringe EC competition rules? Give examples in relation to patent licences.

7. To what extent have intellectual property rights been harmonised within the EC? What is the role of the European Patent Office?

23

COMPETITION LAW AND STATE REGULATION

1. Introduction

This chapter covers the position of public undertakings under Article 90 and the restrictions on state aids (subsidies) in Articles 92 to 94 of the EEC Treaty. The regime providing for a particular category of public undertakings, state monopolies of a commercial character, was examined in Chapter 10 in the context of the free movement of goods.

PUBLIC UNDERTAKINGS

2. The obligation: Article 90(1)

Under Article 90(1), in the case of public undertakings and undertakings to which member states grant special or exclusive rights, member states must neither enact nor maintain in force any measure contrary to the rules provided for in Article 6 and Articles 85 to 94.

3. Categories of undertaking in Article 90(1)

The term 'undertaking' was considered in Chapter 16 in the context of Article 85: *see* 16:**8–10**. In relation to Article 90, the ECJ held in *Italy* v. *Sacchi* (Case 155/73) that even where the main objects of a company are non-economic, it will be considered an undertaking to the extent to which it engages in economic activity. If a local authority, for example, exercises its sovereign powers or acts as a consumer, it will not be considered to be an undertaking for competition purposes, but if it engages in entrepreneurial activities such as carrying on a retail business, it will be considered a public undertaking subject to Articles 85 and 86.

4. The Transparency Directive: Directive 80/723

To avoid inconsistencies arising from different national definitions of public undertakings the ECJ adopted the definition of public undertaking in *France, Italy and the United Kingdom* v. *Commission (the Transparency Directive Case)* (Joined Cases 188–190/80). The Directive (extended in 1985) defines a public undertaking as '. . . any undertaking over which the public authorities may exercise directly or indirectly a dominant influence by virtue of their ownership of it, their financial participation therein, or the rules which govern it': Directive 80/723.

5. Examples of public undertakings

Public undertakings include the following:

Examples
Central and local government (when acting in a commercial context): *see* above, corporations established under public law (e.g. statutory corporations such as British Rail in the UK), public services or authorities (acting in a commercial context), state-controlled undertakings acting under private law (provided the state exerts a dominant influence). *See* also *Aluminium Products* (D1985) in which various producers of aluminium in Eastern Europe claimed that Article 85(2) did not apply to them because under socialist law they were inseparable from the state and were thus entitled to sovereign immunity under international law. The Commission rejected their claim, holding that they were undertakings.

6. The scope of the obligation under Article 90(1)

It is not clear whether the duty of member states is limited to a standstill provision, reinforced by the need to take positive measures to undo prohibitions, with accountability for the behaviour of public undertakings, or whether Article 90 imposes a positive duty on states to act.

Example
Under the green card system of motor insurance a measure gave a national insurance bureau sole responsibility for settling claims for damage caused by foreign vehicles. HELD (ECJ): the measure did not contravene under Article 90(1) (in conjunction with Articles 85 and 86): *Van Ameyde* v. *UCI* (Case 90/76).

Member states are responsible under Article 90(1) independently of any violation of EC law by the undertaking in question. In some cases the undertaking need not itself have acted (e.g. if it has received state aids contrary to Article 92). Where the undertaking has broken EC law (e.g. Article 85) the legal position of the member state is determined not under the same provision as the undertaking but under Article 90(1).

There is no ECJ ruling whether Article 90(1) is directly effective. Arguably, it may be, at least where it relates to a legal provision which is itself directly effective (e.g. Article 86).

7. Application of Article 90(1)

The practical effect of Article 90(1) is that a breach of EC Competition Law does not arise out of the mere existence of state-regulated activity. It depends on how that power is exercised.

Example: A German rule required persons looking for employment to contact potential employers through a state-licensed agency with exclusive powers in this area. HELD (ECJ): a breach of Article 90(1) had occurred where national rules restricted sources of supply without state ability to meet demand: *Höfner v. Macrotron* (Case C-41/90). In other words, a state measure which compelled an undertaking to infringe Article 86 was illegal under Article 90(1).

See also *ERT* v. *DEP* (the *Greek Broadcasting* case) (Case C-260/89) from which it appeared that giving an exclusive right to an undertaking to retransmit foreign programmes to an undertaking already holding exclusive domestic broadcasting rights amounted to an abuse.

There is no ECJ ruling as to whether Article 90(1) is directly effective. Arguably it may be, at least where it relates to a legal provision which is itself directly effective (e.g. Article 86).

In *Merci Convenzionali Porto di Genova* v. *Siderurgica* (Case C-170/90) the ECJ considered the exclusive rights under Italian law for recognised companies to load and unload all ships at Genoa. Dominance was clearly established. Practices arising out of exclusive rights including excessive prices and the failure to use new technology were held to be an abuse: cf. *Société Civile Agricole* (Case C-323/93).

It follows from the developing case law of the ECJ that an exclusive reservation of activities by the state raises a presumption that Article 90(1) has been infringed giving rise to the possibility of a challenge in the national courts by a rival private operator (*see* Weatherill and Beaumont p. 757).

8. The exception for entrusted undertakings and fiscal monopolies: Article 90(2)

Under Article 90(2) undertakings entrusted with the operation of services of general economic interest or having the character of a revenue-producing monopoly are subject to the rules of Treaty except where the performance of particular tasks assigned to the undertakings is likely to be obstructed. A limitation is placed on the exception in that the development of trade must not be affected to such an extent as would be contrary to the interests of the Community: *see Municipality of Almelo* (Case C-393/92).

9. Categories of undertakings in Article 90(2)

Undertakings covered by Article 90(2) are likely to be state-controlled. There are two categories: entrusted undertakings (the more important category) and undertakings with the character of a revenue-producing monopoly.

10. Entrusted undertakings

This category has been strictly defined by the ECJ. The key factor is that the state must have taken legal steps to secure the operation of services by the undertaking in question. This definition excludes an undertaking created by private initiative for the management of intellectual property rights: *BRT* v. *SABAM* (Case 127/73). 'Operation of services' appears to require the organisation of a regular performance, e.g. in relation to public utilities.

The phrase 'of general economic interest' indicates that there must be economic activity even if the aims are social. Examples include telecommunications undertakings, water supply companies, but not a bank transferring its customer's funds from one member state to another: *Züchner* v. *Bayerische Vereinsbank (Bank charges)* (Case 1712/80).

Examples
(of entrusted undertakings in the UK): British Gas, British Rail, regional electricity boards, the BBC, British Airways *but not* British Coal (which produces a commodity rather than services).

11. Undertakings having the character of a revenue-producing monopoly

The main purpose of such undertakings is to raise revenue for the government through exploitation of an exclusive right (e.g. a state monopoly in the supply of alcohol). As such undertakings usually operate as commercial monopolies, they are also regulated by Article 37. The ensuing references to entrusted undertakings should be taken to include fiscal monopolies. The activities of such a monopoly may benefit from the exception in Article 90(2): *see* below, but only to the extent that they relate to a revenue-producing function.

12. The exemption under Article 90(2)

An undertaking seeking to benefit from the exception must show that application of the rules under the Treaty would obstruct the performance of tasks assigned to it. In *Italy* v. *Commission* (Case 41/83) Italy failed to establish that condemnation of British Telecom's activities as contrary to Article 86 would prejudice the specific tasks of BT. It follows that it is only possible to rely on the exception of Article 90(2) after the effects of applying the normal rule become clear. The exception does not, for example, permit the relaxation of any procedural rules.

Usher has commented (in Plender and Usher p. 434) that it appears after *Italy* v. *Commission* that Article 90 is relevant only to those activities of a public undertaking required or imposed by the state. The commercial activities of such an undertaking would be regulated by Articles 85 and 86.

13. Article 90(2) and the national courts

The main issue is the extent to which a claim that a matter is covered by the exception in Article 90(2) interferes with other provisions which normally create rights for individuals before their national courts. There are three leading cases: *Hein* (Case 101/71), *Sacchi* (Case 155/73) and *Inter-Huiles* (Case 172/82).

The approach of the ECJ to the role of the national courts under Article 90(2) has moved away from the restrictive decision in *Hein* (Case 101/71) to more liberal decisions such as *Telemarketing* (Case 311/84): *see* below.

14. *Hein*: Article 90(2) an early, restrictive decision

In *Hein* (*Ministére Public of Luxembourg* v. *Hein née Muller*) the defendants were prosecuted in Luxembourg for the unauthorised use of a wharf contrary to legislation giving special rights to the Société du Port de Mertout. The defendants claimed that the legislation infringed EC competition law. An Article 177 reference was made to the ECJ which interpreted Article 90. The ECJ held that, as against entrusted undertakings, EC provision cannot be invoked by individuals in the national courts.

15. *Sacchi*: Article 90(2) only a limited exception

In *Sacchi* an Italian court referred to the ECJ the question of compatibility with the Treaty of a measure extending the national broadcasting monopoly, RAI. The Court held that the national court must ascertain the existence of abuse. It is the function of the Commission to remedy the abuse within the limits of its powers. Even within the framework of Article 90, Article 86 has direct effect and confers rights on individuals before the national courts.

The Court in *Sacchi* appears to have reaffirmed that the general principles of the Treaty apply to entrusted undertakings, while creating a limited exception in their favour.

16. Application of Article 90(2)

Despite its ruling in *Inter-Huiles* (*Syndicat Nationale des Fabricants Raffineurs d'Huile de Graissage* v. *Inter-Huiles*) (Case 172/82) that Article 90(2) cannot create directly effective rights for individuals, the ECJ has now modified its view: see the decisions in *Ahmed Saeed* (Case 66/86), *ERT v. DEP* (Case C-260/89) and *Belgian Telemarketing* (*Centre Belge d'Etudes de Marché-Telemarketing (CCBEM) SA* v. *Compagnie Luxembourgeoise de Télédiffusion SA et. al.* (Case 311/84)). In the *Belgian Telemarketing* case the ECJ held that national courts may investigate whether the application of Article 86 would obstruct the entrusted undertaking in the performance of its tasks. These later decisions confirm the ECJ's interpretation of Article 90(2) in *Sacchi* that the exception is a limited one.

17. Article 90(3): the powers of the Commission

The Commission is obliged under Article 90(3) to ensure that Article 90 is applied, to which purpose it is empowered to issue directives or decisions. It is also open to the Commission to use its other powers, e.g. under Regulation 17/62. The Commission does not have to wait for an infringement to act under Article 90(3). It may take preventive measures which are legally binding (cf. the Article 169 procedure in which a reasoned opinion is given).

The first directive adopted under Article 90(3) is Directive 80/723 on the transparency of financial relations between member states and public undertakings: *see* 4. Under the Directive member states must keep accounts of such relations for five years and make information available to the Commission on request.

In the *Transparency Directive Case* (Cases 188–190/80) France, Italy and the UK claimed that Directive (80/723) was *ultra vires* and discriminated against public undertakings. Both claims were rejected by the ECJ.

The procedure under the Directive was invoked for the first time in 1983 requiring member states to submit accounts for the previous three years in relation to certain aspects in industries involving public undertakings: motor vehicles, man-made fibres, textile machinery, shipbuilding and tobacco products.

18. The first ECJ decision under Article 90(3)

The first decision of the ECJ under Article 90(3) was *Commission* v. *Hellenic Republic (The Greek Insurance case)* (Case 226/87). The Commission ordered Greece under Article 90(3) to alter its domestic legislation requiring all public property in Greece to be insured by Greek insurance companies in the public sector. When Greece failed to comply, the Commission issued proceedings under Article 169, resulting in a declaration that a decision under Article 90(3) is binding in its entirety on the person to whom it is addressed. As a result the addressee of a decision under Article 90(3) must comply with it until the ECJ suspends its decision or declares it void.

19. Competition in telecommunications

The Commission issued a directive in 1988 under Article 90(3) as part of the process to liberalise competition in the terminal equipment market (Directive 88/301).

The use of Article 190(3) rather than Article 169 as the legal basis of the Directive was challenged by France in *France* v. *Commission* (Case C-202/88). The ECJ held that where the conferral of exclusive rights cannot be justified, the Commission may proceed by way of Directive under Article 90(3). It is likely that Article 90 will be used increasingly in the future to regulate anti-competitive state practices in areas such as energy supply. (*See* Weatherill and Beaumont p. 760.)

STATE AIDS

20. Introduction

The giving of state aids (subsidies) to a particular undertaking or industry distorts competition and undermines the free movement of goods. Nevertheless, such assistance may be a vital element in national regional or economic policy during a recession or period of high unemployment. The EC Treaty regulates state aids in Articles 92 to 94. Article 92(2) prohibits state aids which distort (or threaten to distort) competition by favouring certain undertakings or the production of certain goods, where inter-member trade is affected. Derogations are, however, permitted by Article 92(2) and (3).

Aid which is permissible under Article 92 cannot infringe Article 30 or Article 37. However, provisions which exceed what is necessary may infringe these Articles. See, for example, *Ianelli & Volpi SpA* v. *Meroni* (Case 74/76) (non-discrimination requirements of Article 37 infringed) and also *Commission* v. *Ireland* (Case 249/81) ('Buy Irish' campaign infringed Article 30).

21. Aid compatible with the common market: Article 92(2)

Article 92(2) lays down a number of categories reflecting legitimate goals in which state aid 'shall be compatible with the common market'. These are:

(a) Aid having a social character granted to individual consumers, provided that the aid is granted without discrimination related to the origin of the products concerned;

(b) Aid to make good the damage caused by natural disasters or exceptional circumstances;

(c) Aid granted to the economy of certain areas of the Federal Republic of Germany affected by the division of Germany after the Second World War, in so far as the aid is required to compensate for the economic disadvantages caused by that division.

22. Aid which may be compatible with the common market: Article 92(3)

Article 92(3) lists categories of aid which may be compatible with the common market as follows:

(a) Aid to promote the economic development of areas where the standard of living is abnormally low or where there is serious underemployment

(b) Aid to promote the execution of an important project of common European interest or to remedy a serious disturbance in the economy of a member state

(c) Aid to facilitate the development of certain economic activities or of certain economic areas, where such aid does not adversely affect trading conditions to an extent contrary to the common interest (followed by specific restrictions in relation to state aids to shipbuilding)

(d) Aid to promote cultural conservation, where it does not affect competition in a manner contrary to the common interest (added by TEU)

(e) Such other categories of aid as may be specified by decision of the Council acting by qualified majority on a proposal from the Commission.

23. Procedure

Articles 93 and 94 provide a procedure for the application of Article 92. Under Article 93(1) the Commission must, in co-operation with member states, keep all systems of existing aid under review. Under Article 93(3) the Commission must be notified of any plans to grant or alter aids in sufficient time to enable it to make comments.

If the Commission finds that existing aid is compatible with the common market or is being misused it may require the member state to abolish the aid within a specified time (normally two months if unspecified: *Lorenz GmbH v. Germany* (Case 120/73). Failure to comply with a decision may lead to action before the ECJ: Article 93(2). Decisions may be challenged in the ECJ under

Article 173. It should be noted, however, that Article 92 is not directly effective: *Fédération Nationale* v. *France* (Case C-354/90).

New aids may not be implemented until the Commission has made a final decision: Article 93(3). The ECJ in *Lorenz GmbH* v. *Germany* (Case 120/73) held that Article 93(3) is directly effective. As a result an individual may challenge a state aid in a domestic court where this aid has been granted without notification under Article 93(3) or implemented before the decision of the Commission: *see*, for example, in the UK: *R.* v. *AG, ex parte ICI* (1987 Court of Appeal). *See* also *Ianelli & Volpi SpA* v. *Meroni* (Case 74/76): *see* **26** below.

Exceptionally, a member state may apply to the Commission for a decision that an existing or new aid to be granted is compatible with the common market. Any proceedings initiated by the Commission will be suspended until the Council has made its attitude known: Article 93(2).

Under Article 94 the Council may make regulations concerning the application of Articles 92 and 93, acting by qualified majority on a proposal from the Commission.

24. Compliance

Member states must comply strictly with the requirements of Article 93, in particular the duty to inform the Commission of plans to grant or alter aid. Failure to comply may result in the Commission directing defaulting states to recover the illegal payments, for example the payments made by Renault and Rover in 1989. Such repayment may be recovered despite the legitimate expectations of the party in question: *Commission* v. *Germany* (Case C-5/89).

Firms which have received illegally paid aid have only rarely been allowed to keep it, for example when the Commission has delayed adopting a decision under Article 93: *RSV Maschinenfabrieken en Scheepswerven NV* v. *Commission* (Case 223/85), or where it is impossible to recover the money: *Commission* v. *Belgium* (Case 52/84). Impossibility does not arise where the obligation to repay conflicts with national principles of company law: *Re Tubemeuse: Belgium* v. *Commission* (Case C-142/87).

25. Scope of state aids

Nearly all forms of government activity could be interpreted as a form of aid: infrastructural and environmental controls, for example, may reduce the direct expenditure of industry and lead to a reduction in the cost of a product. Such general benefits are outside the scope of Articles 92 to 94 (although they are covered by Article 102 which provides for consultation with member states and the issuing of directives to remedy distortions in competition caused by differences between the provision laid down by law, regulation or administrative action in the member states).

Under Article 92(1) a state aid may be granted 'in any form whatsoever', with no distinction made between aid granted directly by the state or by public or private bodies: *Steinike und Weinleg* (Case 78/76). A state aid will be judged by its effect, not by its name or policy purpose: *Italy* v. *Commission (Re Aids to the Textile Industry)* (Case 173/73). There are many different types of state aid:

Examples

Preferential interest rates; investment grants or subsidies; purchase of shares above market value; special prices for power: *Kwekerij Gebroedeers van der Kooy* (Cases 67, 68 and 70/85); *but not* a system of minimum pricing (which is subject to Article 30): *Van Tiggele* (Case 82/77): *see* 9:7).

26. Commission policy on state aids

The Commission is placing great emphasis on the applications of the rules on state aids in the approach to completion of the internal market. In its First Report on State Aids in the European Community 1989 the Commission reported a dramatic increase over the last ten years in the number of cases notified and investigated and the number of complaints made by aggrieved competitors. An inventory of aids in the Survey showed that over 108 billion ecus was given in aid each year in the EC, of which the largest part went to manufacturing companies (not to the sectors usually assisted such as agriculture and transport). Such 'special' aids have been granted under Article 92(3)(c). Aid is only permitted where it will contribute to sound economic structures, to make an industry competitive. Regional aids (on a national basis) have been progressively co-ordinated since 1971 when the first formal guidelines on regional aids were introduced. General aids usually fall outside Article 92 and may occasionally be permitted for short periods to counter a serious disturbance in the economy of a member state: Article 92(3).

The legitimacy of a state aid will be determined in most cases by the Commission (apart from the exceptions under Article 92(3)(d) and Article 93(2) which are decided by the Council). Aid which falls within the scope of the mandatory provisions of Article 92(2) must be permitted, whereas aid which falls within the categories under Article 92(3)(a) to (c) is within the discretion of the Commission.

27. The exercise of discretion

The discretion exercised by the Commission covers both the decision on validity and also the extent of the exemption: *Walloon Regional Executive & Glaverbell SA v. Commission* (Case 67/87) in which modernisation aid granted to Glaverbel, manufacturers of glass in Belgium, was held by the ECJ (under Article 173) not to qualify as an important project of European interest under Article 92(3)(b) as it did not form part of a transnational European programme.

In *France* v. *Commission* (Case 102/87) the French government challenged a Commission decision that a loan below market rate provided by a body called the Fonds Industriel de Modernisation (FIM) constituted a state aid which had been illegally granted without notification and it was incompatible with the common market. FIM was itself financed by a savings scheme where the investors received a lower rate of interest in return for tax exemption. The ECJ held that the French government could not argue that the loan was not aid unless it raised issues not considered by the Commission. The ECJ also ruled that inter-member state trade could be affected even if the undertaking to benefit did not export provided that its production competed with imports from other member states.

In *Philip Morris (Holland) BV v. Commission* (Case 730/79), under Article 173, the ECJ upheld a Commission decision refusing to allow the Dutch government to grant aid to Philip Morris, a Dutch cigarette manufacturer, to increase production capacity in competition with a number of other producers of cigarettes within the EC.

28. The Transparency Directive

Directive 80/723 was issued in 1980: *see* **16** above, providing for the transparency of relations in financial matters between states and public undertakings.

29. Rights of individuals

Articles 92 and 94 are *not* directly effective, being dependent on the exercise of discretion by the EC institutions: *Ianelli & Volpi SpA v. Meroni* (Case 74/76). However, Article 93 is directly effective. It follows that an individual may challenge a grant of aid in breach of Article 93(3) but may not act when there has been no such decision on the legality of aid.

Any person to whom a decision on a state aid has been addressed may challenge the decision before the ECJ under Article 173. Where a decision affects a whole industry it may not be challenged by individual members unless they form an organisation which participated in the proceedings leading to the granting of the aid: *Kwekerij van der Kooy* (Cases 67, 68 and 70/85). An individual complaint may be lodged with the Commission if the individual suspects that an illegal state is being granted. Any action or inaction arising may be challenged under Articles 173 and 175: *Irish Cement Ltd. v. Commission* (Case 166/88).

Progress test 23

1. When is a body considered to be a 'public undertaking' under Article 90? Give examples.

2. What obligation is placed on member states in relation to public undertakings?

3. What is meant by the term 'entrusted undertaking'? Give examples of the treatment of such undertakings under Article 90(2).

4. Why is it necessary to regulate the giving of state aids within the EC?

5. When may an individual challenge the giving of a state aid?

6. When are state aids permissible under the EC Treaty?

Part Four

THE SOCIAL DIMENSION

24

SOCIAL POLICY

1. Introduction

The EEC Treaty contained no direct reference to the 'social dimension'. Policies were originally conceived in economic terms. There were passing references in the Preamble to the purpose of the EC which was 'to ensure . . . social progress' and in Article 2 in which the objectives of the EC were stated to include an 'accelerated standard of living'. The European Social Fund was established under Article 123 to facilitate the employment of workers and to increase their geographical and occupational mobility within the EC.

The Paris Summit of 1972 was the starting point for the development of social policy beyond the four freedoms and was followed by the first Social Action Programme in 1974. The Programme set out objectives for full and better employment and for improvement of living and working conditions, leading to a number of employment protection measures, notably the Collective Redundancies Directive 75/129 (*see* **7** below) and the Transfers of Undertakings Directive 77/187 which guaranteed continuity of employment on the transfer of an undertaking. It also provided for worker participation, leading only to limited rights of information and consultation but not to the adoption of the extensive procedures in the draft 'Vredeling' Directive (named after its proposer) or its successors.

The SEA 1986 amended the EEC Treaty and provided an impetus to the development of the social dimension. The Social Chapter was adopted in 1989 as the basis for further employment protection measures.

A Social Chapter based on the Social Charter was originally intended to form part of the amendments to the Treaty by the TEU. After UK opposition the Chapter was contained in a Protocol to the TEU signed by the remaining 11 states apart from the UK: *see* **8** and **9** below.

2. The legal basis for social policy under the EEC Treaty

Prior to amendment by the TEU there were three main areas under which the EC could act in the social sphere:

(a) *The free movement provisions*: *Articles 48–51 (workers) and Articles 52–58 (establishment) and Articles 59–66 (services)* (*see* Chapters 14 and 15).

(b) *The harmonisation provisions: Article 100.* Article 100 provided for the approximation (or harmonisation) of measures to improve social relations (e.g. the proposed Fifth Directive on company law which deals with employee participation). Most of the company law harmonisation has, however, been drawn up under Article 54(3) which provides for the co-ordination of safeguards to protect the interests of member states. Measures based on Article 100 required unanimity for adoption. As a result of the SEA a new Article 100A was added, under which measures to complete the internal market could be adopted by qualified majority (after the TEU under Article 189b). Article 235, requiring unanimity, could also be invoked in harmonisation. It allows action to be taken by the EC if it proves necessary to attain, in the course of the operation of the common market, one of the objectives of the EC, and the Treaty has not provided the necessary powers.

(c) *Provisions related to social policy: Articles 117–122 and Article 130.* Article 117 refers to the promotion of improved living and working conditions and to the 'harmonisation of social systems'. Article 118 obliges the Commission to promote close co-operation between member states in matters such as employment, labour law and working conditions. Both Articles 117 and 118 envisaged opinions and consultation, not legislation.

Under Article 118a member states are required to pay particular attention to encouraging improvements, especially in the working environment, in the health and safety of workers, and to set as their objective the harmonisation of conditions in this area. This Article provided legislative powers (by qualified majority) (after the TEU under Article 189c) to achieve the objective. Under Article 118b the Commission are required to endeavour to develop the dialogue between management and labour at European level.

Article 119 provides the principle of equal pay for men and women for equal work: *see* Chapter 25. Article 120 requires member states to maintain the existing equivalence in paid holiday schemes. Article 121 provides for social security for migrant workers. Article 122 requires the Commission to make reports on particular problems of social conditions.

The provisions for economic and social cohesion in Articles 130a to 130e were strengthened as a result of amendment by the SEA and TEU. Article 130a envisages economic and social cohesion as a prerequisite for, and also a tool of, harmonious development, with EC efforts designed to reduce economic and social disparities in the regions. Article 130d instructs the Commission to draw up a plan to clarify and rationalise the tasks of the structural funds (including the Social Fund and the Regional Development Fund). The Council is also authorised to create a Cohesion Fund to finance contributions to environmental projects and trans-European networks: *see* 26:**33**. Environmental action emerged for the first time as an EC objective in Article 130r. Such action shall aim to preserve, protect and improve the quality of the environment, contribute towards protecting human health and ensure a prudent and rational utilisation of human resources. Article 130r may be seen as an early commitment to the principle of subsidiarity: *see* Chapter 26.

THE SOCIAL CHARTER

3. The Community Workers' Charter and Supplementary Action Programme

Following political discussion in the European Councils of Hanover and Rhodes in 1988 the Commission drew up a draft Social Charter in May 1989. The final draft of the Charter was adopted by eleven heads of state and government in December 1989 at the European Council in Strasbourg in the form of a declaration. The United Kingdom refused to adopt the declaration. The Charter sets out twelve main themes of a social nature. These themes are implemented in a Social Action Programme containing initiatives relating mainly to social security, freedom of movement, employment and working conditions, vocational training and the improvement of the working environment: *see* **6** below.

4. The legal basis of the Charter

The Social Charter itself is not legally binding. However, the implementing directives are binding and have been adopted under a number of different Treaty provisions: *see* below.

5. The fundamental principles of the Social Charter

The fundamental principles of the Social Charter relating to 12 main themes are as follows:

(a) Free movement of workers based on the principles of equal treatment in access of employment and social protection.

(b) Employment and remuneration based on the principle of fair remuneration.

(c) Improvement of living and working conditions.

(d) Social protection based on the rules and practices proper to each country.

(e) Freedom of association and collective bargaining.

(f) Vocational training.

(g) Equal treatment of men and women.

(h) Information, consultation and participation of workers.

(i) Protection of health and safety at the workplace.

(j) Protection of children and adolescents.

(k) Protection of the elderly.

(l) Protection of the disabled.

6. The Action Programme

In November 1989 the Commission published the Action Programme to implement the Social Charter. In its 13 chapters it reviews action already taken under each chapter heading (corresponding, in slightly different order, to those of the Charter with the addition of an opening chapter on the labour market). In all there were 47 new proposals in the Programme, 28 of which required action at EC level. The Charter did not provide for new legislative powers in social policy. Existing powers such as Articles 100A and 235 were to be used outside areas of specific competence such as free movement of persons.

7. Implementation of the Action Programme

The Commission is obliged to prepare annual reports on the implementation of the Programme. To date, progress has been limited. Fifteen of the proposals in the Action Programme have been adopted, mostly under Article 118a, following the liberal, Nordic approach to the meaning of the 'working environment'. In the Nordic states (Denmark, Sweden and Finland) the expression 'working environment' has been interpreted more widely than in the rest of the EC to cover social and psychological aspects of the workplace, with the potential to cover virtually any aspect of employment protection: *see* Charlesworth and Cullen p. 393. This approach is not accepted by the UK: *see* below.

Article 118a requires member states to pay particular attention to encouraging improvements, especially to the working environment, as regards the health and safety of workers. A Framework Directive 89/391 on Health and Safety was adopted prior to detailed implementing directives. The following measures are of particular importance:

(a) *The Pregnancy and Maternity Directive 92/85*
The directive provides for a uniform level of social protection for pregnant workers and workers who have recently given birth or are breastfeeding in terms of maternity leave and health and safety risks. Under Article 10 of the directive a pregnant worker, whether full or part-time, may not be dismissed. Refusal to engage a pregnant woman is not covered by the Directive 92/85 but by Article 3 of Directive 76/207 and subsequent case law such as *Dekker* v. *Stichtung* (Case C-177/88): *see* Chapter 24.

(b) *The Working Time Directive 93/104*
The directive provides, subject to a number of derogations (including executives, those with autonomous decision-making power and certain categories of workers such as hospital workers) for a maximum period of 48 hour week, 11 consecutive hours off out of 24, at least four weeks' paid holiday a year, minimum rest periods and a maximum of 8 hours on the employment of night workers.

The UK has challenged the legal basis of the directive (Article 118a) in *UK* v. *Council* (Case C-84/94), arguing that it is not a health and safety measure which may be passed under Article 118a by qualified majority but a measure harmonising employment conditions under Article 100 or 235, requiring unanimity. The UK is also questioning the basis of a further directive to be adopted under Article 118 which prohibits the employment of children under 15 and regulates strictly employment of children between 15 and 18.

(c) *The Proof of Employment Contract Directive 91/533*
The directive requires employers to inform employees of the conditions applicable to a standard contract. It does not create new rights but is particularly important for part-time, short-term or other atypical workers.

(d) *Directive 92/56 amending the Collective Redundancies Directive 75/129*
The amending directive provides more detailed rights of consultation and extends protection to redundancies arising out of a business closure resulting from a judicial decision.

> *Note*: In *Commission* v. *UK* (Cases C-382, 383/92) the ECJ found that the UK implementation of Directive 75/129 and Directive 77/187 (the 'Acquired Rights' Directive) was defective. New legislation is to be introduced in the UK to introduce a new system of workers' consultation to comply with the Directives.

Some directives remain outstanding from the 1989 Programme, having been blocked by member states. They include:

(a) *The draft directive on parental leave*. The proposed 3 month period of unpaid parental leave has been abandoned in favour of an informal consideration of ways to reconcile family and professional life.

(b) *The draft directive on posted workers*, which sought to establish minimum standards for workers in other member states to avoid undermining labour standards, has been opposed by the UK and by states from which many of the migrant workers come: Ireland, Spain and Portugal.

(c) *Draft directive on part-time or non-standard employment* has been removed from the EC legal basis after UK opposition and moved to the Social Policy Agreement procedures: *see* below.

SOCIAL POLICY UNDER THE TEU

8. The Social Protocol

The 11 signatory states to the Social Charter sought in the Maastricht negotiations to place social policy on a firmer footing by incorporating a Social Chapter in the draft TEU. The UK remained opposed, objecting particularly to the proposed extension of qualified majority voting to the ensuing harmonisation measures. The negotiations on this subject nearly caused the collapse of the IGC. A compromise enabled the Social Chapter to be contained in a Protocol to the Treaty signed by 11 member states excluding the UK. An agreement was annexed to the Protocol providing for the implementation of the Social Charter and application of the Protocol by the 11 on the basis of the 'acquis communautaire'.

9. The UK position

The UK is under no legal obligation as a result of the Social Protocol. An amendment to the EC Treaty would be required to admit the UK to the Protocol. However, it is important to appreciate that much social legislation continues to be adopted under provisions of the Treaty such as Article 118a and thus is binding on the UK (*see* e.g. the Working Time Directive 93/104).

10. Austria, Sweden and Finland

Austria, Sweden and Finland acceded to the EU in 1995 on the basis of acceptance of the 'acquis', presumably, but not explicitly, including the Social Protocol. (The 1994 Act of Accession made adjustments to the system of weighted voting under the Protocol without formally adopting the Protocol itself.) Thus the Protocol now appears to be accepted as binding on 14 member states excluding the UK.

11. The Agreement on Social Policy

The Agreement on Social Policy provides a set of objectives in Article 1 on which legislation may be based. These objectives derive from the Social Charter (but are arguably 'more ambitious' and 'more general', Charlesworth and Cullen p. 391), namely: the promotion of employment, improved living and working conditions, 'proper social protection' (considered by Edward and Lane p. 130 to be a poor translation of 'protection sociale adequate'), dialogue between management and labour, the development of human resources with a view to lasting high employment and the combating of exclusion.

12. Implementation of the Agreement

Article 2 provides for implementation of the Agreement by member states acting under the Agreement. The EC is required to support and complement the activities of member states in health and safety, working conditions, worker information and consultation, sex equality and combatting social exclusion. Participating member states may adopt directives in the Council to advance the objectives of the Agreement. Voting requirements vary and tend to reflect their counterpart provisions under the EC Treaty.

Measures adopted under the Agreement to date are few in number but include Directive 94/95 to establish a European Works Council to promote worker information and participation.

13. The legal status of the Agreement

The precise legal status of the Agreement is uncertain, particularly in relation to the use of the decision-making structure of the EU. Practical problems abound: the UK may not participate in Council discussions on matters under the Agreement, although there is no equivalent restriction in UK involvement through the other institutions. The political compromise at Maastricht has been a achieved at the expense of a legally untidy arrangement which has institutionalised the idea of a 'two-speed Europe'.

14. Medium-term Social Action Programme 1995–97

A medium-term Social Action Programme has been established to run from 1995 to 1997. It is based on various Treaty provisions and will only lead to action under the Social Agreement if full agreement under the Treaty cannot be reached. The current programme is more limited than its predecessors, with the emphasis moving away from employment protection towards job creation, the needs of those who are excluded from the workforce (e.g. the long-term unemployed) and other disadvantaged groups (e.g. the homeless). Areas where future action is indicated include: individual dismissals, pay for holidays and sickness and transfer of occupational pensions between member states.

15. Soft laws

In recent years the EC has made increasing use of 'soft laws' in relation to social policy. These laws may take forms such as non-binding recommendations, memoranda and codes of practice. Examples include the Code of Practice on Sexual Harassment 1992, the Equitable Wage opinion 1993 and a Memorandum on Equal Pay for Work of Equal Value. Although such 'laws' are not binding under Article 189 EC they must not be disregarded by national courts: *see* e.g. *Insitu Cleaning Co.* v. *Heads* (1995) in which the EAT in the UK invoked the EC Code of Practice to identify the types of behaviour which constitute harassment.

16. The 1996 IGC

The Social Affairs Commissioner, Padraig Flynn, has proposed that the 1989 Social Charter should be incorporated into a revised Treaty to be agreed at the IGC. Further, he considers that the Charter should be strengthened by covering new areas of protection including freedom of association, discrimination against the nationals of third countries, and equal treatment on grounds of race, colour, sex, religion, age and disability.

Progress test 24

1. What were the main areas within the EEC Treaty which formed the legal basis for the development of social policy? Why was the legal basis of social policy less extensive than the basis of other policies such as competition?

2. What are the fundamental principles put forward in the Social Charter? How are these principles reflected in the Action Programme?

3. Outline the scope of the directives proposed in relation to the improvement of employment and working conditions. How does the voting system within the Council of Ministers affect the implementation of the Social Charter?

4. Which Treaty provision has proved to be the most effective legal base in the implementation of the Social Charter? Why does the UK object to its use?

5. By what mechanism has the TEU sought to provide for social policy? Is the UK bound by this mechanism?

6. What are 'soft laws'? Do they have any legal force?

25

EQUALITY OF PAY AND TREATMENT

1. Introduction

Under Article 119 of the EEC Treaty each member state is required during the first stage to ensure and subsequently maintain the principle that men and women should receive equal pay for equal work. This obligation reflects both an economic objective (the avoidance of a competitive disadvantage in states implementing the principle) and a social objective (the improvement of living and working conditions of EC citizens): *Defrenne* (Case 43/75): *see* 6:**9**. In addition to Article 119 six directives have been issued relating to equal pay for equal work, the equal value principle, equal treatment for men and women, and equal treatment in social security, occupational pension schemes and self-employment: *see* below.

2. Direct effect of Article 119

In *Defrenne* v. *Sabena* (No. 2) (Case 43/75) Ms Defrenne, an air hostess sued her former employers, Sabena, in the Belgian courts. She relied on Article 119, claiming equal pay on the same basis as male cabin stewards. The ECJ held in an Article 177 reference that Article 119 was directly effective from the date of the judgment both vertically and horizontally, entitling her claim for equal pay to succeed. It is thus clear from *Defrenne* that Article 119 applies equally in both the public and the private sectors.

Employees and surviving spouses of deceased employees may invoke Article 119 directly against employers and trustees: *Coloroll Pension Trustees* v. *Russell* (Case C-200/91).

MEANING OF 'PAY'

3. The Treaty definition

Article 119 provides that 'pay' means 'the ordinary basic or minimum wage or salary or any other consideration, whether in cash or in kind, which the worker receives directly or indirectly, in respect of his employment from his employer.' The ECJ has adopted a liberal interpretation to the question of what constitutes pay. The following have been held, in certain circumstances, to constitute pay:

(a) Non-pay benefits

(b) Supplementary payments

(c) Contributions under a statutory scheme used to calculate other forms of benefit

(d) Contributions under a contractual scheme

(e) Sick pay

(f) Retirement pensions

(g) Redundancy payments

(h) Pensions paid to the spouses of deceased employees.

4. Non-pay benefits ('perks')

In *Garland* v. *British Rail Engineering Ltd* (Case 12/81) the Court held under Article 177 that the grant of special travel facilities to former employees after employment constituted pay, even in the absence of contractual entitlement to such facilities.

5. Supplementary payments

A supplementary payment by employers to male employees under 25 years of age, for the purpose of contribution to an employees' occupational pension scheme, was held (under Article 119) to be pay: *Worringham* v. *Lloyds Bank Ltd* (Case 69/80).

> *Note*: In both *Garland* and *Worringham*, reliance on rights under Article 119 provided the basis for entitlement lacking under UK law, as s.6(1)(a) of the Equal Pay Act 1970 excludes from its scope any provision made, in connection with death or retirement.

6. Contributions paid under a statutory scheme used to calculate other forms of benefit

It is clear from *Defrenne* v. *Belgian State* (No. 1) (Case 80/70) that contributions paid into a *statutory* social security scheme are *not* pay within Article 119. The exclusion of statutory social security schemes from coverage by Article 119 was upheld by the ECJ in *Barber* v. *Guardian Royal Exchange Assurance Group* (Case C-262/88), an ECJ ruling of great importance on a number of points: *see* below.

7. Contributions under a contractual scheme

The ECJ held in *Bilka-Kaufhaus* v. *Weber von Harz* (Case 170/84) that employer's contributions to an occupational pensions scheme under a *contractual* obligation were pay. In this case Ms Weber, a part-time worker, challenged her employer's occupational pension scheme. The scheme was non-contributory, being financed entirely by contributions from the employer. Part-time workers were excluded from benefits unless they had been employed by the firm for at least 15 out of 20 years. There was no such requirement for full-timers. As the majority of part-time employees were women, Ms Weber claimed that the scheme infringed Article 119. The ECJ held that a contractual (but not a statutory scheme) could fall within Article 119. Since the contributions were made by the employer to supplement existing social security schemes, they amounted to consideration paid by the employer to the employee within the meaning of Article 119. This approach is supported by the ECJ in *Barber* (below) and *Bestuur* v. *Beaune* (Case C-7/93).

8. Sick pay

In *Rinner-Kuhn* v. *FWW Spezial Gebäudereinigung GmbH & Co. KG* (Case 171/88) a part-time office cleaner challenged German legislation permitting employers to exclude part-time workers (i.e. those working less than 10 hours a week, most of whom were female) from entitlement to sick pay. While such a claim might appear to be outside Article 119, the ECJ held that national legislation permitting employers to differentiate between two groups of workers, one of which was mainly female, infringed Article 119. This decision underlines the importance of the distinction between national legislation which *obliges* employers to differentiate between employees (outside Article 119) and those where different treatment is *allowed* (within Article 119).

9. Retirement pensions

Retirement schemes within the state social security scheme are outside Article 119, *see* **6** above. However, the ECJ decided in *Barber* v. *Guardian Royal Exchange Assurance Group* (Case 262/88), a decision with important implications for pensions which is set out fully below, that a pension paid under a 'contracted-out' scheme was pay within the meaning of Article 119. Note that it is the prospective periodic payments rather than the employer's contributions which constitute pay: *Neath* v. *Hugh Steeper Ltd* (Case C-152/91): *see* **15** below.

10. Redundancy payments

Redundancy payments were held to be pay within Article 119 by the ECJ in *Barber*, irrespective of whether payment is made under a contract of employment, under statute or on a voluntary basis.

11. Pensions paid to the spouses of deceased employees

The ECJ held in *Ten Oever* (Case C-109/91) that pensions paid to the spouses of deceased employees were pay, but this was modified in *Coloroll Pension Trustees* (Case C-200/91) to exclude single-sex pension schemes.

12. *Barber* v. *Guardian Royal Exchange Assurance Group*: the facts

Mr Barber was a member of a pension fund set up by Guardian Royal Exchange (GRE). The scheme was non-contributory and 'contracted-out' (i.e. a private, non-statutory scheme approved under UK legislation). Under the scheme, the normal pensionable age for women was 57 and for men, 62 years. The terms of Mr Barber's contract of employment provided that in the event of redundancy, members of the pension fund were entitled to an immediate pension on reaching 55 years (men) or 50 years (women). Mr Barber was made redundant in 1980, aged 52. He received from the GRE severance pay under the terms of his contract, statutory redundancy pay and an *ex gratia* payment. He was, however, refused payment of his pension until reaching pensionable age (62 years), although a woman made redundant in similar circumstances would have been entitled to an immediate pension. Mr Barber brought an action before an industrial tribunal, claiming unlawful discrimination contrary to the Sex Discrimination Act 1975 and EC law. The claim failed in the industrial tribunal and in the EAT. The Court of Appeal referred various questions to the ECJ for a preliminary ruling, the action having been taken over by the widow of Mr Barber after his death.

13. *Barber*: the ECJ ruling

The ECJ ruled that:

(a) The benefits paid by an employer to a worker in connection with compulsory redundancy fell within the scope of Article 119, whether they were paid under a contract of employment, by virtue of legislative provisions or on a voluntary basis.

(b) A pension paid under a contracted-out private occupational scheme fell within the scope of Article 119.

(c) Article 119 was infringed where pension rights were deferred to the normal retirement age in a man made compulsorily redundant. Such a breach occurred in relation to a man when a woman made redundant would be entitled to an immediate pension, as a result of the application of an age condition varying according to sex (in the same way as the national statutory pension scheme). In deciding whether there is discrimination between the sexes, the court should consider each element of the remuneration separately, in accordance with the principle of 'transparency' in *Danfoss* (Case 109/88).

(d) Article 119 may be relied upon before the national courts.

(e) The direct effect of Article 119 in relation to equality in pensions claims was limited to entitlement to pensions after the date of the judgment, except for cases pending before the national courts.

14. Temporal effect

Employers were required to harmonise pension ages for men and women in contracted-out schemes from the date of the judgement (in practice, usually at 65 years). This ruling on temporal effect has been incorporated into the TEU by a Protocol. Like *Defrenne*, the decision is not retro-active. cf. *Vroege* (Case C-57/93) which did not limit liability of access to pension schemes in time as the position had been clear since *Bilka-Kaufhaus* (Case 170/84): *see* **19** below.

15. Treatment of actuarial factors in pensions

The decision in *Barber* must be read subject to a number of later ECJ decisions on pensions. In *Neath* v. *Hugh Steeper* (Case C-152/91) the ECJ held that differentiation by the employer in contributions paid under a defined benefits scheme as a result of actuarial factors such as life expectancy are outside Article 119. A similar conclusion was reached on the conversion and transfer of pension rights to a capital sum where these were determined by reference to the funding arrangements. Thus, as Steiner points out (p. 284), actuarial factors allow for a different level of contribution by employees between the sexes in the payment of capital sums and transfer rights, but not in relation to periodic payments under a pension.

EQUAL WORK

16. Equal pay for work of equal value: Directive 75/117

Directive 75/117 was introduced to implement and define the scope of Article 119. Article 1 of the Directive introduces the principle of equal pay for work of equal value.

17. Equal work

It follows from Article 1 of Directive 75/117 that equal work means either the 'same work' or 'work to which an equal value has been attributed'. The 'same work' need not necessarily be identical work. It should include jobs displaying a high degree of similarity, following the submission of Advocate-General Capotorti in *Macarthys* v. *Smith* (Case 129/79). See also *Worringham* and *Humphreys* v. *Lloyds Bank Ltd* (Case 69/80).

18. Work of equal value

To determine whether a man and woman are engaged upon 'like work' a comparison should be made on the basis of an appraisal of work actually performed by employees of different sex within the same establishment or service; such comparisons, however, are not limited to men and women employed contemporaneously: *Macarthys Ltd* v. *Smith* (Case 129/79), nor to employment in the same state. A woman carrying out work of greater value is not entitled to be paid more than a male comparator: *Murphy* v. *Bord Telecom Eirann* (Case 157/86).

19. Direct and indirect discrimination

Discrimination in pay contrary to Article 119 where men and women are engaged in equal work must be based exclusively on the difference of sex of the worker. It may be either direct or indirect: *Jenkins* v. *Kingsgate (Clothing Productions) Ltd* (Case 96/80).

A clear example of direct discrimination may be seen in *Dekker* v. *Stichting Vormingscentrum Voor Jong Volwassenen* (Case C-177/88) in which a pregnant woman was refused a teaching post. The ECJ held that since only a woman could be refused employment on the ground of pregnancy, such a refusal constituted direct discrimination based on sex which could not be justified on the basis of financial loss suffered by the employer.

In several cases the question has arisen of whether a difference in pay between part-time and full-time workers constitutes a breach of Article 119. In *Jenkins v. Kingsgate (Clothing Productions) Ltd* (Case 96/80) part-time workers (all but one of whom were female) were paid 10 per cent less than full-time workers. The ECJ (in an Article 177 reference from the EAT) held that a lower rate of pay for part-time workers did not necessarily infringe Article 119, provided the difference in pay was objectively justified and was in no way related to discrimination based on sex.

In *Enderby* v. *Frenchay Area Health Authority* (Case C-127/92) the ECJ held that where statistics showed a real difference between pay for jobs of equal value where one is almost entirely carried out by women (in this case, speech therapists) and the other by men (pharmacists) the employer must show that the difference is objectively justified on grounds other than sex.

In *Bilka-Kaufhaus GmbH* v. *Weber von Hartz* (Case 170/84) a part-time worker challenged her employer's occupational pension scheme, which discriminated against part-timers. This discrimination was suffered disproportionately by women since most of the part-timers were female. (Male part-timers constituted only 2.8 per cent of the total workforce.) The ECJ (under Article 177) upheld its decision in *Jenkins* and held that, if a considerably smaller proportion of men than women worked part-time, and if the difference in treatment could only be based on sex, the exclusion of part-time workers from an occupational pension scheme would infringe Article 119. Such difference in treatment would only be permissible if objectively justified by factors unrelated to discrimination based on sex: *see* below. The decision in *Bilka* was upheld in *Vroege* (Case C-57/93) and in *Fisscher* (Case C-128/93) (exclusion of married women from occupational pension schemes).

20. Objective justification

In *Bilka-Kaufhaus* v. *Weber von Hartz* (Case 170/84) the ECJ laid down guidelines as to what constitutes an objective justification for measures causing a difference in treatment, where there is indirect discrimination:

'If the national court finds that the measures chosen by Bilka correspond to a real need on the part of the undertaking, are appropriate with a view to achieving the objectives pursued, and are necessary to that end, the fact that the measures affect a greater number of women than men is not sufficient to show that they constitute an infringement of Article 119.'

The guidelines have been strictly applied by the ECJ in *Rinner Kuhn* (Case 171/88) in the context of state legislation. The onus rests on the state to prove that the social policy objectives justify the means selected.

21. Assessment of equal value claims

Article 1(2) of Directive 75/117 provides that where a job classification system is used for determining pay, it must be based on the same criteria for both men and women and exclude any discrimination on grounds of sex. Member states are required under Article 2 of the Directive to introduce into national legal systems the necessary measures to enable all employees who consider themselves wronged by the failure to apply the principle of equal pay to pursue their claims by judicial process after recourse to other competent authorities. Further, under Article 6, member states must take the necessary measures to ensure that the principle of equal pay is applied and that effective means are available to take care that this principle is observed. This need not be by a job evaluation scheme.

In *Commission* v. *United Kingdom (Re Equal Pay for Equal Work)* (Case 61/81) the UK was found to have infringed Articles 1 and 6 of Directive 75/117 by failing to provide a means of assessment of equal value claims in the absence of a job evaluation scheme. A similar ruling was made in *Commission* v. *Luxembourg* (Case 58/81).

In *R* v. *Secretary of State for Employment, ex parte Equal Opportunities Commission* (1994) the House of Lords held that parts of the Employment Protection (Consolidation) Act 1978 contravened Article 119. The threshold conditions which excluded workers employed for fewer than 8 hours a week affected women to a greater extent than men. This indirect discrimination was found not to be objectively justified.

22. Criteria in job evaluation schemes

To avoid being discriminatory, the system for job evaluation must take account of the particular aspects of each sex. Criteria based entirely on the attributes of one sex ran a risk of discrimination.

In *Danfoss (Handels-og Kontorfunktionaernes Forbund* v. *Dansk Arbejdsgiverforening for Danfoss)* (Case 109/89) the Danish Employees' Union challenged the criteria approved by the Danish Employees' Union and applied by the firm, Danfoss, including the criteria of flexibility and seniority. The ECJ held that where neutral criteria (e.g. flexibility) were applied, resulting in systematic discrimination against women workers, they must have been applied in an abusive manner. A system in which the criteria are not clear is described by the Court as lacking in 'transparency'. In such a case the proof of justification rests with the employer. Applying the principle of transparency it would appear that each element of the remuneration package should be considered separately in an equal value claim. See also *Barber* in which the ECJ held that the application of the equal pay principle must be ensured in respect of each element of remuneration and not only on the basis of a comprehensive assessment of the consideration paid to workers.

EQUAL TREATMENT

23. Equal treatment in employment: Directive 76/207

Directive 76/207 provides in Article 1(1) for the principle of equal treatment of men and women as regards access to employment, including promotion, and to vocational training and as regards working conditions, and to social security (on the conditions referred to in paragraph 2). The action provided for in Article 1(2), was taken in Directive 79/7 on statutory schemes and Directive 86/378 occupational schemes. Equal treatment is defined in Article 2 as prohibiting all discrimination on grounds of sex either directly or indirectly by reference in particular to marital or family status. Derogation is permitted under Article 2(2); *see* below. The directive has been invoked particularly in relation to the protection of pregnant women and mothers at work and to retirement ages.

> *Note*: Unlike Directive 75/117 which was adopted under Article 119, Directive 76/207 was based on Article 235 (the general power of the institutions), harmonisation of living and working conditions being outside the scope of the equal pay principle.

24. Pregnancy and maternity

In *Dekker* v. *Stichting* (Case C-177/88) the ECJ held that it was discriminatory to reject a woman as an instructor at a training centre on grounds of pregnancy. Such a rejection could only be made against one sex and thus amounted to direct discrimination.

C.f. *Hertz* (Case 179/88) in which dismissal of a woman suffering from complications of pregnancy during maternity leave was held to be indirect sex discrimination and therefore capable of objective justification.

Webb v. *EMO* (Case C-2/93) considered the dismissal of a pregnant employee who had been hired as a maternity leave replacement. This was found to be direct discrimination contrary to Directive 76/207 interpreted in the light of Directive 92/85 (on pregnant workers and working mothers).

> *Note*: In *Hofmann* v. *Barmer Ersatzkasse* (Case 184/83) the ECJ dismissed the claim of a father of an illegitimate child in Germany for social security payment during a period of unpaid leave to look after a child when a mother would have been entitled to payment, holding that the directive was not concerned with the sharing of family responsibilities but with the biological protection of the mother.

25. Retirement ages

The main provisions of the directive which have been invoked in relation to retirement ages are Article 5 (conditions of work or dismissal) and Article 6 (obligation to provide remedies).

In *Burton* v. *British Railways Board* (Case 19/81) the applicant failed to bring his application within the directive because his voluntary redundancy at the same age as retirement was treated as covered by the Social Security Directive 79/7 which permits a derogation from the equal treatment principle.

However, it is clear after the decision of the ECJ in *Barber* that the calculation of pensionable age for the purpose of redundancy is now regarded as governed by Articles 119: *see* **10** above.

26. Determination of pensionable age 'for other purposes'

In *Marshall* v. *Southampton and South West Area Health Authority* (No. 1) (Case 152/84) the ECJ distinguished *Burton* on the grounds that the benefits in *Marshall* were linked to a national social security scheme. Mrs Marshall relied on Article 5(1) of Directive 76/207 to challenge the policy of the Area Health Authority which required women employees to retire at 60 whereas men could continue until 65. The ECJ held (on a reference from the EAT) that pensionable age was determined for the purpose of retirement, i.e. 'for other purposes' than those specified in Article 7 of Directive 79/7. Thus, it followed that the determination of pensionable age was not covered by the exclusion and Mrs Marshall could rely on Article 5(1): *see* **29** below. The ECJ has applied its approach in *Marshall* in *Roberts* v. *Tate & Lyle Industries Ltd* (Case 151/84).

> *Roberts* v. *Tate & Lyle Industries Ltd*: The applicant challenged the compulsory early retirement scheme operated by her employers, with entitlement to an accelerated pension. HELD (ECJ, Article 177): Such a scheme fell within the scope of Directive 76/207, being a condition governing dismissal. To fix a different age for offering an early pension would be a breach of Article 5.

27. Derogation under Articles 2(2), 2(3) and 2(4)

(a) *Article 2(2)*. Article 2(2) provides for exemption from the equal treatment principle for activities for which the sex of the worker constitutes a determining factor. In *Commission* v. *United Kingdom (Re Equal Treatment for Men and Women)* (Case 165/82) the Commission brought an action against the UK Government for failure to comply with Directive 76/207 in the Sex Discrimination Act 1975 which exempted from equal treatment employment in a private household and in firms employing fewer than six staff. The ECJ held under Article 169:

> (*i*) While individual exemptions might be appropriate in circumstances where the sex of a worker was a determining factor, blanket exemptions were not.
> (*ii*) Article 2(2) did justify the UK in restricting male access to the profession of midwifery under s. 41 of the Sex Discrimination Act 1975.

In *Johnston* v. *Chief Constable of the RUC* (Case 222/84) a female member of the Royal Ulster Constabulary challenged an RUC decision to refuse to renew her contract of employment. The RUC had decided as a matter of policy not to employ any women as full-time members of the RUC Reserve as women were not trained in the use of firearms. HELD (ECJ, Article 177): Any claim for derogation from Directive 76/207 had to be decided in the light only of Directive 76/207 (and not Article 48(3), as claimed by the RUC). There was no public safety exception to Directive 76/207. The national court was to decide how national legislation should be interpreted.

(b) *Article 2(3)*. Article 2(3) provides for the protection of women in relation to pregnancy *but not* men: *Hofman* v. *Barmer Ersatzkasse* (Case 184/83): *see* **24**.

(c) *Article 2(4)*. Article 2(4) permits measures giving 'a specific advantage to women with a view to improving their ability to compete on the labour market and to pursue a career on an equal footing with men': *Kalanke* v. *Frei Hausestadt Bremen* (Case C-450/93) *but not* affirmative action (e.g. quotas).

28. Remedies

Remedies are discussed in Chapter 5 in the context of the direct effect of directives. Article 5 was held to be directly effective but only against a public body: *Marshall*. In *Von Colson* the ECJ held back from deciding that Article 6 of the directive requires member states to provide a mechanism for enforcement. Instead the directive should be invoked as a means of statutory interpretation, i.e. the national courts should interpret national legislation so as to give effect to the directive being implemented. Note the treatment of limitation periods in *Emmott*, etc.: see 6:13.

29. Obligations on member states under Article 3(2)

Article 3(2) requires member states to take the necessary steps to ensure that:

(a) Any laws, regulations and administrative provisions contrary to the principle of equal treatment are abolished.

(b) Any provisions contrary to the principle of equal treatment in collective agreements, individual contracts of employment, internal rules of undertakings or in rules governing the independent professions are annulled or amended: *see Commission* v. *United Kingdom (Re Equal Treatment for Men and Women)* (Case 165/82) in which the UK was held to be in breach of Article 3(2)(a) and (b).

> *Note*: The Social Policy Protocol to the TEU in essence repeats the provisions of Article 119, but includes a further provision which enables member states to maintain or adopt measures which provide for specific advantages, enabling women to pursue vocational training or to prevent or compensate for disadvantages in their professional careers: Article 6.

EQUAL TREATMENT IN MATTERS OF SOCIAL SECURITY

30. Equal treatment in matters of social security: Directive 79/7

Directive 79/7 implements in matters of social security the principle in Directive 76/207 of equal treatment for men and women. Directive 79/7 became directly effective on 23 December 1984, the implementation deadline: *Netherlands* v. *FNV* (Case 71/85). The purpose of the directive is the progressive implementation of the equal treatment principle: Article 1.

31. Personal scope

Article 2 states that the directive applies to the working population, defined as 'self-employed persons, workers and self-employed persons whose activity is interrupted by illness, accident or involuntary unemployment and persons seeking employment' and to 'retired or invalided workers and self-employed persons'. The definition has been interpreted broadly by the ECJ, which accepts its application according to the function of the benefit. In *Drake* v. *Chief Adjudication Officer* (Case 150/85), the ECJ held that it covers all benefits designed to maintain income where any of the risks specified in the directive had been incurred. In *Drake* the applicant had given up work to care for a disabled mother.

The directive does not, however, cover persons who have not been employed and who are not seeking work; nor does it cover persons whose work has not been interrupted by one of the risks in Article 3(1): *see* below. Thus a Dutchman who had given up work to care for a family was treated as voluntarily unemployed at the time of retirement and so not covered: *Achterberg-te Riele and others v. Sociale Verzekeringsbank* (Cases 48, 106, 107/88).

32. The risks covered

Article 3(1) of Directive 79/7 provides that equal treatment principles apply to:

(a) Statutory schemes which provide protection against sickness, invalidity, old age, accidents at work or occupational diseases and unemployment
(b) Social assistance, in so far as it is intended to supplement or replace those statutory schemes.

The directive may be invoked in relation to benefits covered by the directive but payable to third parties: *Drake* (invalidity allowance payable to Mrs Drake's mother). It also applies to schemes exempting persons of pensionable age from prescription charges: *R. v. Secretary of State for Health, ex parte Richardson* (Case C-137/94).

To be covered by the directive the benefit must be 'directly and effectively linked to the protection provided against one of the risks in Article 3(1)': *R v. Secretary of State for Social Security, ex parte Smithson* (Case C-243/90). The ECJ held that housing benefit was not covered; its calculation was partly based on risks listed in Article 3(1).

In *Jackson v. Cresswell* (Cases 63, 64/91) the ECJ held that a general benefit such as supplementary allowance intended as a replacement for a wage was not covered. Survivors' benefits and family benefits (except those granted by way of increases to benefits in statutory schemes covered by the Directive) are excluded: Article 3(2).

33. Meaning of the equal treatment principle

Article 4(1) provides that the principle of equal treatment means that there shall be no discrimination whatsoever on grounds of sex either directly or indirectly by reference to marital or family status, in particular concerning:

(a) The scope of schemes and the conditions of access thereto
(b) The obligation to contribute and the calculation of contributions
(c) The calculation of benefits including increases due in respect of a spouse and for dependents
(d) The conditions governing the duration and retention of entitlement to benefits.

The principle of equal treatment is stated to be without prejudice to the provisions relating to the protection of women on grounds of maternity: Article 4(2). It is likely to be interpreted similarly to Directive 76/207, Article 2(3).

Examples

(1) Refusal to pay an invalidity allowance to a married woman where it was payable to a married man infringed Article 4(1): *Drake (but not* an invalidity benefit where the amount of the allowance was determined by the marital status and income of the spouse or existence of a dependent child: *Teuling* (Case 30/85).

(2) Refusal to pay invalidity benefits to part-time workers most of whom were female (under a Dutch minimum subsistence scheme) also infringed Article 4(1) unless it could be justified by factors unrelated to sex. In this case the amount payable under the scheme to part-timers was linked to the claimant's previous income whereas full-timers could receive a sum which corresponded to the Dutch minimum subsistence allowance: *Ruzius-Wilbrink* (Case 102/88).

34. Exclusion from the equal treatment principle

Member states are permitted under Article 7 to exclude various matters from the principle of equal treatment, namely:

(a) The determination of pensionable age

(b) Pension benefits or other entitlements granted to persons who have brought up children

(c) Old-age or invalidity benefits deriving from a wife's entitlements

(d) Increases in benefits granted to a dependent wife.

As far as the determination of pensionable ages is concerned, the ECJ has ruled that Article 7(1)(a) of the directive cannot justify early retirement at a pensionable age which is discriminatory: *Marshall* (Case 152/84); *Beets Proper* (Case 262/84). Where there is no such discrimination retirement at pensionable age would be covered by the exception: *Burton* v. *BRB* (Case 19/81). However, in *R* v. *Secretary of State for Social Security, ex parte EOC* (Case C-9/91) the ECJ held that Article 7(1) may justify a difference in the number of contributions required for a full pension between men and women. Article 7(1) does not allow a member state which had set the pensionable age for women at 60 and men at 65 to provide that women were exempt from prescription charges at 60 and men only at 65: *R.* v. *Secretary of State for Health, ex parte Richardson* (Case C-137/94).

35. Remedies

Article 6 requires member states to implement the directive by providing adequate remedies. In *McDermott and Cotter* v. *Minister of State for Social Welfare* (Case 286/85) indicates that Directive 79/7 may be relied on to challenge national social security legislation by enabling a woman to claim that she should be treated in the same way as a man, even though this may result in payment of double benefit.

EQUAL TREATMENT IN OCCUPATIONAL PENSION SCHEMES

36. Equal treatment in occupational pension schemes: Directive 86/378

Directive 86/378 was drawn up to implement the principle of equal treatment in relation to occupational pension schemes. It complements Directive 79/7 and passed its implementation date in July 1989. It did not, however, become fully directly effective on that date as member states were allowed until 1 January 1993 to take all the necessary steps to ensure that occupational pension schemes were revised to comply with the principle of equal treatment.

37. Relationship between Directive 86/378 and Article 119

Much of the significance of Directive 86/378 has been lost as a result of the *Barber* decision which held that pensions paid under private occupational pension schemes are 'pay' and are therefore covered by Article 119. Thus, questions relating to matters such as differing retirement ages or pension entitlement for men and women will now be dealt with under Article 119, avoiding the problems of the direct effect of directives. However, certain matters such as survivor's pensions continue to be covered by the Directive: *see* **41** below.

38. The provisions of Directive 86/378

The provisions of Directive 86/378 are set out in almost identical terms to Directive 79/7. Article 2 states that it applies to occupational schemes not governed by Directive 79/7 where the purpose is to supplement or replace the benefits provided by statutory social security schemes. The categories of persons (Article 3) and the risks (Article 4) are the same. However, survivors' and family benefits are not excluded under Directive 86/378, provided these benefits form part of the consideration paid by the employer by reason of the employee's employment: Article 4.

39. Equal treatment under Directive 86/378

A list of examples of provisions which infringe the equal treatment principle is given in Article 6. These include Articles fixing different retirement ages: Article 6(f), and setting different levels of benefits, *except insofar as may be necessary to take account of actuarial calculation factors which differ according to sex*: Article 6(h). The exclusion in relation to actuarial factors is unlikely to be upheld after *Barber*. However, the need to enact legislation to uphold the principle of equality in matters of pension contributions remains, after *Newstead* (Case 192/85). In this case the ECJ treated the obligation to contribute as falling under Articles 117 and 118, not 119.

40. Deferral of the application of the equal treatment principle: Article 9

Article 9, which permits member states to defer the application of the equal treatment principle in relation to the determination of pensionable age for the granting of old-age or retirement pensions, must be read subject to the *Barber* decision. It is clear from *Barber* that such a deferral contravenes Article 119. The only concession made by the ECJ to Article 9 in *Barber* was the ruling that Article 119 (in relation to pensions entitlement) is directly effective from the date of the judgment.

It is not clear what the effect of the *Barber* decision is on Article 9(b) of the directive under which survivors' pensions which do not constitute consideration paid by the employer are exempt from the equal treatment principle. Claims under the directive may only be brought from 1 January 1993, the implementation date.

41. Future changes

The Commission proposes to amend the directive to bring it into line with the decisions in *Barber* and subsequent cases.

EQUAL TREATMENT IN SELF-EMPLOYMENT

42. Equal treatment in self-employment: Directive 86/613

Directive 86/613 is complementary to Directives 76/207 and 79/7. It applies the principle of equal treatment to men and women engaged in an activity in a self-employed capacity or contributing to the pursuit of such an activity, in relation to those aspects not covered by other directives: Article 1.

43. Provisions of Directive 86/613

The Directive applies to all persons pursuing a gainful activity for their own account, including farmers and members of the liberal professions. It also covers their spouses (who are not already employees or partners) where they participate in the activities of the self-employed worker, performing the same or ancillary tasks: Article 2.

44. The equal treatment principle

Article 3 states that the equal treatment principle implies the absence of discrimination on the grounds of sex, either directly or indirectly, by reference in particular to marital or family status. However, this provision is without prejudice to the protection of women during pregnancy and motherhood: Preamble.

45. Establishment of a business

Member states must take all necessary measures to ensure the elimination of all provisions contrary to the principle of equal treatment under Directive 76/207, especially in respect of the establishment, equipment or extension of a business or the launching or extension of any other form of self-employed activity including financial facilities: Article 4.

46. Company formation

Under Article 5, member states must (without prejudice to the specific conditions for access to certain activities applying equally to both sexes) ensure that the conditions for the formation of a company between spouses are not more restrictive than the conditions for the formation of a company between unmarried persons.

47. Contributory social security schemes

Member states must ensure that the spouses who participate in the activities of the self-employed worker are enabled to join a contributory social security scheme voluntarily where they are not protected under the self-employed worker's social security scheme: Article 6.

48. Judicial process of claims

Member states must introduce the necessary measures to enable all persons who consider themselves wronged to apply the principle of equal treatment in self-employed activities to pursue their claims through the judicial process, possibly after recourse to other competent authorities: Article 9.

49. Implementation date

The implementation date for the Directive was 30 June 1989. There was an exception for those states which had to amend their legislation on matrimonial rights and obligations in order to secure the equal treatment principle in the formation of companies, in which case the date was 30 June 1991: Article 12. The Directive is directly effective from the relevant implementation date.

Progress test 25

1. Which objectives underlie the legal obligation in Article 119?

2. Define 'pay' within the meaning of Article 119. Which of the following have been held by the ECJ to constitute 'pay': travel facilities, contributions paid into a statutory social security scheme, contributions paid into an occupational pension scheme, redundancy payments?

3. What is the meaning of 'equal work' under Article 1 of Directive 75/117?

4. In what circumstances are measures causing a difference in treatment based on sex justified?

5. Are member states required to assess equal value claims by means of a job classification scheme? What is the principle of 'transparency' in relation to a remuneration package?

6. Explain the importance of the decision in *Marshall* (Case 152/84) in relation to the determination of pensionable age. How did the decision affect the legal status of directives?

7. In what circumstances are member states allowed to depart from the principle of equal treatment in matters of social security?

8. What is the significance of the *Barber* decision in relation to Directive 86/378 on equal treatment in occupational pension schemes?

9. How does Directive 86/613 provide for equal treatment in self-employment?

26

OTHER POLICIES WITH A SOCIAL DIMENSION

1. Introduction

The EEC Treaty did not provide for a number of policy areas which became increasingly important as public awareness developed. The Paris Summit of 1972 stimulated discussion, calling for an EC environmental policy, as it had for social policy: *see* Chapter 24. Steps have been taken, in some cases under the SEA and, more recently, under the TEU, to establish a clear legal base for policies in relation to the environment, consumer protection, research and technology, education, public health, trans-European networks and energy. This chapter outlines developments in environmental policy and consumer protection. Other policy areas are considered in brief.

THE ENVIRONMENT

2. The legal base before the SEA

Despite the lack of provision in the EEC Treaty the EC adopted three Environmental Action Programmes (EAPs) before the SEA, the first two identifying necessary remedial measures and the third a call for environmental action to assist economic growth through non-polluting industries. Decisions, regulations and over 100 directives were adopted on the environment before the SEA, often under Article 235.

> *Note:* The general power under Article 235 entitles the EC to take appropriate measures to ensure that one of the Treaty objectives is attained, even if there is no specific provision in the Treaty. A measure may only be adopted by the Council acting unanimously on a proposal from the Commission, after consultation with the Commission.

Environmental policy is a major area of development with an ever-increasing body of detailed legislative provision. Students seeking information on individual environmental measures should refer to a specialist text. Implementing legislation is listed in Lasok and Bridge (pp. 711–16).

3. The introduction of a specific policy under the SEA

Environmental threats such as pollution bear little relationship to national boundaries. The SEA, in response to growing recognition of the need for environmental measures at EC and international level, introduced specific provision for environmental policy in Article 130r–130t. The stated objectives in Article 130r were:

(a) to preserve and improve the quality of the environment

(b) to contribute towards protection of human health

(c) to ensure a prudent and rational utilisation of natural resources.

Under Article 130r measures were to be taken on a preventative basis, with rectification of the problem at source a priority; the polluter should pay for the damage caused. Environmental policy was to be seen as a constituent of the EC's other policies. Article 130r was limited by the first (indirect) reference to subsidiarity: the EC was required to take action on the environment where the objectives of the policy could be better achieved at EC level than at the level of the member states. Environmental measures could also be adopted under Article 100a if they were necessary for the functioning of the internal market.

Commission v. Council (The Titanium Dioxide Directive Case) (Case C-300/89) arose out of Directive 89/48 on titanium dioxide waste. The ECJ held that the principle under Article 2 of the SEA that environmental protection must be seen as a component of other policies meant that a measure would not be covered by Article 130s simply because it concerned the environment. It followed that the Directive was essentially a harmonisation measure and should have been adopted under Article 100a (which required the co-operation procedure) and not under Article 130s. The measure was annulled.

The present legal position is uncertain after the ECJ reached the opposite conclusion in *Commission v. Council* (Case C-155/91), namely that the Waste Directive 91/56 was validly founded on Article 130s rather than Article 100a.

4. Environmental policy under the TEU

The TEU maintains the principles introduced by the SEA, enhancing the provision of environmental policy by including it as one of the policies of the Union: Article 3k. Articles 130r, 130s and 130t were amended accordingly. The principle that the polluter should pay is addressed to member states rather than individuals or corporations. 'This', write Lasok and Bridge (p. 170), 'is the weakness of Maastricht'.

After amendment, Article 130r(2) provides that 'Environmental protection requirements must be integrated into the definition and implementation of other Community policies'. Thus it is no longer necessary to rely on the general power under Article 235. Environmental policy must take into account regional variations within the EC, availability of scientific and technical data, the costs and benefits of action or inaction and the economic and social development of the EC.

5. Implementation of environmental policy

Environmental policy since 1973 has been expressed in a series of Environmental Action Programmes (EAPs): *see* 2 above. The legislation implementing the EAPS mainly covers the following areas:

(a) Aquatic and air pollution (e.g. Directive 75/324 on CFCs)

(b) Noise abatement (e.g. Directive 80/51, as amended, on aircraft noise)

(c) Chemical pollution (e.g. Directive 77/728 on the labelling of paints, Directive 89/530 on emission of trace elements)

(d) Protection of the natural environment (e.g. Regulations 3528/86 and 2158/92 on protection of the forest from rain and fire, Directive 76/160 on bathing water).

The fourth programme (1987–1992) set out environmental policy as integral with other policies to complete the internal market.

6. Protection of the natural environment

While all the areas under the EAPs are important the protection of the natural environment has been particularly controversial. One of the most significant measures in this category is Directive 85/337 which provides a set of guidelines in relation to the use of land. Under the guidelines local planning authorities should assess the effects of certain public and private proposals on the environment as part of the procedure for seeking planning permission. Environmental impact assessments should be carried out for projects listed in the two annexes to the Directive where the project is likely to have an impact on the local environment due to size, nature or location. Annex 1 list projects such as power stations and major road projects which must be assessed. Annex 2 list smaller projects where the member states have a discretion to assess if they consider it necessary. National defence projects are excluded.

The Directive is addressed to national planning authorities rather than to member states. It was implemented in the UK by the Town and Country Planning Regulations 1988 and 14 further regulations. The directive was held by the Irish Court in *Brown* v. *An Bord Pleanola* (1990) not to be directly effective, thus depriving individuals (if the Irish interpretation is correct) of the opportunity to rely on the directive.

7. Monitoring of environmental policy

Monitoring the implementation of environmental policy rests with the EC, primarily through the Commission, although the Court of Auditors and the European Environmental Agency are also involved. The European Environmental Agency and its related Monitoring and Information Network were set up in 1990 to provide a permanent system for monitoring and information collection. Two major directives have resulted from the monitoring process: Directive 85/337 on the environmental impact of certain projects (*see* 6 above) and

Directive 90/313 on public access to environmental information in relation to the condition of air, soil, water, animal and plant life, and natural habitats.

8. Enforcement

Responsibility for enforcement is borne by the Commission which may use the Article 169 procedure to bring an action against a defaulting member state in the ECJ. Failure to observe a judgement under Article 169 may, after the TEU, lead to the imposition of a fine: Article 171. Action by the Commission has been limited by lack of resources. It has been difficult to establish conclusively that the member state is in breach, particularly where the state relies on meeting the directive by existing law: *see* e.g. *Commission* v. *Germany* (Case 131/88).

While uncertainty surrounds the possible direct effect of environmental measures the scope for application of the *Francovich* principle is apparent. Failure to implement a directive adequately in circumstances which satisfy the conditions in *Francovich* will enable individuals to claim compensation against the state concerned: *see* Chapter 6 (e.g. where a state does not implement a water quality directive and an individual as a result suffers loss through illness caused by bathing in polluted water).

9. The fifth Environmental Action Programme

The fifth EAP was adopted in 1993 and will run until 2000. It aims to provide guidelines on environmental policy for regional and local authorities and other groups by increasing participation in the drafting of environmental legislation. Five target sectors are selected for particular attention: industry, energy, transport, agriculture and tourism. A feature of the Programme is the shift of emphasis from regulatory measures to economic and fiscal measures such as tax incentives.

> *Note*: The Eco-Management and Audit Scheme Regulation 1993 came into force in April 1995. The purpose of the scheme is to encourage the voluntary assessment of environmental performance by manufacturing and other companies to identify feasible targets for improvement in performance. The Eco-Label Regulation 880/92 is also in force and involves a similar voluntary scheme to assess whether the product may be labelled 'eco-worthy'.

10. International developments

International agreements on the environment may be concluded either by the EC or concurrently with the member states under Article 130r(5). Treaties concluded include: the Helsinki Convention on the Protection of Marine Environment 1983, the Barcelona Convention for the Protection of the Mediterranean Sea against Pollution 1985, the Vienna Convention for the Protection of the Ozone Layer 1988, and the Rio de Janeiro Earth Summit Conventions signed at the UN Conference on Environment and Development 1992. Many problems of ratification remain.

CONSUMER PROTECTION

11. Introduction

The EEC Treaty contained no explicit provision for consumer protection, the underlying assumption being that free competition would inevitably benefit the consumer. Thus consumers were mentioned only twice prior to amendment by the SEA:

(a) In Article 30, stating that products under the CAP should reach the consumer at fair prices.

(b) In Article 85(3) (competition rules), stating that one of the criteria for granting exemption to an otherwise invalid agreement is that the agreement should contribute to improving production or distribution of goods while allowing consumers a fair share of the benefit.

The SEA stimulated the development of EC consumer protection by providing an improved mechanism for internal market directives under Article 100a. However, consumer protection did not become a specific policy until the amendments made by the TEU.

12. Programmes of consumer protection

Following the 1972 Summit the First Consumer Programme was adopted in 1975 setting out a plan for implementation of the 5 fundamental consumer rights:

(a) The protection of health and safety

(b) The protection of consumers' economic interests

(c) Consumers' rights to information and education

(d) Consumers' right to redress

(e) Consumers' right to representation and participation.

The Second Programme in 1981 recognised in addition the need for consumer protection in the field of services. Harmonisation following both programmes was achieved under Article 100: *see* **3–8** below. The Third Programme in 1986 and the Fourth in 1990 supported the internal market programme and emphasised the harmonisation of consumer protection through the recognition of standards: *see* **19** below.

13. The Three Year Action Plans

The consumer protection policy was 'relaunched' in 1989 with the creation of the Consumer Policy Service and the identification of a number of priority areas including the integration of consumer policy into other policy areas, representation of consumers at EC level and promotion of general safety of goods and services and of access to legal redress. These themes were taken up in two Three Year Action Plans. The first in 1990 focused on the consumer measures needed for the completion of the internal market and the second in 1993 on access of consumers to justice and the resolution of consumer disputes in the single market.

HARMONISATION BEFORE THE SEA

14. Harmonisation under Article 100

A package of 18 measures under Article 100 to harmonise consumer protection was adopted by 1976 covering products such as motor vehicles and cosmetics. These measures were based on the assumption that national differences in consumer protection legislation could lead to distortion of competition. Harmonisation under Article 100 was slow as unanimity was required for the Council to adopt a directive.

15. Product liability: Directive 85/374

After many years of debate Directive 85/374 was adopted. The Directive imposes strict liability on producers for damage caused by defective products: Article 1. The term 'producer' covers manufacturers, importers and (where the producer cannot be named) the supplier of the product. The injured person must prove the damage, the defect and the causal relationship between the defect and the damage: Article 4. Various defences are available under Article 7. The Product Liability Directive was implemented in the UK by Part I of the Consumer Protection Act 1987.

16. Other directives adopted under Article 100

Other directives adopted under Article 100 include:

(a) The Misleading Advertising Directive (84/450) which aims to protect businesses and the general public against the effects of misleading advertisements

(b) The Doorstep Selling Directive (85/577) which introduces a seven-day cooling-off period for certain contracts concluded at the consumer's home or workplace

(c) The Consumer Credit Directive (87/102) which provides a similar level of protection in consumer credit transactions to that enjoyed by consumers in the UK under the Consumer Credit Act 1974.

HARMONISATION AFTER THE SEA 1986

17. Harmonisation under Article 100A

Although the SEA did not specifically provide for a consumer policy it added a requirement in Article 100A(3) that the Commission when making internal market proposals concerning health, safety, environmental protection and consumer protection take as a base 'a high level of protection' (undefined). To speed up the pace of harmonisation of consumer protection, most directives in this field after the SEA were adopted under Article 100A of the EEC Treaty, requiring only a qualified majority. As a result an extensive programme of directives was adopted as part of the 1992 programme.

18. Toy safety: Directive 88/378

The Toy Safety Directive harmonised the standards for selling toys and should prevent dangerous toys from being sold within the EC. The standards are to be drawn up by the European standards body, CEN (Comité Européan de Normalisation). There are two approaches to attaining the requisite standard:

(a) Conformity with the relevant national standard (in the UK the CEN standards will be adopted as the relevant national standards)

(b) Conformity with an approved model, i.e. by obtaining an EC type-approval certificate.

All toys supplied in the EC must bear the EC mark ('CE'), confirming compliance with **(a)** or **(b)** *above*. The name, trade mark and mark and address of the manufacturer or importer must also be displayed. In the UK the Directive was implemented by the Toy [Safety] Regulations which came into effect on 1 January 1991.

Note: The Toy Safety Directive was adopted as part of the EC's new approach to technical harmonisation and standards, agreed in 1985. There are two bodies responsible for drawing up EC standards: CEN and CENELEC (Comité Européan de Normalisation Electro-technique). Directives forming part of the programme are limited to setting the essential requirements for health, safety, consumer protection and the environment, with the technical details drawn up by CEN or CENELEC as European standards. Goods bearing the 'CE' mark may be freely traded within the EC and may not be refused access to any EC market on technical grounds. Other 'new approach' directives cover construction productions, machinery safety, personal protective equipment and gas appliances.

19. Other directives adopted

A number of directives have been adopted, mostly under Article 100A, including:

(a) *Price indication*: Directive 88/314 and 315 amending Directive 79/581, requiring the display of selling prices and (in certain cases) unit prices of food and non-food products.

(b) *Units of measurement*: Directive 89/617, extending the use of metric units throughout the EC and requiring imperial units to be phased out with certain exceptions (e.g. the mile for road signs and the pint for beer and milk).

(c) *Dangerous imitations*: Directive 87/357, harmonising national legislation on dangerous foods imitations.

(d) *Low voltage*: Directive 73/23 harmonising standards for the safety of electrical products operating within defined low voltage limits.

(e) *Household products containing radioactive substances*: Euratom Directive 80/836 prescribing prior approval schemes to member states for household products containing radioactive substances.

(f) *Package travel*: Directive 90/314, adopted in June 1990 for implementation by the end of 1992, established minimum safeguards for consumer protection on package travel, package holidays and package tours.

> *Note*: A recommendation was issued in 1988 on payment systems (85/590) proposing common rules on the rights and liabilities of payment card issuers and card holders.

20. The Unfair Contract Terms Directive 93/113

The Unfair Contract Terms Directive was adopted in 1993 and came into force at the end of 1994. It applies to all contracts entered into on or after 1 January 1995 between a seller or supplier of services and a consumer for the supply of goods or services. A contract term covered by the Directive (i.e. not an individually negotiated term) will be regarded as unfair if, contrary to the requirement of good faith, it can cause a significant imbalance in the parties' rights and obligations to the detriment of the consumer. The Directive has been implemented in the UK by regulations which will exist alongside the Unfair Contract Terms Act 1977. In some areas the standards of the directive are lower than the 1977 Act.

21. Consumer protection under the TEU

The TEU promoted consumer protection to the status of a policy of the Union. Article 129a of the EC Treaty states that a high level of consumer protection is to be achieved through:

(a) Internal market measures under Article 100a

(b) Specific action to support and supplement the policy pursued by the member states to protect health, safety and economic interests of consumers and to provide adequate information to consumers.

The co-decision procedure under Article 189b must be followed after consultation with the ESC for measures in both categories. Action taken under Article 129a does not prevent a member state from adopting a more stringent consumer protection measure provided it is compatible with the Treaty.

22. Legal position in the absence of EC rules

Where there are no EC common or harmonised rules on consumer protection, member states are free to adopt the measures they consider necessary. *See*, for example, *The State (Italy)* v. *Ciacoma Caldana* (Case 187/84) in which the ECJ held that national measures could be adopted in the absence of common or harmonised general rules on the classification, packaging and labelling of dangerous preparations.

An EC measure may expressly allow national measures which impose higher standards. In *Buet* v. *Ministre Public* (Case 328/87) French law imposed a total ban on the doorstep selling of educational material. Directive 85/577 gave consumers the right to withdraw from certain contracts concluded at home (while permitting national measures which afford a higher degree of consumer protection). The ECJ held that such a ban did not infringe Article 30: *see* 12:**14** and **15** on the relationship between Article 30 and consumer protection.

OTHER POLICIES: RESEARCH AND TECHNOLOGY

23. Before the SEA

As with so many policy areas the EEC Treaty lacked a specific policy on research and technology. Guidelines were adopted in 1974 for the co-ordination of national policies in various areas including the participation in the European Science Foundation and development of an EC programme for scientific and technological research.

The EC has funded a number of research programmes such as the European Strategic Programme for Research and Development in Information Technology (ESPRIT). Other programmes cover areas including the environment and life sciences, biomedicine and agriculture. Agreements providing for co-operation in research were adopted in relation to the former Eastern bloc countries and the former EFTA states.

24. Research and development under the SEA and TEU

The first explicit provision for a research policy was made in the SEA in Title VI for Research and Technological Development. This provision was retained in the TEU with little change. Article 130h of the TEU states that 'The Community and the member states shall co-ordinate their research and technological development activities so as to ensure that national policies and Community policies are mutually consistent'.

EDUCATION

25. Before the TEU

Although the EEC Treaty did not provide specifically for Educational Policy it referred in Article 41 to co-ordination in vocational training in agriculture and in Article 128 to laying down general principles to implement a common vocational training policy. An Education Action Programme was initiated in 1974, leading to various reports and pilot studies. The increasing awareness of the social dimension was reflected in the development of an education policy. The Commission issued guidelines for education and training in 1989. Education featured under the EEC Treaty in relation to:

(a) The recognition of professional qualifications: *see* 15.**28** on the mutual recognition of qualifications

(b) Residence rights of students: Directive 93/96 (replacing Directive 90/366): *see* 15.**39**

(c) Education as a social advantage in social security: *see* 16.**17**.

26. Under the TEU

While the SEA had little effect on education with the exception of the adoption of Directive 90/366 (*see* above), the TEU added to the EC's activities a contribution to education and training. Title VIII was given over to Education, Vocational Training and Youth. While the European dimension is to be emphasised, full responsibility for teaching content rests with the member states.

27. Programmes of financial assistance

One of the most successful aspects of the EC's education policy has been the adoption of programmes providing financial assistance to students and others. Of these, the ERASMUS programme has provided for co-operation between universities, by supporting staff and student mobility and exchange: *see* 15:**37**. From 1995 support for these activities has moved to the SOCRATES programme. SOCRATES has extended the LINGUA programme for the promotion of foreign language skills to include distance learning though the EC information network known as EURYDICE.

COMETT, established in 1986, represents a programme for co-operation between industry and universities particularly in relation to technology. TEMPUS and PHARE were introduced in 1990 to provide educational assistance to students in the former Eastern bloc countries to study at an EC university.

28. Culture

Prior to the TEU there was no policy for culture, although it was raised in a number of different contexts such as the protection of national treasures under Article 36 and of cultural values in relation to Sunday trading. The TEU, in somewhat vague terminology, includes in the EC's activities the 'flowering of the cultures of the member states'. While co-operation between states is to be encouraged the EC must respect their national and regional diversity while bringing the common heritage to the fore: Article 128(1). Cultural factors are to be taken into account in other action under the Treaty: Article 128(4).

29. Public health

Public health occurs in the EEC/EC Treaty in the context of derogations from the free movement of goods (Article 36), persons (48(3)) and services (Article 66). Some mention is also made in relation to health and safety under Article 118 which requires co-operation between member states in areas including occupational hygiene and the prevention of occupational accidents and diseases.

The TEU provides for primary responsibility for public health to remain with the member states, encouraging co-operation between states: TEU Article 129. It also provides that health protection requirements form a consistent part of the EC's other policies: Article 129(1). The EC may issue non-binding recommendations but may not engage in harmonisation of national law: Article 129(4). EC action should be directed at disease prevention through the promotion of research and co-operation: Article 129(3).

TRANSPORT

30. Under the EEC Treaty

nany other policy areas transport was made the subject of a specific n (Title IV) in the EEC Treaty which stated in Article 74 that the objectives reaty were to be pursued within the framework of a common transport This foresight on the part of the drafters of the Rome Treaty did not lead activity on the part of the Council which was required under Article 75 own:

nmon rules on transport

nditions for non-resident carriers

asures to improve transport safety

ny other appropriate provision.

31. Decisions of the ECJ

Matters came to a head in *Commission* v. *Council* (Case 22/70) in relation to the European Road Transport Agreement (*see* 3.12) which held that the EC has had international capacity in matters of road transport since the 1969 Council regulation providing for common rules to implement a transport policy. The agreement concluded by the member states in 1970 was allowed to stand only because it had been largely negotiated before the 1969 regulation.

Inaction by the EC institutions nevertheless continued. In *Commission* v. *French Republic* (Case 167/73) the ECJ held that Transport was not limited under the Treaty to Title IV. In *Parliament* v. *Council* (Case 13/83) the ECH stated that 'There is not yet a coherent set of rules which may be regarded as a common transport policy' and found that the failure to implement parts of Title IV amounted to a breach of the Treaty.

32. Under the SEA

It was clear that remaining restrictions in transport would have to be removed in order to complete the internal market. A Common transport policy at last emerged, with a programme of directives on areas such as technical specifications for vehicles and transport by rail, sea and air. It has been apparent from competition decisions of the ECJ and regulations that competition rules under Article 85 and 86 apply to transport.

33. Under the TEU

The TEU has introduced a number of new aspects to transport policy, notably trans-European networks. These are European networks in transport, telecommunications and energy infrastructures. Financial support may be available through feasibility studies and subsidies, and through the Cohesion Fund for Transport Infrastructures. Other consequences of the TEU include the need to integrate environmental policy with other policies such as transport and the entrusting of transport safety matters to the Council. Despite progress it is clear that a common transport policy is emerging but remains far less developed than other policy areas such as the environment.

ENERGY

34. Energy

An energy policy was not provided in the original founding treaties although decisions relating to energy were taken under the ECSC and Euratom Treaties. The main incentive to develop a policy was the oil crisis of 1970, although little progress was made until a framework regulation in 1978 on the granting of financial support for alternative energy projects. A series of implementing measures followed.

The Council adopted resolutions on Community energy policies in 1980 and 1986 setting out objectives for 1990 and 1995 to limit reliance on oil and reduce oil imports, to improve energy efficiency and to increase the contribution from new and renewable sources. The Commission issued guidelines in 1991 for the completion of the internal market in electricity and gas to be reviewed in 1996. The Commission has supported programmes such as THERMIC (renewable energy sources) and SAVE (energy conservation), both of which have been implemented by directives.

In 1991 the EC signed the European Energy Charter and started international negotiations for a Basic Agreement on energy, competition rules, access to capital, intellectual property, technology transfer and dispute resolution. The external dimension of the energy policy is developing with energy-producing countries through nuclear co-operation, commercial agreements and technical assistance. Former Eastern bloc countries are benefiting from technical assistance through the TACIS and PHARE programmes.

Progress test 26

1. Under what legal bases were environmental measures taken before the SEA?

2. How did the SEA develop environmental policy?

3. What new principles were introduced by the TEU and what are their limitations?

4. What are the main areas in which environmental policy has developed? What are environmental impact assessments and why are they important?

5. Which body bears responsibility for the enforcement of EC environmental policy and how is enforcement achieved?

6. What part was played by programmes and action plans in the development of consumer protection in the EC?

7. What were the main directives adopted under Article 100 relating to consumer protection? Why was harmonisation under Article 100 difficult to achieve?

8. What change was made in the harmonisation of consumer protection measures as a result of the SEA?

9. Outline the main features of Directive 88/378 on Toy Safety. What is the function of CEN?

10. What is the main feature of Directive 93/113 on Unfair Contract Terms? What problem does the Directive pose for UK law?

11. What change was introduced into consumer protection by the TEU?

12. How has the EC sought to develop its policy on research and technology?

13. What features do the policies on education, culture and public health have in common?

14. How does treatment of transport policy in the EC Treaty differ from most other policy areas considered in this chapter?

15. How actively was transport policy developed prior to the TEU?

16. How is the EC contributing to energy conservation and the development of renewable energy sources?

Part Five

THE FUTURE

27

THE FUTURE OF THE EUROPEAN UNION

1. Introduction

This chapter outlines some of the important issues which face the EU in the immediate future, particularly in relation to the 1996 IGC, and considers areas of possible development after the IGC.

THE 1996 IGC

2. Institutional changes

Further discussion of the so-called 'democratic deficit' whereby legislation continues to be adopted by the unelected Council rather than the Parliament (EP) is inevitable. The EP is not pressing for full legislative powers at present, perceiving it to be an unrealistic goal. Instead, more modest proposals such as the right for the EP to initiate legislation are likely to be discussed. Greater scrutiny by the EP of the activities of the other institutions may also emerge. The European Council at Cannes in June 1995 stated that preparations for the IGC should focus on issues which would enable the EU to respond to new challenges facing Europe and its citizens including ways to make the institutions of the EU more efficient, democratic and open.

The EP has consistently maintained that institutional questions such as the number of MEPs and the role of qualified majority voting must precede further enlargement. In previous years, often in response to a sudden need, such changes have been made on an *ad hoc* basis. The European Council appears to have accepted this need, stating at Cannes that the Reflection Group preparing for the IGC will set out possible improvements in the operation of the institutions in the light of the future enlargement of the Union for consideration by the Heads of Government.

The larger member states are concerned about the dilution of power in the Council as a result of enlargement to 20 members. Redefinition of what constitutes a qualified majority is likely. The number of Commissioners may also change. Procedures for the adoption of legislation, particularly the co- decision procedure, will be under review. So far each major Treaty revision (the SEA and the TEU) has produced a significant new procedure.

3. Subsidiarity

The operation of the subsidiarity principle will be examined to see whether it may be put into practice more effectively. This principle has taken on particular significance in relation to the future nature of the EU itself and the question of the EU's federal direction. While some states see subsidiarity as supporting the move to a more federal system, other see the principle as a check. Any move to strengthen the role of the EU by moving matters currently within the second or third pillars of inter-governmental co-operation to legal control under the Treaty are likely to be resisted by certain states, particularly by the UK, as unacceptably federalist and contrary to the principle of subsidiarity.

4. The Social Protocol

The operation of the Social Protocol outside the Treaty is bound to be considered. Since the Protocol was adopted at Maastricht, Austria, Finland and Sweden have also accepted the obligations of the Protocol. Thus the only member state outside its scope remains the UK where the question of future adherence to the Protocol is a controversial party political issue. Whether legislation in future will be based on Article 118a (health and safety) to include the UK or on the Social Protocol is unclear.

5. EMU and a multi-speed Europe

While the EU has continued to support the timetable set at Maastricht for entry into the third stage of EMU by 1999 at the latest, economic commentators have regularly cast doubt on the practicality of its achievement. It is to be hoped that the IGC will clarify the commitment in a realistic way. There are obvious implications for differing levels of integration once full EMU is reached, with scope for a small number of states at the heart (France and Germany), a larger number involved to a lesser degree (including Italy, Spain, and the UK and Denmark if decisions to proceed to EMU are taken) and an outer circle of former Eastern bloc states (following possible EU accession).

6. The Common Foreign and Security Policy (CFSP)

Under the TEU the CFSP replaced European political co-operation, a policy initiated in 1970 as the forerunner of a possible EC foreign policy. The CFSP, the second pillar of the Union, is not regulated by the legal regime of the EC Treaty. It requires inter-governmental co-operation on European security and makes the development of a European Defence Policy more likely. However, there are major differences between the member states as to the extent to which the EU should become a military power. There is general agreement within the EU that all the EU member states should become members of NATO through the Council of the Western European Union (an international organisation with a role largely limited to defence within NATO).

7. Justice and home affairs

Justice and home affairs constitute the third pillar under the TEU and, like the CFSP, are regulated by intergovernmental co-operation rather than EC law. Article K of the TEU lists matters of common concern to the member states under this pillar including asylum policy, immigration from third countries, combating drug addiction, international fraud, illegal residence and work, and co-operation on customs and police matters (particularly terrorism and drug trafficking).

In areas of common concern member states are encouraged to consult each other in the Council. There are many uncertainties about the role of the EC institutions in relation to the regulation of internal security. The European Council has called on member states to adopt the Europol Convention which provides for an EU-wide system for exchanging information within a European Police Office. Ways to improve internal security will be considered at the IGC.

8. Developing policy areas

A number of new policy areas were identified and given a legal base in the TEU. These include education, culture, consumer protection, trans-European networks, industry, technology and the environment: *see* Chapter 29. Of these, environmental law is particularly significant, with the accession of the former EFTA states. This may lead to a strengthening of environmental provision but could also lead to harmonisation at a lower level with scope for higher standards: *see* Charlesworth and Cullen p. 464. Technological advances particularly in communications have led to demands for regulation at European or possibly international level.

ENLARGEMENT OF THE EU

9. The EU, the EEA and Eastern Europe

The 1995 enlargement of the EU to include the three EEA states, Austria, Finland and Sweden, was relatively straightforward. All three states enjoy a tradition of democracy and were seen as economically stable. All are net contributors to the EU budget. In contrast the possible accession of the newly independent states of the former USSR and its satellites poses difficult problems for the EU and the applicant states.

The current measures (trade agreements, Partnership and Co-operation Agreements and Europe Agreements) were considered in Chapter 1. These agreements should be seen as temporary and transitional in character, acting in many cases as a preparation for full EU membership. The main problems relate to the economic circumstances of the applicant states and to their short experience of democratic procedures. The EU has made it clear that political stability and progress towards economic reform are required before negotiations for full membership may start.

The agreements entered into with the former Eastern bloc states involve varying degrees of integration with the EU regime. Under the agreements financial assistance from the EU has been substantial through programmes such as TACIS (Technical and Financial Assistance), assisting the movement from centrally planned to market economies.

In December 1994 the European Council declared that associated states of central and Eastern Europe (i.e. those with Europe Agreements) may join the EU as soon as the necessary conditions are fulfilled. Accession negotiations may begin when the 1996 IGC has been concluded.

10. The next round of enlargement

There is an existing commitment to include Cyprus and Malta in the next round of enlargement.

11. The study of EC law in a changing world

The study of EC law is stimulating, not least because it reflects rapidly changing developments within Europe and the world. Any student of the subject will benefit from learning about the structures and policies of the evolving European Union and should be better placed as a result to appreciate decision-making at EC level and its implications in a wide range of areas.

Progress test 27

1. Which issues of institutional reform are likely to be discussed at the 1996 IGC?

2. What are the uncertainties over the future role of the Social Protocol?

3. What is the likely effect on integration if the third stage of EMU is achieved?

4. To what extent has a common foreign and security policy been developed within the EU?

5. What mechanisms have been adopted between the EU and former Soviet bloc states to provide for closer integration?

APPENDIX 1
WHERE TO FIND THE LAW

1. Primary and secondary legislation

EC legislation can be divided into primary legislation, in the form of treaties (e.g. the EEC Treaty and the Single European Act) and secondary legislation in the form of regulations, directives and decisions of the EC institutions; *see* **3**.

2. The *Official Journal (OJ)*

All legislation and important notices are published in the *Official Journal* of the European Communities. Proposed legislation appears in the 'C' section of the *OJ* and adopted secondary legislation in the 'L' section.

3. Law reports

The official version of proceedings in the ECJ and CFI appears in the European Court Reports (ECR) and an unofficial version in the Common Market Law Reports (CMLR) also covering decisions in the national courts with an EC element.

4. Databases

A number of databases in EC law exist, including CELEX, SPEARHEAD and LEXIS.

(a) *CELEX.* The official database in EC law is known as CELEX. It provides the full text of materials and is divided into sectors covering primary legislation, secondary legislation (as published in the *OJ*), reports of cases before the ECJ and CFI, Commission legislative proposals, questions in the European Parliament and national legislation implementing EC directives, national decisions and publications on EC law.

(b) *JUSTIS* and *EUROLAW*. CELEX is also available in CD-Rom form through the JUSTIS Service from (i) Context Legal Services; this version is not full text but provides a gateway to the official version; and (ii) EUROLAW, a full text official version from ILI (Informe London Information).

(c) *SPEARHEAD.* A limited version of CELEX is available through Profile Information Services Ltd. This system makes use of SPEARHEAD, the single market on-line database of the Department of Trade and Industry, enabling the user to gain access to the full text of legislation. It is also available in CD-Rom from ILI.

(d) *LEXIS*. The best-known on-line commercial database is LEXIS. EC law coverage includes law reports (European Court Reports and European Commercial Cases), unreported decisions and, where available, opinions of the advocates general. LEXIS also covers Commission competition decisions.

Access to the CELEX database is now available through LEXIS, although some documents are not available in full text form.

5. European Documentation Centres (EDCs)

EDCs comprise major collections of EC documentation, including access to CELEX. The 45 EDCs are based mainly in university libraries. While EDCs provide an academic service within their own institutions, they also serve the needs of the local community.

6. European Information Centres

Twenty-one European Information Centres have been established by the Commission throughout the UK to provide advice for small businesses.

7. EC Information Offices in the UK

Information on the activities and publications of the EC institutions may be obtained from:

The Commission Information Office, 8 Storey's Gate, London SW1P 3AT (tel. 0171-973 1992) and from: The European Parliament Information Office, 2 Queen Anne's Gate, London SW1H 9AA (tel. 0171-222 0411).

APPENDIX 2
BIBLIOGRAPHY

1. Main sources of EC law

Official Journal ('L' and 'C' Series): See Appendix I.
European Court Reports (ECR): *Common Market Law Reports* (CMLR); *See* Appendix I.
Encyclopaedia of European Community Law (Sweet & Maxwell, looseleaf): the constitutive treaties and secondary legislation (annotated).
Halsbury's Laws of England, volumes 51 and 52 (ed. Vaughan) (Butterworths, 4th edition).
Bulletin of the European Communities: reports on EC activities with supplements on specific areas.
Commission, *General Report on the Activities of the European Communities* (annual).
Commission, *Report on Competition Policy* (annual).

2. Periodicals

Cahiers de Droit Europeen (CDE).
Common Market Law Review (CMLRev.)
European Business Law Review (EBLR)
European Competition Law Review (ECLR)
European Intellectual Property Review (EIPR)
European Law Review (ELRev)
Journal of Common Market Studies (JCMS)
Journal of World Trade Law (JWTL)
Legal Issues of European Integration (LIEI)
Yearbook of European Law (YEL)

FURTHER READING

3. Statutes, case studies and materials

Foster, *EC Legislation*, 6th edition (Blackstone Press, 1995–96).
Pollard and Ross, *European Community Law: Text and Materials* (Butterworth, 1994).
Tillotson, *European Community Law: Text, Cases and Materials* (Cavendish, 1993).
Weatherill, *Cases and Materials on EC Law*, 2nd edn. (Blackstone Press, 1994).

4. General

Arnull, *The General Principles of EEC Law and the Individual* (Leicester University Press, 1990).
Brown and Jacobs, *The Court of Justice of the European Communities*, 4th edn. (Sweet & Maxwell, 1994).

Charlesworth and Cullen, *European Community Law* (Pitman, 1994).

Edward and Lane, *European Community Law: an Introduction*, 2nd edn. (Butterworth, 1995).

Hartley, *The Foundation of European Community Law*, 2nd edn. (Oxford, Clarendon Press, 1994).

Lasok and Bridge, *Law and Institutions of the European Union*, 6th edn. (Butterworths, 1994).

Mathijsen, *A Guide to European Community Law*, 6th edn. (Sweet & Maxwell, 1995).

O'Keefe and Twomey, *Legal Issues of the Maastricht Treaty* (Chancery, 1994).

Shaw, *European Community Law* (Macmillan, 1993).

Steiner, *EC Law*, 4th edn. (Blackstone Press, 1994).

Weatherill and Beaumont, *EC Law*, (Penguin, 1993).

Wyatt and Dashwood, *European Community Law*, 3rd edn. (Sweet & Maxwell, 1993).

5. Competition law

Goyder, *EC Competition Law*, 2nd edn. (Oxford, Clarendon Press, 1993).

Korah, *An Introductory Guide to EEC Competition Law and Practice* (ESC Publishing, 1990).

Singleton, *Introduction to Competition Law* (Pitman, 1992).

Whish, *Competition Law*, 3rd edn. (Butterworth, 1993).

6. Other aspects of substantive law and procedure

Kramer, *EEC Treaty and Environmental Protection* (Sweet & Maxwell 1991).

Nielson and Szyszczak, *The Social Dimension of the European Community* (Handelshojskolens Forlag, 1991).

Usher, *Legal Aspects of Agriculture in the European Communities* (Oxford, Clarendon Press, 1988).

Note: where authors are cited in the text, e.g. Wyatt and Dashwood p. 20, the reference is to the Bibliography above.

INDEX